STRATEGIC MANAGEMENT
IN MULTINATIONAL COMPANIES

Other Titles of Interest

DAVIS, S. M.
Managing and Organizing Multinational Corporations

EILON, S.
Aspects of Management, 2nd ed.
Management Assertions and Aversions
Management Control, 2nd ed.

HUSSEY, D. E.
Introducing Corporate Planning, 3rd ed.
Corporate Planning: Theory and Practice, 2nd ed.
The Truth about Corporate Planning

McNAMEE, P.
Tools and Techniques for Strategic Management

TAYLOR, B. & HUSSEY, D. E.
The Realities of Planning

A Related Journal
LONG RANGE PLANNING*

The Journal of the Society for Strategic and Long Range Planning and of the European Planning Federation

Editor: Professor Bernard Taylor, The Administrative Staff College, Greenlands, Henley-on-Thames, Oxon RG9 EAU, UK

The leading international journal in the field of long-range planning, which aims to focus the attention of senior managers, administrators, and academics on the concepts and techniques involved in the development and implementation of strategy and plans.

*Free specimen copy gladly sent on request.

STRATEGIC MANAGEMENT IN MULTINATIONAL COMPANIES

by

YVES DOZ
INSEAD, Fontainebleau

PERGAMON PRESS

OXFORD · NEW YORK · BEIJING · FRANKFURT
SÃO PAULO · SYDNEY · TOKYO · TORONTO

U.K.	Pergamon Press, Headington Hill Hall, Oxford OX3 0BW, England
U.S.A.	Pergamon Press, Maxwell House, Fairview Park, Elmsford, New York 10523, U.S.A.
PEOPLE'S REPUBLIC OF CHINA	Pergamon Press, Qianmen Hotel, Beijing, People's Republic of China
FEDERAL REPUBLIC OF GERMANY	Pergamon Press, Hammerweg 6, D-6242 Kronberg, Federal Republic of Germany
BRAZIL	Pergamon Editora, Rua Eça de Queiros, 346, CEP 04011, São Paulo, Brazil
AUSTRALIA	Pergamon Press Australia, P.O. Box 544, Potts Point, N.S.W. 2011, Australia
JAPAN	Pergamon Press, 8th Floor, Matsuoka Central Building, 1-7-1 Nishishinjuku, Shinjuku-ku, Tokyo 160, Japan
CANADA	Pergamon Press Canada, Suite 104, 150 Consumers Road, Willowdale, Ontario M2J 1P9, Canada

Copyright © 1986 Yves Doz

First edition 1986
Reprinted 1987

Library of Congress Cataloging in Publication Data
Doz, Yves L.
Strategic management in multinational companies.
1. International business enterprises—Management.
2. International business enterprises—Planning.
I. Title.
HD62.4.D69   1985   659.4'012   85-9282

British Library Cataloguing in Publication Data
Doz, Yves
Strategic management in multinational companies.
1. International business enterprises—Management
2. Corporate planning
I. Title
658.4'012   HD69.17
ISBN 0-08-031808-8 (Hardcover)
ISBN 0-08-031807-X (Flexicover)

#12079501

Printed in Great Britain by A. Wheaton & Co. Ltd., Exeter

To Nicole, Marianne and Gabriel

Acknowledgements

I am deeply indebted to many individuals for their generous support in developing this book.

The industry and company studies on which the book is based were supported by the Division of Research of the Harvard Business School. In particular, I am grateful to Walt Salmon and John McArthur who gave me the time and the resources to carry out extensive field research while on the Harvard Business School Faculty. Joseph Bower, Raymond Vernon and Michael Yoshino were constant sources of intellectual stimulation and support. I am also grateful to INSEAD which supported the completion of this work.

Many colleagues and friends read draft chapters of this book and made extremely valuable comments, in particular Richard Caves, Michel Crozier, Donald Laurie, Richard Meyer, Edith Penrose, C. K. Prahalad, Jose de la Torre and Louis T. Wells. Robert N. Ross helped me greatly to organise and edit the manuscript. Danielle Chouet typed the first drafts with great dedication, while Alison James, at INSEAD, has guided the preparation of the manuscript with great skills.

In spite of all this help, I am entirely responsible for the accuracy of my information and the soundness of my analysis.

Contents

LIST OF TABLES   xi

LIST OF FIGURES   xii

INTRODUCTION   1

1. **Industry Characteristics and Strategic Choices**   12
   The Multinational Business Strategies Defined   12
       Multinational Integration   12
       National Responsiveness   16
       Multifocal Strategies   18
   Industry Economics and Multinational Business Strategies   19
       Economies of Scale   19
       Economies of Experience   21
       Economies of Location   22
       Product Differentiation   22
       Technology   23
       Export Channels and Intensity of Selling Task   24
       Access to Capital   25
   Conclusion: Economic and Competitive Determinants of Integration   28

2. **Multinational Integration and Host Government Policies**   35
   Host Government Concerns Toward Multinational Companies   35
   Host Government Policies Toward Multinational Strategies   38
       Policies Toward Multinational Integration   38
       Policies Toward National Responsiveness Strategies   44
       Policies Toward Multifocal Strategies   48
   Multinational Strategies, National Policies, and Resulting Industry Structures   49
   Conclusion: Toward a Framework   52

3. **Competition in Global Industries: The Automobile Industry**   57
   Structural Characteristics of the Automobile Industry: Competitive Imperatives   60
       Economies of Scale in Production   60
       Economies of Scale in Distribution   63
       Similarity Among Geographical Markets   64
       Factor Costs and Productivity Differences   65
       Free Trade Policies   65
   Firms' Strategies: The Search for Competitiveness   66
       Integration Strategies   66

viii   *Contents*

Quasi-integration Strategies   70
Geographical Expansion Strategies   73
Specialization Strategies   74
Flexibility Strategies   75
National Policies: Facing the Competitive Imperatives   77
Limits to Interdependency   77
Benefits from Interdependency   80
Support for the National Industry   81
Conclusion: National Policy Choices   83
Conclusion: Competition in a Global Industry   85

4. **Compromise in Government-controlled Industries: The
    Telecommunication Equipment Industry**   89

The Historical Dominance of Political Imperatives   90
State-owned Customers' Demands on Equipment Manufacturers   90
Direct Government Influence on Suppliers of Equipment   95
*Bargaining Power, Market Maturity, Product Technology and the Balance
  between National Responsiveness and Integration*   96
Conclusion: Technology and the Political Imperative   100
Multinational Strategies for Government-controlled Industries   102
Strategic Alternatives: Technological Leadership vs. National Responsiveness   104
Conclusion   107
Government Policies   110
Government Policies in Innovating Countries   110
Policies for Technological Adaption   111
Technology Transfer Recipients   113
Conclusion   115

5. **Coexistence in Mixed-structure Industries: Computers
    and Microelectronics**   118

A Difficult Trade-off Between Political and Economic Priorities   118
Reasons for Government Control   118
The Economic Imperative as a Damper to Government Intervention   121
Host Government's Dilemma   125
The Dilemma of National Strategies   125
Selective Support of National Companies to Compete Internationally   126
Protection and Support of a Broad Base National Industry   128
Multinational Alliances   132
Multinational Business Strategies   137
Multinational Integration   137
Multifocal Strategy and Multinational Alliance   141
National Responsiveness   143
Conclusion   144

6. **The Spread of Global Competition**   146

Industry Structures, Strategies, and Firm Performance   148
Industry Structures Compared: A Summary   148
Firm's Performance and Choice of Strategy   152
Implications for MNC Management   153
Globalization vs. Localization   154
Competitive Strength and Bargaining Power   156
Strategic Segmentation   158
Strategic Clarity vs. Administrative Complexity   159
Implications for Industrial Policies   160
International Industry Structures: A Host Government Perspective   160

Bargaining Power of Host Governments 162
Negotiating with MNCs 163

7. **Managing an Integrated Multinational Business** 166

Integration Strategies: The Managerial Tasks 166
Managing and Developing the Integrated Network Effectively 168
  Manufacturing and Logistics Management 168
  Research and Development Management 170
  Marketing Management: Balancing Local Needs and Headquarters
    Demands 173
Effective Representation of Host Country Partners: Government and Labor 174
  Host Government Representation 174
  Labor Relations 175
Structuring Headquarter Subsidiary Relationships 178
  Fostering Clarity in the Organization: Building Visibility to Subunit
    Performance 179
  Fostering Unity: Building Communication Channels 183
  Formal Management Structures 187
Conclusion 188

8. **Managing a Nationally Responsive Multinational
    Business** 191

Issues and Tasks 191
Managing Resource Allocation 192
  Uniformity of Planning, Budgeting and Control Systems 193
  Measurements and Incentives 194
  Peer Control 195
  Direct Top Management Involvement 196
  Conclusion 197
Management of Technology 198
  Impediments to the Central Management of Technology 198
  Two Examples: ITT and BBC 199
  Conclusion 202
Exports Coordination 202
  Export Coordination as a Source of Competitive Advantage 202
  Coordinating Exports 203
  Transfer of Knowledge and Skills 205
Decentralized Strategy and Headquarters Control 206
  The Pitfalls of a Decentralized Strategy 206
  Central Management Overlay 208
  The Need for Central Guidance 210
Conclusion 211

9. **Managing a Multifocal Strategy** 214

The Issues and the Tasks 214
Leverage Points for Top Management 222
Using Tools Toward a Multifocal Organization 225
Conclusion 232

10. **Conclusion:
    Strategic Control and the Future of Multinational
    Companies** 234

Index 241

List of Tables

1.1	Evolution of Number of Basic Major Components for the IVECO product range	15
1.2	Impact of Industry Structure characteristics on the choice of the Strategy for Multinational Businesses	26–27
2.1	Patterns of International Competition in Mixed Structure Industries	53
3.1	Imported Passenger Cars as Percent of Total New Car Registrations	58
3.2	Hypothetical Die Cost Calculation	62
3.3	Sensitivity of Car Variable Manufacturing Costs to Scale	63
4.1	Characteristics of Major Product Segments: Telecommunication Equipment Industry	91
4.2	Evolution of Host Government Demands in a Government-Controlled market	99
4.3	Conditions of Access to the International Switching Equipment Market (1975–85)	103
5.1	Public Assistance to the Computer Industry	129
5.2	Private and Public Sector Computer System Market Shares in selected European Countries 1971–75	130
5.3	National Policies	136
6.1	Sample of industries and Extent of Government Control (Percentage)	147
9.1	Typical Repertoire of Administrative Mechanisms to Carry Out Top Management Tasks demanded by Multifocal Strategy	222

List of Figures

I.1   Manufacturing dependencies: IBM Corporation   6

1.1   Integration pattern of Ford of Europe for Fiesta Car Line   14

2.1   Customers, Market Shares and Multinational Strategies: hypothetical relationships   54

2.2   Customers, Market Shares and Strategies: Industries studied in detail   55

3.1   Growth of Japanese Car Exports and Domestic Registrations   79

4.1   Simplified sketch of a Telephone Network   90

4.2   MNC Bargaining Power   97

4.3   Technology and Market Presence in the World's Telephone Switching Industry   104

4.4   Comparisons between two multinational strategies for government-controlled businesses   109

6.1   Customers, market Shares and Multinational Strategies   149

8.1   Simplified sketch of ITT Structure   200

Introduction

This book is about the strategic integration of multinational companies (MNCs) in the context of national pressures for fragmentation. As international competition intensifies, the need for global competitive advantage is tempered by the needs and wishes of host nations and by the diversity among their markets. Needs for national responsiveness and needs for international integration often conflict, and managers within multinational companies are continually faced by the problems of managing the tensions that result. Conflicting demands must constantly be traded off.

Its purpose, based on extensive detailed research in selected multinationals, is to analyze the types of strategic choices and organizational capabilities that underly the success (or explain the failure) of MNCs in trading-off needs for responsiveness and needs for integration. Success in managing such trade-offs is the key to MNC survival and success in the 1980s.

Until the 1960s, MNCs typically operated fairly autonomous national subsidiaries, each catering for its own national market. Management tasks at MNC headquarters usually remained simple and limited in scope (mainly finance and treasury functions, technology transfers, and, sometimes, export coordination). Competitive pressures were mild, national markets were protected by tariff barriers, and the position of the firms in each national market was often negotiated with the government rather than decided by international competition. A strategy of *national responsiveness* was pursued.

To succeed against local competition, MNC subsidiaries could draw on unique intangible assets provided by their mother company. Such assets were usually based on knowhow and information not easily or cheaply available to local firms. New product and manufacturing process technology developed centrally was made available to the various subsidiaries. Marketing skills for product differentiation were also available centrally, and MNCs in the food and beverage industries, for instance, succeeded in branding and differentiating what were previously staple goods in most countries. By scanning the world for raw material supplies and potential export markets—at a much lower cost of information than national companies—MNCs could further their advantages. Professional management and

1

standardized administrative procedures also allowed them, at least in theory, to maximize operational efficiency and minimize administrative costs.

Since most of the unique intangible assets of mother companies could hardly be transferred by market mechanisms, given their "public good" nature and the difficulty of transactions in knowledge, they contributed to the spread of MNCs worldwide.[1]* Patent protection conceived to create a market for technology seldom fully applied internationally; for some products and countries, such as drugs in Italy, it did not apply at all. Once these assets had been developed at great cost in one location (e.g., technology in the parent company's labs), transferring them abroad only involved marginal costs, particularly once the initial network of foreign subsidiaries had been established.[2] Yet, for the MNC to recover its initial investment, it was essential to keep them proprietary, hence the "internalization" of their use through fully owned foreign subsidiaries rather than licences or joint ventures.[3]

Further, full control of subsidiaries in different countries provided competitive strength: it was possible to respond to competitive activity not where foreign competitors initiated it, but where they could be hurt most. IBM, for example could not only fight the Japanese computer manufacturers in the United States, but also could use its Japanese subsidiary to attack them in Japan, where they had most to lose. Strength in competitive rivalry was, therefore, another motive to expand internationally via controlled subsidiaries, rather than via licensing and other forms of technology transfer.

Over time, the markets for such intangible assets as technology became less imperfect, and alternatives to the MNC developed. Some technology leaders licensed their technology rather than exploit it internationally, either for fear it would upset the fragile equilibrium of existing oligopolies and therefore investments might never pay off (e.g., Pilkington's licensing of float glass), or because the innovating company lacked interest in active foreign investment (e.g., RCA in television tubes) or perceived excessive risks or difficulty in penetrating foreign markets on its own (e.g., Corning's licensing of optical fiber technologies to major glass and telecom cable manufacturers in Europe and Japan). Technology transfers contributed to the emergence of strong potentially global competitors in many industries, particularly when they were orchestrated and coordinated, as in Japan. The history of Japanese post-World War II development is the most obvious example of the emergence of new global competitors.[4] Concurrently, trade liberalization removed the forbidding protection that sheltered most national markets and exposed national industries to renewed international competition. In particular, the markets of mature industrial countries were

---

*Superscript numbers are to references at the end of the chapter.

open to imports from Japan and other more recently industrialized countries. In many industries, prices offered by these new suppliers were lower than that of established companies, and their quality often higher.

In the quest for the lower costs and better efficiencies needed to fend off such global competition, large multinational companies often integrated their operations across borders. They adopted an *integration strategy* with the main purpose of reducing their manufacturing costs. Instead of separately manufacturing a complete product range in each country, they specialized their plants so that each national subsidiary produced only a small part of a common product range and procured the large part of the product range it did not manufacture from sister companies located in other countries. The decrease in manufacturing costs to be gained from larger "focused" factories and longer run-lengths more than offset increased transportation costs. When end-products were complex (e.g., automobiles, integrated circuits, or television sets), specialization also developed by stages in the manufacturing process to exploit different economies of scale at the various stages and different factor input mixes. Despite a dearth of empirical data, it seems that significant numbers of major European and American multinationals integrated international operations in the 1970s, and more were in the process of doing so by the late 1970s. By the early 1980s, according to some sources, about half of MNC exports may be intra-MNC transactions, denoting extensive integration of manufacturing and sourcing.[5]

In integrating their operations, the MNCs have added several sources of competitive advantage to the internalization of intangible assets and to strength in global rivalry. First, they have increased their oligopoly power by exploiting scale and experience effects beyond the size of national markets and, therefore, raised the barriers to entry to the industries in which they participate. They have also made it increasingly difficult for national firms (i.e., producing and selling only in one country) to survive in global industries. Second, they have placed themselves in the best position to exploit the growing discrepancy between a relatively efficient market for goods (created by free trade) and very imperfect markets for production factors. MNCs can, more easily than national firms, exploit differences in labor cost among countries. Third, they can also exploit differences in tax rates and structures and set transfer prices within the integrated system so as to show high profits in low-tax countries only. MNCs can also exploit to their advantage differences in capital costs and exchange rates, as well as government policies that affect factor costs or the specific cost of doing business, for the firm, and in the country (e.g., subsidies, favorable credit terms, export guarantees, etc.). The specialized and integrated nature of operations in each individual country also makes hostile host government action less rewarding and less likely.[6] Integration thus provides MNCs with the potential to maximize their total system-wide margin between prices and costs, to exploit imperfections in labor and financial markets, and to improve bargaining power with host governments.

At the same time, integration increases the risks for the MNC. First, it becomes vulnerable to national disruptions (such as labor unrest or changes in government policies) that can have impact on its whole integrated network. Second, exchange rate fluctuations may play havoc with integration strategies. Third, home and host governments may try to use it as a far-reaching tool of foreign policy, imposing restrictions and performance requirements, or requesting ventures that may weaken the company's overall competitiveness. To some extent, bargaining power works both ways, also in favor of host governments in whose countries critical parts of the integrated network are located.

Finally, the management task is also complicated: instead of the distant control of autonomous subsidiaries where key decisions are made locally, as a function of local circumstances, towards local optima, decisions in the integrated network have to contribute to a sytem-wide optimum within the diverse constraints of operating interdependently in multiple countries. In many industries the adoption of large-scale highly efficient manufacturing technologies has also reduced the capability of the firm to adjust to local or temporary fluctuations, and this may lead to significant opportunity costs. (Ford, for instance, after having fully integrated its European operations in the 1970s, has lately been moving toward a more flexible manufacturing set-up.)

Integration strategies have been implemented most extensively in Western Europe where free trade and free investment prevail—the consequences of the European Economic Community—and where high manufacturing labor costs combine with a large market over a small geographic expanse to maximize the benefits of integration strategies. In some industries, such as electronics, however, integration encompasses global plants in countries where labor is efficient and inexpensive, mostly in the Far East. Since integration is most prevalent in Western Europe, however, our analysis of the tensions between national responsiveness and global integration within multinational companies is centred on Western Europe.

Tensions between national responsiveness and global integration affect many industries whose companies employ a major share of national capital and manpower, account for most of the value added in manufacturing and introduce most of the significant innovations. These industries manufacture such products as automobiles and trucks, electronic data processing equipment, nuclear reactors and electrical power systems, telecommunication equipment, aircraft, mechanical components (for instance, bearings or industrial motors), electronic components, chemicals and consumer durables. Many of these industries are related to national defense; all are intimately involved in national welfare.

Freer trade and lower growth make national responsiveness and multinational integration conflict more directly. Freer trade opened the opportunity for integration of operations within multinational companies; it became possible to serve a national market from a plant located in another, and, in turn, to develop an integrated production system serving a number of national markets from a number of foreign plants. Slower growth and the maturing of demand in many industries made the firms increasingly sensitive to cost savings and efficiency increases, in order to compete effectively for a stable market.

Slower growth, accompanied by rising unemployment and falling standards of living, often makes national governments more sensitive to location decisions by multinational companies. Countries are competing for jobs and investments. Lesser growth has prompted some governments to try to recoup via industrial policies the loss of control in their national economies that they fear freer trade and growing interdependence will bring. Such policies make discrepancies in factor markets all the greater, and therefore provide further incentives for MNCs to integrate their operations. More direct government interventions in industry structure often leads to direct negotiations between governments and companies. Governments often demand more responsiveness from major foreign companies operating on their soil at the very moment when the integration of their national operations into global networks removes such responsiveness from the purview of national subsidiary managers. Rather than on local accommodations, the result of negotiations between multinational firms and nation states is now dependent on their overall bargaining power.

The opportunity for a MNC to integrate the operation, or to increase the national responsiveness of a particular multinational business,* varies with three sets of variables:

1. The underlying economic and technical characteristics of the business, such as cost structures for various manufacturing scales and technologies of the various stages in the addition of value, its particular distribution set-ups, the cost of R & D, the sensitivity of costs to locations, etc.;
2. The particular set of host country conditions and government policies that this business is facing, worldwide; and
3. The competitive position of the business *vis-à-vis* national and multinational competitors.

The objective of this book is twofold. First, it analyzes the strategic choices open to multinational companies confronted with tensions between national responsiveness and multinational integration. As suggested above, the economic characteristics of an industry, the capabilities and policies of

---

* "Business" is taken here in the sense of a product or service, or set of related products and services, which share R & D manufacturing and distribution facilities or services, i.e., in the same sense as in the now familiar "strategic business unit" concept.

nation states, and the current competitive posture of the firm in the industry interact to structure the strategic choices open to the firm to compete in that industry.

Second, whatever the choice made in principle, it must be reflected in the structure and management process of the firm. The second objective of the book results from the issue of translating a desired strategic orientation into an actual management process. Two aspects complicate this issue.

First, any big MNC is intrinsically complex. It has multiple layers of managers and, in most cases, multiple businesses—it develops products, manufactures and sells them, and services them in multiple countries. The staggering complexity of the interaction of subunits within an integrated MNC can be grasped from the network of manufacturing interdependencies (transfer of products and knowledge) within IBM, presented in Fig. I.1. A choice in principle, be it national responsiveness or integration, or a mix of both, therefore, cannot be reflected in top management criteria only; it has to be embedded in a complex industrial and managerial structure so that the myriad choices made daily within the organization fall in line with

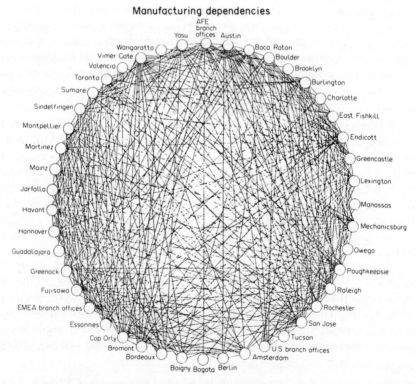

FIG. I.1   Manufacturing dependencies. IBM Corporation.

the chosen strategic orientation. In other words, in the large multinational company a strategic choice remains meaningless unless it is embedded into the management process that links executives from various functions, from various businesses and from various locations (in particular the head-quarters executives with those of the far-flung subsidiaries).

Second, and even more taxing, the choice between national responsiveness and global integration can seldom be of the "one or the other" variety. In most situations it is "how much of one and how much of the other". Therefore, responsiveness priorities cannot be allowed to drive out concern for integration and vice versa; some asymmetric balance has to be struck, leading to "more of one than of the other". Again, the complexity of the MNC means that such balance is necessarily embedded in managerial and administrative processes rather than merely decreed from the top.

One implication of the two aspects discussed briefly above is that there is an organizational cost to the management of complexity. Internalizing transactions to exploit better unique competitive advantages results in the added cost of building and maintaining the complex structure* and management processes that administer the internalized transactions—lack of internal control within such complex structures may also result in operating inefficiency and suboptimal choices.

An analysis of the choices between national responsiveness and multinational integration would be incomplete if no attention were devoted to the managerial costs of complex multinational operations and if no recommendations were sought on how to embody overall choices of strategic direction into the configuration and management of the network relationships linking the various subunits of the firm.

The second objective of this book, therefore, is to provide a managerial understanding of strategic choices rather than merely an analytical one. Such an understanding reintroduces the costs, constraints and capabilities of the administrative process into an analysis that could otherwise become far divorced from the organizational reality. In sum, the choice of strategy, and its successful implementation, are subject to an organizational capability constraint.

The greater its organizational capability, the more strategic options a firm can consider. While MNC managers can act to improve their bargaining power *vis-à-vis* host governments on their competitive position, their most direct leverage point remains to increase the strategic capability of their firms. By strategic capability we mean developing the administrative procedures and management processes that allow them to cope successfully with a wider range of strategic situations: differing industry characteristics, different forms of government intervention and extents of bargaining power, and different competitive situations.

*Economists would say "hierarchy", but this term can be misleading since MNCs are often characterized by multiple intricated hierarchies that constitute a so-called matrix structure.

The argument presented in this book draws on a series of industry analyses and detailed studies of individual companies carried out between 1976 and 1982.

Six major industries were analyzed in detail: automobiles, trucks, microelectronics, data processing equipment, telecommunications systems and heavy electrical engineering. All these industries are submitted to intense economic and competitive pressures for international integration: similarity of worldwide needs, economies of scale, and experience, intensity of research and development activities, cost pressures and intense competition for existing customers and new markets on a global scale are compelling forces in favor of global integration. All six industries are important to the national development and independence of host countries.*

A deliberately purposive sample was selected on economic and competitive variables. Industries were selected where economic and competitive factors would provide strong incentives for multinational firms to integrate their operations. Industries where the economic benefits of integration would be insignificant or negative (e.g., many prepared food products or service industries) were deliberately excluded.

Government importance as a customer for these industries varies greatly, from almost exclusive public sector sales in electrical equipment to almost none for automobiles. These six industries were chosen to maximize the differences in direct government control over their markets. There are also many such differences within each of these industries. Passenger cars are sold primarily to private customers, four-wheel drive vehicles mainly to the military. Telephone switching equipment is sold mostly to postal authorities, branch exchanges mainly to business users, and so forth. The selection of industries ensured that each industry would be narrow enough economically to be a single competitive arena and yet broad enough for its economic and political characteristics to be reflected in the strategies and organizations of the participating firms. A narrow economic definition was selected to ensure that firms identified as participants in the industry would compete for the same market with substitutable products, services and technologies. A broad industry definition, such as "non-electrical machinery", would not be meaningful economically; it encompasses a wide range of markets and firms and multiple competitive environments. A very narrow definition, such as "high intensity lamps", might not be significant strategically and organizationally. Major multinationals in the lamp business, such as Philips, or ITT or GTE-Sylvania, may not identify high-

---

* Industries such as oil and petrochemicals or steel may be considered as even more critical to national independence. They have not been considered in this study—nor have other resource-based industries—because they necessarily imply integrated multinational production systems from raw material sources through intermediates to end product. The sample was designed not to include industries for which raw material availability could be the determining location factor.

intensity lamps as a separate business with its own strategy and organization, independent from that of related businesses.

A second sample of industries was subsequently selected to provide an independent test of the tentative hypotheses developed in studying the first sample. It included television tubes and sets, agricultural tractors, aircraft engines, and civilian and military aircraft. The structure of each of these industries was analyzed from published documents and industry sources. The strategies followed by the various international competitors were identified and analyzed using published data and selective interviews.

For each of the first six industries the management processes of at least one multinational competitor following each type of strategy identified (international integration, national responsiveness, multifocal) was analyzed in detail. Cooperation was usually sought from several competitors following similar strategies, and one was ultimately selected. Between twelve and one hundred interviews were carried out in each of the companies selected for in-depth study. Internal documents such as product plans, investment requests, organization manuals, budget forms, etc., were also obtained and studied for most cases. Among the companies that generously cooperated for a detailed study were IBM, Ford and General Motors, Fiat, C2I-Honeywell Bull, Philips, Brown Boveri, Massey Ferguson,* LM Ericsson and General Telephone and Electronics. Several more companies on which detailed information was collected wish to remain anonymous. Interview data were cross-checked and referenced and a detailed research case was written on each company. Data on specific companies that appear in this book have all been cleared with the management of the company, unless the data draw on referenced published sources only.

I am well aware of the limitations and difficulties of this type of research. The factual richness of interview data cannot all be reduced into a few operational hypotheses or propositions and still be preserved. Detailed presentation of the various cases would have led to a book of unacceptable length and would have made tedious reading. I have made the deliberate choice in this book of a middle-ground solution: individual cases are referred to, but not presented in detail. Readers interested in the detail of specific companies and issues may turn to the cases that have been published.† All the arguments developed here have not been reduced to measurable variables and testable hypotheses, although a subset of propositions has been formally tested.

Chapters 1 and 2 outline the analytical framework and provide a general discussion of how the interaction between the economic characteristics of

---

* I am indebted to Peter Mathias, then doctoral student at Harvard Business School, for his study of Massey Ferguson.
† Except for those cases which have to remain confidential, references are made to this material throughout the book when appropriate.

an industry, the government policies that influence the industry, and the firms' competitive postures shape the strategic choices available to the firm. Chapter 1 assesses the relative benefits of alternative multinational strategies from an economic and competitive perspective. Chapter 2 complements this approach by taking host government concerns into account and develops an integrative framework to account for the interaction between competitive and political factors. Chapters 3, 4 and 5 present an application of the framework to three industries: automobiles, telecommunication switching equipment, and electronic data processing equipment and components respectively. These industries have been chosen because they provide three typical examples of generic market structures: global market competition in automobiles, nationally administered markets in telecommunications equipment, and mixed structure markets in electronic data processing, some market segments being open to international competition, other segments being protected nationally. Chapter 6 generalizes the applicability of the framework by analyzing data from the overall sample of industries and companies. Chapters 7, 8 and 9 draw the managerial implications of strategic choices by analyzing in detail the organizational, administrative and managerial issues faced in following various types of strategies. The concluding chapter proposes an approach to increase a firm's strategic capability.

Hoping to appeal to practising managers in MNCs, public policy-makers, students and educators, I have tried to make this book readable in style, avoiding theoretical abstractions and the complex language that provide only the trappings of objectivity and not the essence of it. My hope is that the framework outlined here should be helpful to managers formulating strategies and designing organizational structures and management systems for multinational businesses. The framework should also be helpful to government officials negotiating with multinational companies, particularly by pointing out how MNC strategic and organizational choices make the companies more or less amenable to one type of cooperation with host governments or another. This should help government officials in selecting which multinationals to negotiate with, given their policy objectives. Finally, students of the multinational company should find here a framework which integrates separate theories of the international business literature—industry analysis and oligopoly theory, theories of foreign direct investment, host country relationships, organizational design and management processes—into a managerial understanding of the multinational company.

References

1. See S. M. Hymer, *The International Operations of National Firms* (Cambridge, Massachusetts: M.I.T. Press, 1976), based on the author's 1960 Ph.D. thesis; Raymond Vernon, "International Trade in the Product Cycle", in *Quarterly Journal of Economics*, May 1966;

W. M. Gruber, R. Vernon and S. Mehta, "The R & D Factor in International Investment of U.S. Industries", in *Journal of Political Economy*, February 1967; and M. P. Claudon, *International Trade and Technology: Models of Dynamic Comparative Advantage* (Washington D.C.: University of America, 1977). For a summary of various theories explaining the growth of multinational enterprises see P. J. Buckley and M. Casson, *The Future of the Multinational Enterprise* (New York: Holmes and Meier, 1976).

2. See R. Vernon, "The Product Cycle Hypothesis in a New International Environment", *Oxford Bulletin of Economics and Statistics*, Vol. 41, No. 4, Nov. 1979, and R. Vernon and W. M. Davidson, "Foreign Production of Technology-intensive Products by U.S.-based Multinational Enterprises" (Boston: Harvard Business School Working Paper, HBS 79–5, 1979).

3. See J. H. Dunning, *International Production and the Multinational Enterprises* (London: George Allen & Unwin, 1981), chapter 2.

4. Among the many books which deal with the development of the Japanese in competition in international industries, some of the most informative are Y. Tsurumi, *The Japanese Are Coming* (Cambridge: Ballinger 1978), M. Y. Yoshino, *Japan's Multinational Enterprises* (Cambridge: Harvard University Press, 1976), and L. G. Franko, *Réplique Occidentale aux Multinationales Japonaises* (Paris, Presses Universitaires de France, 1983). For a broader background see J. P. Lehmann, *The Roots of Modern Japan* (London: Macmillan, 1981).

5. J. H. Dunning and R. D. Pearce, *The World's Largest Enterprises* (Farnborough: Gower, 1981).

6. For evidence on integration as a source of MNC bargaining strength, in the context of Latin America, see N. Fagre and L. T. Wells (Jr), "Bargaining Power of Multinationals and Host Governments", in *Journal of International Business Studies*, Vol. 3.2, Fall 1982.

1

Industry Characteristics and Strategic Choices

Confronted with tensions between needs for integration and needs for national responsiveness, multinational companies can behave in any of several ways. Some integrate their operations across borders, others let their subsidiaries in various countries behave almost as if they were national companies. *Multinational integration* and *national responsiveness* constitute generic choices which express a clear strategy, placing global efficiency over national attention to one set of priorities—integration or responsiveness—one strategy usually remains preferred to the other, and patterns of strategic decisions reflect such preference over time. Some companies, however, try to *avoid developing a clear pattern of preference* for national responsiveness or worldwide integration, but attempt to *combine elements of both in an ad hoc way*. National responsiveness and integration priorities are traded-off flexibly. The strategies of such companies can be labeled *multifocal*.

One strategy or another is more or less attractive as a function of the underlying economic characteristics of the industry in which it is implemented, of the extent and form of government intervention into that industry, and of the competitive posture of the firm. In this chapter the generic types of multinational strategies are defined and their applicability as a function of the economic characteristics of an industry are analyzed. In the next chapter the interaction between industry structure, host government intervention and competitive postures are analyzed.

The Multinational Business Strategies Defined
Multinational Integration

Multinational integration is defined as the specialization of plants across borders into an integrated multinational production/distribution network. Integration may involve product or process specialization. In a product specialization approach, instead of producing complete product ranges to satisfy the needs of each national market, the MNC manufactures in each country only part of a common multinational product range, but for the global market. Each national subsidiary distributes the complete product range but procures that substantial portion of the product range it does not produce from sister national subsidiaries. The narrow segment of the product range it does produce it supplies to all other subsidiaries. Process specialization in a multistage manufacturing process involves the specialization of plants by stages in a product's manufacturing process. Most typical of process specification was the farming-out, first to "border plants" in Mexico, then to the Far East, of circuits finishing and bonding— a labor-intensive operation—by U.S. semiconductor manufacturers. The automobile industry has also widely practiced both process and product specialization, leading to regional or global integration, as can be illustrated with the evolution of Ford's operations in Europe.

Ford of Europe's Fiesta project illustrates particularly well Ford's strategy of integration. Figure 1.1 shows how the total Fiesta production capacity of 2650 units per day (as of 1977) was shared—both for components and end products—among several European countries. Various considerations had guided the assignment of tasks to the various subsidiaries. Cars were assembled in Spain, not only because the government made it a condition of entry to the Spanish market, but also because assembly labor costs in Spain were about half that of Germany, where Ford's other major assembly center in continental Europe was located. Spain therefore provided a low-cost manufacturing location for exports to Italy and France. Engines were manufactured in Spain because of local content regulations which required 65% of the value added to be created locally, given Ford's export volumes.[1] The Bordeaux component plant in France had been expanded because of strong pressures from the French government for an increase in value added in France, given Ford's significant sales in that country. Lower costs also made expansion in France more attractive than in Germany. A comparable mix of economic and political reasons led to the choices affecting Germany and Great Britain. An analysis of IBM's integrated manufacturing network in Europe would show comparable patterns and reasons for specific location choices. In a similar fashion, many other MNCs integrated their European operations in the 1970s.[2]

The main benefit of integration is seen by MNC managers as the opportunity to reduce costs. Several factors usually contribute to lower costs. Although it is difficult to assess the benefits of integration in general, a close look at another example—the Industrial Vehicle Corporation (IVECO)—shows many of them. IVECO was an integration venture between Fiat's commercial vehicle activities in Italy (known as VISpA), the Magirus truck division of Klockner Humboldt Deutz in Germany, and Fiat's commercial vehicle subsidiary in France, UNIC. After a legal and financial merger of the three entities, actual integration started in 1975, with the ambition to simplify the product range and increase manufactur-

electrophoresis anticorrosion surface treatment. Parts and components were allocated to categories according to their needed production volume (short runs below 25 units per day, medium runs of 50 to 250 units per day, and long runs over 300 units per day).

The proven Fiat expertise in automation and process engineering had been applied to determine the best production methods for various parts at various volumes. In short-run production, numerical control machines were used; in medium- and long-run production, computer-controlled transfer machines were introduced. The rationalization plan had thus been accompanied by substantial capital investment programs that were to continue until 1982, at which time IVECO expected to have the most modern, most efficient set of manufacturing facilities in Europe. *In toto*, almost $1 billion was devoted to new investments between 1975 and 1982.

Production integration was complemented by product line simplification. A common product range was engineered with more truck types made from fewer components. Table 1.1 portrays the decrease in the number of distinct types.

TABLE 1.1   *Evolution of Number of Basic Major Components for the IVECO Product Range*

	1969	1972-73	1978–80
Engines: water cooled	31	20	13
(air cooled)*	(6)	(6)	(6)
Gearboxes	18	14	(not comparable)†
Rear axles	19	18	13‡
Front axles	15	13	12‡
Cabs	16	14	12‡

*Magirus only, engines purchased from Klockner Humbolt Deutz.
 Modular engine construction around a single basic type.
†Magirus purchases gearboxes and transmissions from the outside and has numerous types for all-wheel-drive vehicles made in small numbers.
‡Including Magirus types, whereas 1969 and 1972-73 figures exclude them; straight comparison of numbers across columns thus does not portray full extent of rationalization
Source: IVECO.

Between 1975 and 1978 labor productivity increased by 30% at VISpA, 19% at Magirus and 70% at UNIC. Further increases of 20%, 14% and 15% respectively, were achieved between 1978 and 1982.

In all cases, integration strategies result in centralized management, since key decisions affecting operations in one country—such as production programming, sales volumes, changes in production processes, plant expansion or reduction, new product introductions and acquisitions—also affect other countries directly. Each subsidiary plays a well-defined part in the integrated multinational system, particularly for manufacturing, engineering and research and development. Headquarter coordination and control of subsidiary activities are considerable. Beyond fulfilling their roles in the system, subsidiary managers obviously provide input—in the form of data, analysis, suggestions and feedback—into the major decisions affecting their subsidiaries, but the decisions are not theirs. Decisions are taken from the perspective of overall systemwide optimization, subject to economic and political constraints. Therefore, some decisions may be detrimental to individual subsidiaries taken in isolation and obviously differ from the decisions that an independent national firm would have taken.

National Responsiveness

Contrary to the strategies of integration, national responsiveness allows the subsidiaries to behave as if they were national companies. Subsidiaries are thus free to respond to host governments' demands as their managers see fit; MNC headquarters seldom intervene in the decisions made by their national subsidiaries. Typically, subsidiaries manufacture a relatively complete product range in each country so that intersubsidiary trade is not significant. In a national responsiveness strategy, there are few pressures on the subsidiaries to maximize economic efficiency for the MNC as a whole. Optimization takes place locally, in each subsidiary.

The affiliation of a subsidiary to a multinational company is bound to make it different from a national company, however, even with no manufacturing integration, intersubsidiary trade or centralized management. For instance, even when subsidiaries are independent profit centers with full autonomy over national price and product decisions, the multinational can still offset gains and losses among subsidiaries. Therefore, its subsidiaries may be willing to take higher risks (for potentially higher returns) than a typical national firm.[3] Furthermore, headquarters still build the knowhow and assume the risk sharing that provide a competitive advantage to their subsidiaries over national firms. First, financial risks may be shared, financing coordinated and treasury functions jointly managed among subsidiaries. Second, a MNC can coordinate R & D efforts among subsidiaries, avoid duplications and spread R & D cost amortization over the larger volume generated by multiple national markets. A domestic national competitor having to amortize comparable costs on a smaller volume is at a disadvantage. Third, multinationals can afford to maintain a wider export network than can most national competitors. The sheer size of the MNC's operation, compared to that of a national company, may justify the maintenance of effective well-staffed export subsidiaries, regional offices, local agents and representatives, competent service teams, training staffs and installation experts. This alone could increase the overall sales of the MNC on the world export markets. Further, the availability of several alternate sources for similar equipment within the same multinational company is a major advantage for sales to many Third World and Eastern Europe markets. Bilateral trade agreements most often guide sales to these markets, and sales are conditioned by financing arrangements. It is clear that since nationally responsive MNCs can supply essentially similar goods from alternate sources located in different countries, they are in a better position to take advantage of such bilateral trade agreements and financing arrangements than either national companies or integrated MNCs.

Provided they achieve a measure of central control in pricing and marketing policies, and can differentiate their policies from country to country, nationally responsive MNCs can also increase their competitive resilience. Rather than competing independently in each national market, MNCs may coordinate their actions to maximize competitive impact. Goodyear, for example, could react to Michelin's entry into the U.S. tire market by competing more aggressively in Europe, and particularly in France, where Michelin was dominant, so as to deprive Michelin of the financial resources needed in its effort to gain a large share of the U.S. market, Goodyear's largest and most profitable market. Had Goodyear fought back primarily in the United States, it might have hurt itself more than Michelin.[4] National firms which cannot retaliate in their competitor's home markets are therefore put at a competitive disadvantage over nationally responsive MNCs, provided the latter can coordinate policies among their subsidiaries so as to enhance the competitive posture of the whole company, not only of each subsidiary independently. Global competition therefore limits the full extent of autonomous national responsiveness by the individual subsidiaries.

MNCs can also gather and exploit data on supplies and purchasing opportunities worldwide, at a lower cost than national firms, and use their total size to gain bargaining power against suppliers. Finally, since it has comparable operations in different countries, the nationally responsive MNC can transfer skills between subsidiaries, particularly for plant process engineering and for marketing. Moreover, the multiplicity of similar operations broadening the corporate experience is likely to give the MNC a distinct advantage over firms restricted to one country.

National responsiveness, therefore, does not eliminate a need for headquarter coordination of selected tasks—financing, R & D, export sales, pricing, purchasing, process engineering and marketing. Long-term success of the company over purely national competitors is rooted in this ability to exploit common capabilities and proprietary knowledge in multiple national markets, and often to coordinate its competitive actions across boundaries.[5]

Multifocal Strategies

Some firms do not choose between the benefits of integration and the flexibility of national responsiveness. By selecting a *multifocal strategy* they avoid becoming locked into a particular choice and seek both the benefits of integration and the flexibility of responsiveness. In such firms the relative merits of responsiveness and integration are given due consideration for each major decision. Some *ad hoc* solution emerges from the policy discussions of conflicting priorities implicit in that particular decision. A multifocal strategy tries to provide something for everyone.

The firm is willing to maintain production and R & D facilities in each market it serves, and to enter into collaboration with local firms or host governments as called for by local conditions. Yet a multifocal strategy still pursues opportunities for integration to the extent permitted by the variety of local arrangements made to adapt best to market conditions and to obtain host government support. The management of a firm following a multifocal strategy recognizes that sacrifices of optimal efficiency have to be made in order to sustain market access in many countries critical to its global strategy, each country with its particular market needs, and/or host government priorities.

Without an overriding priority it becomes necessary to shift priorities in decision making rapidly, from one country to another, from one decision to the next. Therefore, an ability to consider issues from multiple points of view must be built into the organization. In some cases important decisions are few enough to allow top management to decide in substance—based on conflicting inputs—and ensure they follow a consistent pattern. Swedish telecommunication equipment maker LM Ericsson, for instance, was a one-industry company which faced relatively infrequent critical decisions and whose top management was thoroughly familiar with the products, technologies and competitive conditions.[6]

Often, however, it is difficult for top management to make all key decisions wisely. The very nature of the constraints brought by host governments makes the central determination of an acceptable trade-off difficult, and not amenable to easy analysis. Evolving demands that become fully revealed only through close interaction with the host government can hardly be dealt with centrally. A sense for these and, perhaps, some measure of influence over their formulation, can only be acquired by direct ongoing contacts with host government officials, the type of contacts most easily developed by nationally responsive subsidiaries. Yet the advantages of integration cannot be ignored, since a multifocal strategy represents an attempt to respond to such concerns without renouncing opportunities for integration. The choice of responses implies some involvement by corporate executives and product division managers. Yet corporate managers on their own can seldom confirm or challenge the information provided by subsidiary managers. When a national subsidiary manager claims that his plans rest on the words of local intermediaries or on his relationships with government officials, it is difficult for other managers to determine the soundness of his assumptions. Similarly, when a subsidiary manager complains that a decision made at the corporate or worldwide product group level is going to jeopardize his relationships with the local customers, there is no way of knowing whether he is right. Discrepancies between governments' public logic and rhetoric and the facts, or the reality of policy, make it even more difficult for corporate or regional managers to understand the situation.

Multifocal strategies, because they aim at a constantly fluctuating balance between the imperatives, create an ambiguous form of management. They institutionalize constant tensions within the organization between the drive for economic success, based on a clear strategy, and the need to consider major uncertainties springing from host governments. When decisions are numerous and diverse, they must be delegated, with country managers and worldwide managers sharing in their making. Conditions which lead to effective decision making, or prevent it, in multifocal organizations can be created by top management, as will be analyzed in Chapter 9.

Whether multinational managers opt for integration or responsiveness, or try to combine both into a multifocal strategy, hinges partly on the economic characteristics of the industries in which they compete.

Industry, Economics and Multinational Business Strategies

Industry economics characteristics can make multinational integration, national responsiveness or multifocal strategies more or less attractive to multinational companies. Economies of scale, experience, and location, the basis for product differentiation, product and process technology, the maintenance of export and distribution channels controlled by the firm, and the firm's access to capital, are most critical in making a strategy attractive. This list is not surprising; this is the basis for oligopolistic competitive advantages, and theories of foreign investment tell us that multinational companies have been successful largely to the extent they exploited these advantages from country to country.[7] However, some of these advantages apply only via integration, whereas others are based on multinationality, irrespective of integration.

*Economies of Scale**

MNCs following a strategy of integration can best benefit from econo-

---

*Economies of scale, experience and location are usually at work in some combination. The actual production. costs for a particular product are thus a resultant of their combined influence. Though some generalizations are possible as to the likely direction of their impact on the relative cost positions of firms following different strategies, an assessment of actual cost differences needs a careful study of specific firms in an industry.

mies of scale in production. By specializing their plants across borders, they can achieve very large production volume at a single site for a particular product or component. National companies are likely to have a smaller overall market. They may not achieve similar economies of scale, although they too produce in a single location.

Several studies document the less than optimal scale of most manufacturers in Europe—national and multinational—as well as the potential cost savings offered by integration of production.[8] Automobile manufacturers, for example, fall short of exploiting all available economies of scale.[9] Similar conclusions have been reached about such different industries as petrochemicals, television tubes, electrical generators, and farm equipment.[10] In petrochemicals, for instance, Pomper showed that integration could save 20% on the manufacturing costs of a typical multinational firm.[11] Recent developments in manufacturing automation may, however, limit, and even reverse, the general trend toward growing economies of scale. Evidence from the machinery and automobile industry suggest that the flexibility offered by computer-assisted manufacturing can be obtained at a relatively low added cost, leading many manufacturers to forgo the marginally decreasing returns of higher scale in favor of flexibility and versatility in their manufacturing operation. Similarly, in the chemical industry, smaller scale more versatile production methods may become feasible in the near future. Substantial investment costs, training requirements and social consequences of computer-assisted flexible manufacturing may, however, limit the speed with which new manufacturing methods are adopted.

Where economies of scale are significant, multinationals following a strategy of national responsiveness often find themselves at an even greater disadvantage, compared to integrated multinationals, than national companies. They make a given product or component in many national subsidiaries in much smaller quantities than the large single plant of an integrated MNC. Their subsidiaries are also sometimes smaller than national companies, particularly in continental Europe (in many other countries, available evidence suggests that foreign subsidiaries are larger than their domestic competitors).[12] Companies following a multifocal strategy fall somewhere between integrated and nationally responsive MNCs according to the extent to which they integrate their operations.

The specific cost disadvantage incurred by a firm will vary with the positions of competitors in different national markets. A dominant national supplier in a very large national market may enjoy a better cost position than a small integrated MNC with lower overall sales volumes scattered in a number of countries. Yet, in most cases, the presence of substantial economies of scale in an industry is likely to benefit integrated MNCs most and nonintegrated ones least, with large developed countries' national suppliers falling between these two extreme positions.*

Economies of scale in distribution or servicing—particularly when service speed is critical to users—on the contrary tend to favor national or even local firms with high local market shares justifying high service density and intensive distribution. In such cases integrated manufacturing firms may delegate sales and service to strong dense local dealers, as do suppliers of trucks and earth-moving equipment.

Economies of Experience

Assuming that manufacturing operations are efficient and well managed, the average unit cost of a product to a company usually falls by a constant percentage each time its total historical cumulative production volume doubles.† This effect is known as economies of experience. Cost decreases for each doubling of cumulative volume typically range from 15% to 25%, but vary with the industry.[13] Some economies of experience are location specific. When a given work force becomes more productive over time, production in a different location with a new work force may derive little benefit from its experience. Other location-specific factors, such as the breaking-in of new manufacturing equipment, may account for a large part of the total experience effect.

Some economies of experience may be transferred within a company from plant to plant, however. For example, the tenth subsidiary starting to manufacture a given product in a nationally responsive MNC usually starts with an initial unit cost much lower than that of the first subsidiary. Its unit costs, at a similar cumulative volume manufactured locally, are also likely to be much lower than that of an independent national competitor. Much of the success of Philips in consumer products in Europe, before the development of the EEC, was based on the firm's ability to replicate efficiently organized plants from country to country. Economies of experience are thus likely to benefit integrated MNCs most, but also to give some advantage to nationally responsive ones over purely national competitors, unless the national competitors are much larger than the MNC subsidiaries.

---

*It is further assumed here that each firm successfully achieves the economies of scale made possible by its competitive posture. This assumption is not necessarily warranted. British Leyland, in the auto industry, for instance, for long had its production scattered among over thirty plants in the United Kingdom, and was far from fully exploiting its potential for economies of scale. Many national companies resulting from the forced merger of smaller firms have failed to exploit economies of scale made possible by the merger, hamstrung with social problems (e.g., plants which could not be closed or converted) or plagued by poor management (e.g., political operators rather than professional managers).

† This applies only to the value added to the product within the firms, costs of components and distribution costs may vary independently.

Economies of Location

Factor cost differences among countries also favor integrated MNCs over national companies of nationally responsive MNCs active in high factor cost countries. Integrated MNCs can locate factor intensive operations in low factor cost countries, such as semiconductor assembly and packaging operations in South East Asia. Transfers within multinational companies' production networks accounted for 70% of Singapore's 1970 exports. Figures for other Asian countries were lower, but still often between 10% and 20%.[14] Most Far Eastern countries had set up various incentives to attract integrated MNCs; for instance, duty-free industrial sites known as "Free Processing Zones".[15] In some cases the home countries of MNCs also had taken special measures to facilitate integration; for instance, the United States in favor of the electronics industry. Again, factory automation decreases the location of advantage of integrated MNCs, since labor cost differences become less significant—and the education and skills of available labor more important.

Product Differentiation

Product differentiation can take place internationally along three dimensions. For some products, differentiation may take place between similar customers across borders. Such product differentiation often results from the need for a large number of subtypes. Among consumer goods, a striking example is that of the ski industry: the homogenous worldwide market is separated into a series of multinational segments according to the types of skiing, the proficiency and size of the skier, and the price brackets. In such circumstances, pooling demand from several national markets and building a large plant in one country to manufacture some subtypes efficiently results in substantial savings, assuming strong economies of scale and experience. Integration strategies thus have the better pay-off.

Differentiation is also sometimes created by skillful advertising and marketing, particularly for some consumer goods. Where marketing approaches and product differentiation methods can be made common to several national markets, marketing knowledge and experience, as well as heavily advertised brands, can be transferred from country to country. For many consumer products, however, intrinsic product differentiation between countries can make integration of manufacturing unattractive: food companies, for instance, seldom integrate their operations.[16]

Those which tried met with little success; for such products as soups, sauces, biscuits, and prepared food, national taste and cooking habits differences call for national responsiveness. Nationally responsive MNCs, however, can transfer their marketing expertise from country to country and, in some cases, exploit worldwide brands—Nestlé's "Nescafé" is a striking example, with a similar brand used worldwide and many different national tastes. Furthermore, economies of scale in production seldom outweigh added transportation costs—given a high bulk to price ratio—in the food industry.

Integration is possible when staple goods are involved (e.g., fruit juices) or when differentiated products are marketed through extensive advertising (e.g., breakfast cereals in Europe). In some cases advertising is used to justify integration and turn it into a strength. Heineken, for instance, prides itself in the U.S. market to offer an imported product brewed in Holland, whereas some competitors—such as Löwenbrau—have licensed their products to U.S breweries. This image of imported products allows Heineken to obtain a price premium that more than offsets the added cost of shipping beer across the Atlantic.[17]

Integration is also possible when the same product is marketed in different ways in different countries, and differentiation can be achieved via features and product positioning. Japanese copier and camera manufacturers, for instance, have often sold their products in different ways in various countries and sometimes under several brands (e.g., their own and local distributors' brands). They have also positioned the same product differently according to the characteristics of each national market.

Finally, in some products, intensive interaction is needed with local customers whose needs are specific. National companies are then at an advantage, as is found in some speciality food products, residential construction, or in schoolbook publishing. Multinationals seldom enjoy a large share of these sectors.

Technology

Overall, high technology intensity (measured by the percentage of the company's revenues allocated to R & D expenses) favors MNCs that can spread their R & D expenses over larger production volume than smaller national firms. Though inventions seldom take place in MNCs, these firms account for a large share of innovations—the application of new inventions to products and processes—and play a key role in the diffusion of such innovations.[18] Tentative evidence also suggests that R & D efforts do contribute decisively to international success, and that, therefore, there is a feedback effect between technological intensity and multinationality that tends, over time, to increase the competitive advantage of a firm.[19]

Furthermore, technology usually can be safely exploited only via direct investments which preserve its proprietary nature. Beyond its importance in contributing to the multinationality of major firms, technology also interacts with scale and experience to favor integrated multinational companies. First, integration may provide a volume sufficient to adopt intrinsically more efficient productive processes. When SKF integrated its

European operations, for instance, it could shift from batch production to continuous automated production of bearings, at great savings.[20] Second, changes in product technology have often increased the efficient scale of production. Electrical power generators provide an example. Over the years, since the 1920s, when their design had been perfected, electrical power generators increased in size incrementally and gained in efficiency regularly. Higher unit power had been obtained through incremental size increases by adding compressor and turbine stages, a process that could be carried out in existing plants of electrical equipment suppliers. By the late 1960s, however, nuclear reactors started to replace conventional fossil fuel boilers as the generators' steam supply sources. The efficient size of these reactors corresponds to an output of 1000 or more Megawatts (MWe), substantially more than the 600 MWe typical of the most recent fossil fuel powered generators. Doubling turbogenerator unit power was not feasible, except by reducing the rotating speed from 3000 rpm to 1800 or 1500 rpm. To generate the same power slower turning generators had to be much larger. Existing manufacturers' yards could not handle the larger turbogenerators. Further, the overall turbogenerator market would be smaller in units, and the minimum manufacturing plant's efficient size (measured in yearly MWe capacity output) much higher.[21] In such technical evolutions, the industry economics became increasingly favorable to the integrated MNCs to the detriment of other types of competitors.

Export Channels and Intensity of Selling Task

Large MNCs can spread the large fixed costs of maintaining extensive export channels over a larger volume. In contrast, unable to afford its own sales network, a smaller national firm would have to resort to independent agents and importers, with lesser control on the distribution of its products and probably higher distribution costs and weaker marketing efforts. Nationally responsive MNCs also benefit from export contract allocation flexibility that can make access to Third World and socialist countries much easier. They can supply similar products from several countries and take advantage of trade agreements, favorable financing and cultural and diplomatic ties.

The nature of the selling task and the structure of distribution channels may also confer an advantage to one or another type of firm. Easy to penetrate distribution channels (e.g., U.S. mass merchandisers) make integration strategies more feasible, while control of distribution by manufacturers (e.g., the consumer electronics stores in Japan) limits the potential of such strategies. When no permanent distribution channels are in place (e.g., selling aircraft to airlines or electrical power stations to developing countries), national firms can be more successful at competing against multinationals. On the contrary, when selling implies intensive interaction with fragmented customers at the local level—or/and intensive servicing of dispersed equipment—multinational competitors may be at a disadvantage *vis-à-vis* well-entrenched local firms. In the elevator industry, for example, the segment of large fast elevators for high towers is much easier to penetrate for a multinational than that of the small slow elevators for small residential or office buildings. The first segment is concentrated, with large contracts negotiated by sophisticated professional customers, and the installations are often large enough to justify stationing or training people for on-site maintenance. Conversely, the market for small elevators is fragmented among contractors, local housing authorities and town officials, and servicing requires a field force, the efficiency of which is dependent on the level of market share at the regional level.

Control of distribution channels is also essential for the MNC to foster its competitive position, since only owned distribution can guarantee that competitive actions can be coordinated among countries, and that actions that temporarily impinge on the results in one or another national market can be taken without conflict of interest with third parties or distributing partners.

Access to Capital

MNCs may have a lower cost of capital than local national companies, since international lenders may desire to hold debts denominated in the currency of MNCs' home countries rather than that of host countries. Multinational diversification may also be valued by some investors.[22] In that case, nonintegrated MNCs are at somewhat of an advantage over integrated ones, other things being equal: their autonomous subsidiaries represent more of a genuine diversification and the stability of their earnings is less affected by shifts in exchange rates than that of integrated MNCs.[23]

Table 1.2 below summarizes this section's argument by showing how the industry economic characteristics described above push multinational companies toward integration or responsiveness. Also mentioned in Table 1.2 is the relative advantage of nationally responsive firms *vis-à-vis* purely national firms. The relative weight to be given to the factors analyzed above and shown in Table 1.2 depends on their contribution to the value added in the business and on their potential effect in discriminating between competitors. Various stages in the value creation process, from research to after-sales service, may both contribute quite differently to the full product cost, and also be more (or less) sensitive to the factors analyzed above. The most important factors, in selecting a strategy of integration or one of responsiveness in managing an international business, are those which affect the value-added structure significantly and differentially according to what type of strategy is followed. While the differential impact can be

TABLE 1.2 *Impact of industry structure characteristics on the choice of the strategy for multinational businesses*

Industry characteristics	Integrated multinationals	Nationally responsive multinationals	National companies
1. Economies of scale	Very favorable when M.E.S. exceeds size of individual national markets.	Same as for national companies, but add vulnerability to forced merger of subsidiaries into national champions.	Unfavorable, except when low enough to be fully exploited within national market
2. Economies of experience			
– location specific	very favorable, large plants	unfavorable	unfavorable
– firm specific	favorable	favorable (replication capability)	unfavorable
3. Economies of location	favorable (flexibility to locate in low factor cost areas)	unfavorable	unfavorable (unless country well endowed with cheap production factors)
4. Product Differentiation			
– by country	Very unfavorable (diversity among countries)	Favourable (different homogeneous national markets)	favorable
– by customer sets and product types	favorable (similar segments in different countries)	unfavorable (heterogeneous national markets)	unfavorable
– by both country and customer set	unfavourable	unfavorable (fragmented markets)	favorable (fragmented markets)

summarized as in Table 1.2, the absolute impact depends on the particular value-added structure of a business and, hence, is situational.

Conclusion: Economic and Competitive Determinants of Integration

The competitive advantages of integrated and nonintegrated MNCs over national firms are of a different nature. Most advantages of nonintegrated firms are knowledge-based: superior technology, worldwide scanning capabilities for low cost purchases and for markets, industrial experience and marketing expertise to be replicated from country to country and management knowhow. All these constitute intangible assets that the MNC can transfer from country to country at a low cost but that national companies would find extremely costly to acquire or develop independently.

Integrated MNCs benefit from the same assets. They also benefit from the more usual advantages of the large firm with specialized branch plants.[24] In particular, absolute scale of production can be made higher by pooling demand from various national markets. Furthermore, integrated MNCs can thrive on the imperfection of the international market for production factors.[25] Labor costs vary more internationally than domestically (e.g., the labor cost difference is greater between Michigan and Sri Lanka than between Michigan and Alabama). Capital costs may also vary from country to country, particularly as some countries subsidize foreign investments. In fact, in their rivalry to attract MNCs or develop their own industry, national governments add to the imperfections of factor markets by general policies (e.g., undervalued currencies or advantageous tax rates) and by specific interventions (e.g., grants to foreign investors or research contracts to cooperating MNCs).

Nationally responsive MNCs, however, benefit from a series of advantages not equally available to integrated ones. They can more flexibly negotiate with host governments to reach a wide range of compromises, whereas the opportunties for cooperation between integrated MNCs and their host governments are often more limited in scope, as will be discussed in detail in Chapter 2. Less integrated MNCs are also less vulnerable to political and financial disturbances, since they usually supply the same products from multiple geographic locations, each producing a range of products; and are also less dependent on the evolution of exchange rates between sourcing locations and users' markets than integrated firms.

The relative importance of the various factors which allow MNCs to build monopoly power, obviously changes from industry to industry and, therefore, competitive advantage will accrue to one type of firm or another in different industries. The nature of demand and the cost structure in an industry are the major determinants of the relative importance of various sources of competitive advantage. Furthermore, in the same industry over time, the most critical competitive factors are likely to change, and therefore confer an advantage to firms following one type of strategy or another. Let us first consider static differences between industries, and then the likely dynamic evolution of an industry structure over time.

MNCs, integrated or not, strive on high technology: the MNC can spread its R & D costs over several national markets and therefore have lower R & D expenses per unit of production, compared to a smaller national firm. Many researchers have pointed to the strong link between technology-intensive industries and strong MNC presence in those industries.[26] Similarly, MNCs thrive on other sources of product differentiation such as strong brands and intense advertising. Many studies have pointed to the correlation between marketing intensity and the presence of MNCs in an industry.[27]

To these factors integrated MNCs add cost sensitivity to scale and capital-intensity. Integrated MNCs, therefore, are likely to be present in industries where manufacturing represents the major cost of product and whose manufacturing process is amenable to low-cost high-volume operations, such as ball bearings or motor cars. Furthermore, integration most often assumes a homogenous worldwide—or at least regional—demand for similar products. Prices and distribution channels can vary widely, however.

Therefore, not all industries in which there is a significant multinational presence are affected to a similar extent by integration forces. In many industries strong differences between geographical markets, extensive product differentiation and well-segmented customer groups lead integrated and nonintegrated multinationals to compete in a differentiated way. Integrated ones provide low cost production through their efficient production systems; nonintegrated ones show superior adaptive flexibility; and they capture different market segments. In the European home appliance industry, for instance, some firms pursue an integration strategy designed to achieve low costs (e.g., Philips, Merloni), whereas others develop differentiated products and sell them at a higher price (e.g., Siemens, Miele). By acquiring reputable national brands and integrating manufacturing Europewide, Electrolux tries to achieve both.

In many cases, geographical differentiation is combined with market segmentation, as we see in the book publishing industry where integrated MNCs and local firms coexist in the industry. There is a small overall market for art books, little national differentiation, and significant expenses such as research, photography, and reproduction common to editions in several languages. Printing and binding costs and quality also differ greatly from country to country. In art books, multinational integration strategies prevail. The art book segment of the publishing industry is entirely different from high-school textbooks, in which there is complete differentiation across boundaries, no joint expenses, and wide national markets. In school books, autonomous national companies prevail. Similarly, in the drug industry, some product segments are dominated by integrated companies, others by nationally responsive ones, still others by independent national companies, according to product differentiation and market segmentation. Many MNCs are led towards complex multifocal strategies.[28]

There are, therefore, industries where national firms, nonintegrated and integrated MNCs coexist, serving different market segments from a different competitive posture.[29] Customers in different market segments have sufficiently different purchasing priorities to allow firms following multiple strategies to coexist. Furthermore, in some industries the most efficient multinational firm may create a price umbrella under which many less than optimal companies may survive, making lower profits than the most efficient firm. This may help explain the widely-observed high profitability of MNC subsidiaries compared to local firms.[30] Specific evidence gathered in this research suggests that both in the computer industry and in the telecommunication switching business such price umbrellas existed at least until the late 1970s.

Finally, some industries are unlikely to be populated by MNCs, particularly when needed skills are hardly transferable from country to country, when intensive interaction with nationally differentiated customers is required, when a large part of the total costs have to be incurred locally, when technologies are widely available or nationally differentiated, and when economies of scale are insignificant compared to national market sizes. Residential housing, for instance, fits that model and is unlikely to be quickly penetrated by multinational firms. What multinational presence there is in that business is based more on financing land development and introducing suburban development management and marketing (e.g., such as "Levitt towns") in multiple countries than on the actual construction of houses itself.

Moving to more dynamic aspects, it is obvious that except in resource-based activities few companies, if any, started as integrated multinationals, few industries as global industries, and—at least until quite recently—few products were introduced globally. It is, therefore, interesting to consider not only the static advantage characteristics confer to one strategy or another, but also to understand what may trigger the evolution of an industry toward global competition and the choice of integration strategies by most industry participants.

The most widely recognized dynamic model of the evolution of an international industry is the "product life cycle" concept developed by R. Vernon.[31] It postulates that demand for a given product moves from an innovating country (usually the United States, with a large well-developed solvable market for consumer and industrial goods and large innovative firms with the technical and financial resources needed to introduce and market new products) to other countries over time as they develop, and that the location of manufacturing follows the move of demand with some lag.

Higher demand growth and lower manufacturing costs in the imitating countries allows them to capture the competitive advantage from the innovating country. Therefore, the innovating country moves from an early position of exporter to that of importer. Over the decades successive layers of newly industrialized countries capture the competitive advantage for the product. Whereas, early on, the product was a high technology item the development and sale of which required intensive interactions with customers, and the local servicing of which was critical, as the product matures lower manufacturing costs (generating lower prices and greater demand) become the critical competitive variable and process innovation prevails over product innovation.[32] Better product reliability reduces the need for intensive local servicing, and users' familiarity that for active selling. The product thus becomes amenable to mass distribution via distant channels.

This product life cycle model has been widely used to explain the internationalization of different industries, particularly in the electronics field.[33] The emergence of multinational companies in non-resource based industries has also been explained from this model. As demand for a product moves from country to country, the innovating firm first supplies such demand from its domestic plant via export. Threats of entry by other competitors, trade barriers and national demands for local production, or the concern to avoid the cost of distant shipments, or the opportunity to produce at a lower cost, lead to a perceived need to start production in the importing countries. Given the uncertainties and risk of trading technology, the innovating firm is likely to initiate production locally by itself, rather than licence a local firm. Over time, it therefore develops into a MNC.[34]

Why does it then integrate operations?

First, free trade made integration feasible, as a strategic option. Free trade alone seldom led to integration, however.[35]

In some cases, vision may lead to integration. In the elevator industry, for example, according to the disguised case of DAAG, one manager in one company had the vision to recognize that he could change the nature of his industry from national and fragmented to European and integrated, and set out to build a competitive advantage for his firm based on early integration.[36]

Most often, however, integration seems to have been a response to competitive pressures. As a product matures internationally, its technology becomes more easily available and its demand more homogeneous, and efficient producers based in low-cost countries shift the basis of competition toward low price. When price competition dominates, the possible competitive advantage of the MNC shifts from knowledge-based assets to access to more end product and production factor markets than national firms. To increase production volume in each location, and exploit factor cost differences, and therefore defend its competitive posture, the MNC integrates its operations.

The convergence between major world markets has provided a further impetus to integration. It is first a convergence in time: the income distributions in North America, Europe and Japan are getting closer, generating simultaneous rather than sequential market development for consumer goods in the United States, Europe and Japan, as witnessed, for example, by home video systems markets. It is also a convergence of consumers' tastes and habits, in which markets converge to similar products and the basis for product differentiation shift from national differences to worldwide consumer groups. A current example is that of the automobile industry whose markets in Europe, the United States and Japan are increasingly similar, in terms of which product characteristics they value and can afford. Although differences remain in penetration rates (e.g., video recorders) or in segment size (e.g., cars and cameras) between countries, and therefore market sizes are not directly in proportion with population, the same products can be sold in all simultaneously.

The consolidation of distribution channels into large mass merchandising outfits also facilitates the penetration of national markets from distant manufacturing location. The role of Sears in introducing Japanese television sets and French radial tires on the U.S. market is well known.[37] Decreases in the cost of long distance transportation and communication also made integration increasingly feasible.

Finally, the existence of subsidiaries already in place in many countries facilitates the simultaneous introduction of new products in many national markets and the divorce between manufacturing and marketing location. The global scanning, sourcing, manufacturing and distributing capabilities of existing multinationals allow them to plan an efficient integrated network for their new products from the start rather than to evolve toward it.[38]

There is no systematic and complete empirical evidence on exactly which MNCs have integrated their operations in which business. There is, however, a convergence of disparate findings to suggest that integration is taking place, predictably, in maturing high technology industries with standardized products and processes that are sensitive to economies of scale.[39]

It is important, however, to remember that integration strategies are difficult management choices, not economic necessity.[40] In many European industries, integration strategies appeared only with the spur of foreign import competition. Worldwide industries are made, not born. Governments have also a key role in permitting or forbidding the globalization of an industry. In the sample of industries selected for the research reported here, economic characteristics heavily favor multinational integration. Yet far from all the multinational companies studied integrated their operations. The policies and interventions of European governments limit the attractiveness and benefits of integration for many multinational firms. Before examining in detail the findings on specific industries, let us first analyze the possible consequences of government interventions on multinational strategies.

References

1. Yves Doz Ford in Spain (B1) and Ford Bobcat (A1) cases, distributed by Harvard Business School Case Services (HBSCS No. 4–380–098 and 4–380–093).
2. Although data on integration are incomplete and no overall survey has been carried out, supporting evidence can be found in J. H. Dunning and R. D. Pearce, *The World's Largest Enterprises* (Farnborough: Gower, 1981), and in P. J. Buckley and R. I. Pearce, "Overseas Production and Exporting by the World's Largest Enterprises—A Study in Sourcing Policy", University of Reading Discussion Paper in International Investment, No. 39, Sept. 1977. See also N. Hood and S. Young, *European Development Strategies of US-owned Manufacturing Companies Located in Scotland* (Edinburgh: Her Majesty's Stationery Office, 1980).
3. R. E. Caves, "Causes of Direct Investment: Foreign Firms' Shares in Canadian and United Kingdom Manufacturing Industries", *Review of Economics and Statistics*, vol. 56 (August 1974), pp. 279–293.
4. M. Vd. Poel, D. Héau and J. de la Torré, "Michelin III", INSEAD case study, 1983 (distributed by INSEAD, Fontainbleau, France).
5. See, for instance, John H. Dunning, "Technology, U.S. Investment and European Economic Growth", in C. P. Kindleberger (ed.), *The International Corporation* (Cambridge, Mass.: The M.I.T. Press, 1970). See also Edwin Mansfield, "Technology and Technological Change", in John H. Dunning (ed.), *Economic Analysis and the Multinational Enterprise* (London: George Allen & Unwin Ltd., 1974), Richard E. Caves, "International Corporations: The Industrial Economics of Foreign Investment", in *Economica* (February 1971), pp. 1–27. See also "Industrial Organization", in John H. Dunning (ed.), *Economic Analysis and the Multinational Enterprise*.
6. For detailed analysis see Y. Doz, *Government Control and Multinational Strategic Management* (New York: Praeger, 1979), chapter 7.
7. See ref. 5 above.
8. See Nicholas Owen, "Scale Economies in the EEC: An Approach Based on Intra EEC Trade", in *European Economic Review*, No. 7 (February 1976), pp. 143–163.
9. See Euroeconomics "Motor Industry Report", presented at the European Motor Industry Conference, Frankfurt, 1977. Report dated 29 September 1977.
10. Industry studies stressing economies of scale also abound; see, for instance, for farm equipment, R. T. Kudrle, *Agricultural Tractors: A World Industry Study* (Cambridge, Mass.: Ballinger, 1975). For color TV see "The Television Set Industry in 1979: Japan and Europe". (Available from the Harvard Business School Case Services, Boston HBSCS No. 1–380–191.)
11. C. Pomper, *International Investment Planning: An Integrated Approach* (New York: North Holland, 1976).
12. For European evidence see N. Hood and S. Young, *European Development Strategies of U.S.-owned Manufacturing Companies Located in Scotland*. See also Commission of the European Communities, *Situation et Perspective des Gros Equipements Electroméca- niques et Nucléaires Liés à la Production d'Energie de la Communauté, SEC (7512770)* (Brussels: Commission of the European Communities, 1975).
13. See Boston Consulting Group, *Perspectives on Experience* (Boston: Boston Consulting Group, 1976).
14. See Nicholas Harman, "The Sovereign Municipality", *The Economist*, 20 December 1979.
15. See R. Pennant-Rea, "A Survey of Foreign Investment in Asia", *The Economist*, 23 June 1979.
16. C. A. Bartlett, "Multinational Structural Evolution: The Changing Decision Environ-

ment in International Divisions" (unpublished doctoral dissertation Harvard Graduate School of Business Administration, 1979).

17. A. Khodjamirian and J. de la Torré, "Heineken (A)" (unpublished INSEAD case study, 1983).
18. See E. Mansfield, "Technology and Technological Change", in J. H. Dunning (editor), *Economic Analysis and the Multinational Enterprise*.
19. R. E. Caves, "International Corporations: The Industrial Economics of Foreign Investment", *Economica*, p. 38.
20. "SKF Reintegrates Internationally", in *Multinational Business*, No. 4, 1976.
21. Y. Doz, *Government Control and Multinational Strategic Management*, Chapter 4.
22. A. M. Rugman, *International Diversification and the Multinational Enterprise* (Lexington, MA: Lexington Books, 1979).
23. M. Jilling, *Foreign Exchange Risk Management in U.S. Multinational Corporations* (Ann Arbor: UMI Research Press, 1978).
24. See F. M. Scherer, E. Kaufer and R. D. Murphy, with F. Bougeon Maassen, *The Economics of Multiplant Operation: An International Comparisons Study* (Cambridge; Harvard University Press, 1975).
25. See J. P. Neary, "International Factor Mobility, Minimum Wage Rates and Factor Price Equalization: A Synthesis", Seminar Paper No. 158, Institute for International Economic Studies, University of Stockholm.
26. See E. Mansfield, "Technology and Technological Change", op. cit., see also T. A. Pugel, *International Market Linkages and U.S. Manufacturing: Prices, Profits and Patterns* (Cambridge: Ballinger, 1978) and S. Lall, "Monopolistic Advantages and Foreign Involvement by U.S. Manufacturing Industry" in *Oxford Economic Papers*, 32, March 1980.
27. See, for instance, T. Horst: *At home abroad: A study of The Domestic and Foreign Operations of the American Food Processing Industry* (Cambridge, MA: Ballinger, 1974).
28. See, for instance, C. Bartlett, "Multinational Structural Evolution . . .", op. cit.
29. For instance in the computer, aerospace, semiconductor and telecommunication equipment industries, as described in later chapters.
30. See, for instance, J. H. Dunning and R. D. Pearce, *U.S. Industry in Britain* (Boulder, Co.: Westview Press, 1977), and D. J. C. Forsyth, *U.S. Investment in Scotland* (New York: Praeger, 1972).
31. See R. Vernon, "International Investment and International Trade in the Product Cycle", in *Quarterly Journal of Economics*, Vol. 80, 1966, pp. 190–207.
32. See R. H. Hayes and W. J. Abernathy, "Managing Our Way to Economic Decline" in *Harvard Business Review*, July–August, 1980.
33. For a summary of various studies, see Louis T. Wells, Jr (ed.), *The Product Life Cycle and International Trade* (Boston: Division of Research, Graduate School of Business Administration, Harvard University, 1972).
34. See R. Vernon, op. cit.
35. See N. Owens, "Scale Economies", op. cit.
36. This example is described in detail in the DAAG Europe case (Harvard Business School Case Services, HBSCS No. 9–374–037).
37. See, for colour TV, "The U.S. Television Set Market, prior to 1970" (Harvard Business School case study, HBSCS No. 1–380–180); for tyres, see Michelin II (INSEAD case study, mimeo, 1980, revised 1982).
38. See R. Vernon, "The Product Cycle Hypothesis is a New International Environment", in *Oxford Bulletin of Economics and Statistics* , Vol. 41, No. 4 pp. 255–267 Nov. 1979.
39. See N. Hood and S. Young, "European Development Strategies . . .", op. cit., and J. H. Dunning and R. D. Pearce, *The World's Largest Enterprises*, op. cit., and J. H. Dunning, "Toward an Eclectic Theory of International Production: Some Empirical Tests", in *Journal of International Business Studies*, Spring-Summer, 1980, pp. 9–25.
40. See C. K. Prahalad and Y. Doz, "An Approach to Strategic Control in MNCs" in *Sloan Management Review*, Vol. 22, No. 4, Summer 1981, pp. 5–14.

2

Multinational Integration and Host Government Policies

Host governments are not indifferent to the choice of strategy by multinational companies. Integration strategies, in particular, are of much concern to government officials. Governments have often attempted to limit the integration of multinational operations, or to gain control over integration. This chapter first presents briefly the issues raised by multinational integration strategies from the perspective of host governments and the reasons why governments may limit integration. Then it analyzes the nature of relationships multinationals following one type of strategy or another develop with host governments, and the industry structures that are likely to result from the interaction between industry economic variables and political variables.

Host Government Concerns Toward Multinational Companies

Multinational companies complicate the implementation of national policies, particularly when they integrate their operations across borders. Integration very narrowly limits the ability of MNC subsidiaries to respond autonomously to individual national policies as an integrated multinational corporation's requirements for success are quite different from those of autonomous subsidiaries. Nor can such a firm yield to one government's demands without possibly incurring the wrath of others and becoming an arena for intergovernmental conflicts. From the point of view of the British government, for instance, a multinational company whose strategic decisions are controlled by the French state or German unions would be even more troubling than one controlled by private foreign interest. Integrated MNCs cannot let individual governments gain a strong say in their decisions without putting their very ability to remain integrated in jeopardy.

Furthermore, since integrated subsidiaries are strongly influenced by many factors outside the purview of their host government, it is more difficult for the host government to predict their responses to its policies.[1]

Since the integrated multinational sells its products in many national markets, manufactures them in multiple countries, and obtains its raw materials from various sources, it can respond to government intervention in one country by drawing more heavily on other countries. Changes in relative factor prices among countries, or in the relative attractiveness of various countries, can lead to fast realignments of activities in the integrated network. Furthermore, easy access to multiple financial markets, central allocation of exports from the subsidiaries, sharing of research and development work, and variations in transfer prices and remittances between subsidiaries and headquarters can, according to the critics of the integrated MNC, defeat the purposes of almost any government intervention.[2]

There is little evidence, however, to suggest that the above concerns are fully justified. Factories are seldom mobile and hence realignments in integrated networks are difficult, except when only light assembly operations are concerned, such as in the case of the recent closing of Texas Instruments' El Salvador plant. Governments can monitor fund transfers and assess their justification. Faster variations than long-term factor price evolutions strongly influence factor cost differences between countries, currency fluctuations or interest rates shifts, for instance. It remains true, however, that superior access to information about more investment alternatives, at a lower cost, may also make multinational firms' responses to economic policies less predictable than domestic companies'.

More generally, the centrally coordinated multinational activities required by integration raise serious concerns among host government officials, preoccupied with the disappearance of "national decision centers" within the multinational companies. Seldom can the best interest of the MNC as a whole coincide with that of each of its subsidiaries, considered separately, for each and every strategic decision affecting them. In the long term, however, integration may be the only way for subsidiaries hard-pressed by efficient competitors to survive.

MNC integration thus places host governments in a difficult predicament: it may be possible to achieve international competitiveness or to preserve national responsiveness, but not both. Government officials prefer control, but can they strive for control at the expense of jobs? MNCs executives face the same dilemma from the opposite perspective: they may intuitively prefer integration, but should integration be pursued when it results in higher tensions with their host governments and may eventually lead to expropriation and eviction? Should they thus integrate operations across borders in a search for increased competitiveness, leave each subsidiary autonomous and free to behave as a national company would, or try to achieve some of the benefits of *both* integration for competitiveness and autonomy for responsiveness?

Governments have resisted mounting pressures for integration in many industries, though their priorities and constraints in opposing integration have varied. First, the provisions of the Rome Treaty make it difficult to rule out the integration of multinational companies within the European Economic Community. Governments have therefore accepted the inevitability of integration and mostly taken measures to bolster the competitiveness of their own national firms in an internationalizing industry. For instance, domestic consolidations and mergers have been frequent in such industries as chemicals and automobiles as these industries were becoming global.

The market power of state-owned customers is used to protect national industries. Where state-controlled customers dominate the market—in telephone switching equipment, for instance—they have usually succeeded in forestalling the integration of their suppliers. In such industries the power of MNCs has been eroding steadily. Most developed countries now supply the bulk of their needs for telecommunication equipment from domestic companies, some with minority MNC ownership, some purely national. The surviving multinational suppliers compete much as autonomous national companies and only companies following strategies of national responsiveness are tolerated in these industries. The more a product is closely related to national defense, and the larger the share of the market controlled by public customers, the more likely local production becomes, even when great cost disadvantages are incurred against the world price. Fighter aircraft often provide the extreme case where independently developed types or licence-produced aircraft are manufactured at great cost in small quantities in a number of different countries.

Partial government control over markets raises even more difficult trade-offs, both for governments and multinational companies. Governments may be tempted to use whatever leverage they have to support local companies. Yet the domestic public sector market may not be large enough to sustain even a marginally viable competitor, as the French came to acknowledge in their ill-fated attempt to nurture C2I as an autonomous national champion in the computer industry. Despite continuous subsidies, the firm's potential for competitiveness remained dim, industry economics favored integrated MNCs too strongly.[3] By 1976, C2I was merged with the French affiliate of Honeywell, to form C2I-Honeywell Bull. In 1981–82 the equity participation of Honeywell was reduced, but by 1983 the French company retains close technical links with Honeywell. Throughout its history, the French group required substantial government subsidies. International Computers Ltd., in England, with a long-established position in the computer industry, and extensive government purchasing preference was better able than C2I to withstand competition, but remained by and large dependent on public sector orders in Britain. In the late 1970s its future became questioned and an alliance with Japanese computer manufacturer Fujitsu was sought. Increasingly, ICL became dependent on Fujitsu's products and it lost some of its technical and industrial autonomy. In 1984 ICL was then taken over by Standard Telephones and Cables, a British telecommunication equipment firm partly owned by ITT.

Despite the difficulties faced in maintaining autonomous national champions, governments seldom let integrated MNCs alone serve the market segments they controlled. A mix of privileged access to these markets, government-funded research programs, assistance for exports and other forms of subsidies are often used to attract MNCs into cooperation with governments. Among European countries' governments, the French in particular have been adept in this approach. Such cooperation often takes the shape of joint ventures, typical examples of which are C2I–Honeywell Bull, a joint venture between the U.S. General Electric and the French national aeroengine maker SNECMA in jet engines called Compagnie Française des Moteurs, and the MATRA Harris Semiconductors agreement in microelectronics.[4]

Obviously the costs and benefits to host governments of the presence on their markets of multinational firms following one type of strategy or another vary: a nationally responsive MNC does not offer the same mix of advantages nor does it cause the same concern as an integrated MNC. The very nature of relationships is different, so are the policy choices open to governments; these are explored below.

Host Governments' Policies Toward Multinational Strategies

Policies Toward Multinational Integration

Integration may be expected to bring MNCs higher efficiency and returns than could have been achieved by not integrating their operations. Improvements in labor and capital productivity can be substantial, as in the case of IVECO discussed in Chapter 1 or in the ball bearing industry. Integration is often the means of survival for MNCs in mature industries, particularly in Europe.

Integration is often an alternative to relocation to lower labor cost countries; it maintains employment in Europe. In the early 1970s ITT— much exposed to government demands in Europe because of its extensive telecommunications equipment activities—decided not to move its semiconductor operations away from Europe, but to automate them. Except for semiconductors incorporated only into telecommunication equipment (production of which largely remained with autonomous national telecommunication equipment subsidiaries), semiconductor production was integrated among ITT subsidiaries in various countries, and significant investment made to automate production processes. By 1975 ITT's semiconductor sales per employee in Europe were $50,000 vs. $30,000 on average for major competitors producing in Europe. Similarly, Philips has been integrating its European TV tube and set manufacturing operations, rather than relocating them away from Europe. In its most efficient plants—like the Aachen tube plant in West Germany—it achieved cost levels competitive with those of manufacturers in the Far East.[5]

In industries less exposed to intense competition and still developing, integration strategies may make multinationals perform better and more profitably than nonintegrated ones or than national companies. In such cases governments usually bring in MNCs to share with them some of the benefits of integration. The relationship that develops between an integrated MNC and a host country may be seen as one where the MNC incurs some *cost of citizenship* in exchange for the host government's continued license to the MNC to maintain its integration. Success in such a relationship hinges on the MNC's and the government's ability to exchange value so that the perceived utility of both is increased. In other words, they are sharing the economic rent derived from the monopoly power integration creates.

Despite the allegations of some MNC critics to the contrary, the host governments wield the power to limit the extent of, or even to dismantle, the MNC integrated manufacturing and trade networks with more regulations and restrictions on foreign investments and market access. In such situations, managers of integrated MNC may eschew economic performance maximization in order to ensure a sufficient level of satisfaction to host governments through citizenship costs. *Costs of citizenship* can take a variety of forms; they are seldom stated very explicitly.

The most obvious cost of citizenship would be differential taxes. Yet most countries do not discriminate between national and foreign investments except by taxing repatriations of dividends and, in some cases, payments of royalties by foreign subsidiaries. Their taxes usually do not consider integrated multinational companies differently from nonintegrated ones; only import tariffs do so explicitly except when specific provisions exist to exempt certain integrated MNCs imports, such as the reimport of components processed abroad by the U.S. electronics industry.

Normally, costs of citizenship are also incurred through subtler resource transfers than differential taxes only. Some flexibility is left to the MNC to select the means of transfer by which to reach a compromise satisfactory to both host government officials and MNC executives. Governments do not seem unduly worried about potential allocative distortions introduced by MNC selection of the means of transferring resources. To a large extent, MNC executives can decide what groups in the country will benefit from their companies' presence. They may decide how to structure flows of intersubsidiary trade, where to locate plants, where to carry out research and development, who to train, and (to some extent) where to pay taxes. The government, left on its own, might come out differently on these choices. Typical patterns of behavior by integrated MNCs on those choices are summarized below.

Employment

Some multinational companies deliberately show much restraint in their employment policies. A few make commitments to full employment without collective lay-offs; these commitments sometimes reflect the values of the company's founders or its executives' desire to create loyalty to the company at all levels. The most striking example is IBM, which started such policies in the United States in accordance with the values of its founder, Thomas Watson Sr. IBM later found that they contributed to good citizenship abroad as well. IBM's fast growth facilitated the implementation of such policies. At times, however, rapid increases in productivity (particularly in the manufacture of integrated circuits) and sudden technological evolutions have created tensions in various countries. Policies of internal retraining and relocation of production avoided lay-offs, however. The large proportion among IBM's employees of highly skilled technicians and sales and service personnel, whose activities are relatively independent of short-run fluctuations in revenues and growth, made the implementation of a full employment policy easier. Such a policy would be more difficult to apply in a company where direct manufacturing labor is more important, and for a company in a more mature, more cyclical, industry than computers. Ford, for instance, laid off significant numbers of workers in Europe in the trough of the 1974–75 recession.

As labor laws may make lay-offs increasingly difficult and costly in most European countries, the usefulness of MNC's employment policies may well wane as all companies are made to follow similar policies.

Trade

Some of the adverse consequences of integration on host countries can be alleviated if integration does not favor some countries which become net exporters within the integrated system over others which become net importers. The bargaining on location and the fear that MNCs may leave when they find lower cost locations are eliminated by a commitment on the part of the MNC to balanced trade: to each country its share, and no haggling. Though no major company has made a firm commitment to balanced trade, IBM has been a pioneer again in considering explicitly its operations' effects on host countries' trade balances. Where it has no plants, it buys more from national suppliers to offset its equipment sales or leases and tries to expand its plants so that trade remains balanced.

On the other hand, negotiations between General Motors and its unions in Germany resulted in GM being committed to make new investments in Germany that would match the amounts invested in Spain, where labor costs are much lower. Maintenance of employment and concern for balanced trades usually make the integration pattern for MNCs less than optimal. Research on the automobile industry suggests that a cost penalty of about 15% is incurred as a result of cumulative union constraints and government measures, compared to an optimally integrated European production network.[6]

The absence of such policies where free trade prevails raises much concern among governments. For instance, in the spring of 1979 several European countries were wooing Ford, outbidding each other with higher subsidies to attract the car maker. Strong calls for a balanced trade policy that would limit competition among governments and for restraint on their part in promising assistance were voiced by U.S. and EEC officials. Yet certain countries, such as Ireland, saw special incentives to MNC investments as a cornerstone of their industrial development policies.

Although it is easy to condemn these bargaining practices, it is difficult for governments and MNCs alike not to be tempted into them.[7] Conversely, when countries control access to their domestic market, they try to coax MNCs into exporting as a condition for market access, as did Spain with Ford.[8]

Area of location with the country

Integrated MNCs often invest more readily than domestic companies in depressed development areas, possibly because their managers and administrative systems are better able to manage successfully geographically scattered operations than managers of non-integrated multinationals or domestic companies. In France, foreign companies have invested in the provinces, for instance Texas Instruments, Ford, Motorola and IBM invested in the industrially underdeveloped south. In Britain, foreign companies located in Scotland and Wales more willingly than domestic companies.[9] Again, this often made their production networks less than economically optimal. Moreover, locations by foreign MNCs in development areas often had exemplary value for domestic companies.

Location of research and development activities

Willingness to set up research and development labs in various countries and to employ highly skilled local nationals in their own country is a strong point for integrated MNCs. The cost to the MNC of such dispersion of R & D facilities is difficult to assess. In some cases it can be a straight benefit, for instance the employment of outstanding Indian engineers and scientists in their own country at Indian salaries is certainly a saving for MNCs. Still, there is evidence that dissociating research and development activities from the major geographical market and fragmenting them into dispersed labs result in significant coordination costs. Some researchers also suggest that this makes sensitiveness to market demands more difficult to achieve.[10] Left to their own volition, most MNCs would locate research and development activities in their own home country only, except for the adaptation of their products and services for foreign markets. Some, headquartered in small countries (e.g., The Netherlands or Switzerland) might wish to locate in the leading technological markets with the most demanding users (usually the United States).

Transparent financial transfers

The French subsidiary of a very large multinational studied in the research was barely breaking even, according to the accounting methods of the company, whereas a more accurate system with better corrections for inflation and exchange rate accounting would have shown profits close to $100 million. As we have seen, integration provides the MNC with a variety of opportunities to affect financial results in a country through intersubsidiary fund flows manipulation or—as in the case mentioned above—with mere dangers of grossly inaccurate accounting, particularly with high inflation rates and sharp exchange rates fluctuations. Some integrated companies deliberately eschew opportunities for financial optimization in order to show restraint *vis-à-vis* host governments and to behave as if they were national companies: tax is paid where income is created, as far as can be accurately determined.

Training

In countries where training opportunities are few, MNC subsidiaries are often seen as training grounds for good international managers. For instance, in Europe, ex-ITT or ex-IBM managers are considered a rare, valuable breed.

The good citizenship policies described above usually enhance the acceptability of integrated MNCs to host governments. They may directly reduce the profitability of the company, and as such constitute citizenship costs. Beyond these substantive policies some integrated MNCs carefully orchestrate campaigns to enhance their acceptability. They may contribute to scientific research and education, either financially or by applying their skills and technologies to areas of concern to host governments. Again, IBM is a prime example here, from its contribution to educational institutions to the maintenance of a nonintegrated military division working closely with the French government.[11] Rather than the cost of suboptimization within their systems, such moves involve contributions at the fringe of the system. Their motivations are sometimes ambiguous, since they usually contribute to promote the image of the firm, and often its equipment. For instance, scientists trained to use a particular equipment may orient equipment purchases toward its manufacturer.

Conclusion

The extent to which these means are used to transfer resources to host governments varies within clear limits. First, an upper limit on the transfer of resources is usually set by the rent the MNC derives from integration. As integration is often a defensive move against price competition, such rent is not necessarily large. Even after integration, the company's competitive position may remain too weak for it to afford heavy citizenship costs. Governments expect more from a profitable leading company that integrated to draw maximum benefits from its size than they do from a marginal MNC whose only chance for survival is integration.

The exchange of value between the MNC and the host government may be more or less explicit. For instance, IBM's policies are satisfactory enough to governments for direct explicit negotiations to be seldom needed. Indirect negotiations can take place through public pronouncements that are seen as signals by each party. For instance, IBM's French subsidiary's general manager announced in 1979 that, should the French administration continue to favor C2I-HB past the period for which it made formal commitment to Honeywell, new IBM investments in France could be curtailed. The French Ministry of Industry official in charge of data processing commented that France was not a "planned economy" and customers (assumedly including state-controlled ones) were free to select their suppliers. By late 1979 the issue had not been resolved, but it was clear the French no longer helped C2I-HB massively. Some national customers such as the national railroad company had stubbornly opposed using anything but IBM equipment, but public purchases were still sufficiently balanced (IBM still had a 30% share of the public market, against C2I-HB's 50%) for the government to announce credibly a "hands-off" policy in the future. IBM's announcements were a reminder that this policy should be implemented. C2I-HB again became strongly favored by the government following the 1981 elections in which the Socialist party gained a majority in the Parliament.

In some other cases the agreement can be hammered out in great detail between the government and the MNC. When Ford invested in Spain, its European staffs prepared a very detailed proposal and a list of negotiation items and requests to the Spanish government, such as subsidies and tax exemptions, and Ford's proposal stated very precisely export and local content plans.

Even when the terms of the expected exchange are not made fully explicit, integrated MNCs tend to be clear parties in negotiations with host governments, since their decisions tend to be cast in straight economic terms. Strategic choices in integrated MNCs are usually made on a substantive analytical basis and they try to assess the worldwide consequences of alternative courses of action as comprehensively as possible.

This analytical choice process can take into consideration clearly spelled-out government constraints, but is inflexible to ongoing bargaining over time. At the time of an initial investment in a country, the terms of the exchange can thus be made explicit. It is clear to governments negotiating with Ford, for instance, that decisions are reached by the company management largely on marginal return comparisons among investment alternatives.

The very nature of integration helps to stabilize ongoing relationships between integrated MNCs and host governments. A break has adverse consequences for both parties: in the case of expropriation or nationalization, the host government finds itself stuck with a plant of little use outside the MNC manufacturing networks and the MNC finds itself deprived of a key part of its production network. Neither side wins.

Conversely, integrated MNCs are likely to resist any government move that would give national government-controlled agents—or the government itself—a direct say in the making of strategic decisions. Their subsidiaries are too interdependent to tolerate interference by external forces that might lead to decisions favorable to one subsidiary and detrimental to others. Faced with demands that would give a say to governments in key decisions, for instance by appointing government representatives on the subsidiary's board, the MNC is likely to divest or to isolate the involved subsidiary by a partial restructuring of its production network, where the subsidiary remains dependent on others, but not others on it. This usually decreases the economic benefits of integration both for the MNC and the host country. Allegedly, the desire not to establish the precedent of a nonintegrated subsidiary played some role in IBM's withdrawal from India.

Integration strategies are likely to prevail, therefore, where their economic benefits are strong (where they can generate a durable competitive advantage) and where governments are more concerned with economic and social performance than with direct control. Where direct control is a strong issue, national responsiveness tends to prevail, irrespective of the potential benefits of integration.

Policies Toward National Responsiveness Strategies

Most sources of competitive advantage of nonintegrated MNCs are easily tolerable by host governments of developed countries. First, subsidiaries of nonintegrated MNCs are available to cooperate with host governments in high technology ventures.* Governments are quite often

*Technology transfer issues are obviously a major concern of host governments, but mostly in developing countries. Available data suggest that most technology transfers by MNCs take place between OECD countries, and that cooperation between national and multinational firms for the development of new products and technologies becomes increasingly frequent. Recently, however, the U.S. government has shown increasing concern with cooperation between U.S. and foreign firms: in high technology fields, proposed policy measures would make genuine cooperation between U.S. multinationals and foreign firms very difficult.

willing to subsidize new technological developments, but lack competent partners domestically and are loathe to enlist integrated MNCs. According to their views, subsidies to integrated MNCs could be diverted to create skills and technical jobs in other countries instead of the subsidizing one. Host countries also fear that once an integrated MNC is invited into a high technology joint venture, national control over the new technologies would be lost.

To governments concerned with technological capability and responsiveness, nationally responsive MNCs offer an attractive outlet. Their subsidiaries may carry out government-sponsored research and development projects autonomously. Should their research efforts lead to marketable products, they can also diversify in response to government incentives or requests. Such decisions as to develop new products or technologies, or to engage in new production, can often be taken at the national subsidiary level, as regional or worldwide headquarters will usually not challenge local developments unless they duplicate work already being carried out in other subsidiaries. In that case, having access to the MNC technology can spare large resources to the host country.

Second, the coordination of exports between subsidiaries can usually work to their mutual benefit and increase exports from their host countries. The MNC network of agents and sales subsidiaries in export markets, their international image and reputation, and their competence and experience in selling, installing and maintaining equipment in Third World countries cannot be easily matched by purely national companies. Coordination of exports among subsidiaries may also enable the MNC to sell more, overall, on the international markets than a collection of independent national companies could. It can even out workloads and allocate contracts to the various subsidiaries taking into consideration the preferences of the customer, the possible delivery delays, and therefore the activity of each of its subsidiaries is thus likely to be larger and more steady than that of independent companies.

Third, concerns about subsidiary financing and MNC decision making have led host governments to request MNCs to set up joint ventures with national investors or to float subsidiary equity to the public. Nationally responsive MNCs can usually comply flexibly. As an example, Brown Boveri's or ITT's European subsidiaries are not fully parent-owned, although the parent usually remains their largest shareholder. Partnerships with major local companies prevail in developing countries, but unfortunately this is no panacea to host government concerns. In its eagerness for sizeable short-term profits, the national partner often takes the national interest, or the short-term interest of the joint venture itself, less into consideration than does the MNC.

In joint ventures or partly-owned subsidiaries, strategic choices are made primarily at the national level, but since the subsidiaries remain dependent upon technology and skill transfers from their parent, and upon its network for export sales, a relatively balanced situation can develop where both the MNC and local interests may find satisfaction, and feel they share power over the subsidiary.

Further, joint ventures with integrated MNCs provide less of a potential solution to government concerns. Extensive cross-shipments between integrated MNCs' subsidiaries provide additional opportunity for slanting individual subsidiaries' results or tampering with transfer prices. Without integration, the major flows are financial, as they involve payment of fees between subsidiaries for technology transfer or other services, or for the subcontracting of export sales, interest payments, and profit remittances. These are usually less important in amount, and easier to control, than the extensive cross-shipments in integrated MNCs, to which it is often difficult to attribute a realistic market price.

Nonintegrated MNCs often offer another advantage to governments: the managers. Whereas managers of integrated MNCs' subsidiaries often seem stateless and devoted to their company only, managers of nationally responsive MNCs are usually more rooted in the national environment and culture. They are often local nationals who deal comfortably with government officials and local industrialists to whom it is usually clear that subsidiary managers enjoy much strategic autonomy, in contrast with subsidiary managers in integrated MNCs. Furthermore, the dependence of the subsidiary on its national market makes subsidiary managers cultivate a web of business relationships within the country, and their lesser mobility also facilitates the development of long-term relationships. At Brown Boveri, Nestlé, or CPC International, concerns for wide, good, diversified relations at the national level were very strong among subsidiary managers. Mr. Koch, the head of the Brown Boveri's French affiliate CEM, was sufficiently well recognized in the French business environment to be elected chairman of the French electrical equipment industry association.

The advantages in dealing with host governments described above can also become a source of vulnerability to the nationally responsive MNC. Operations of the affiliate can be continued easily, once severed from the MNC, the only drawbacks being the difficulty of exporting autonomously and the end of technology transfers. If subsidiary's activities and the government policies are concerned with supplying the domestic market, and one "adequate" technology has been secured, these drawbacks may not deter the host government. Because it was quite possible for the Brazilian telecommunications authority Telebras to expropriate the subsidiaries of ITT and LM Ericsson, Telebras did not need to expropriate either one: the threat was real enough to gain clout in demanding that the MNCs transform their Brazilian affiliates into joint ventures.[19]

Pursuing export markets raises more difficult questions for the government. For instance, at the initiative of the French government, the French group Thomson-CSF acquired one French subsidiary of ITT and the LM

Ericsson subsidiary in 1976. After three years, export successes had been relatively few, except in two circumstances: (1) when Thomson-CSF proposed its own equipment (instead of that made under license from ITT or LM Ericsson); and (2) where sales were secured through direct intergovernmental contracts had gone directly to the makers of original equipment, LM Ericsson or ITT.* Furthermore, Thomson CSF's switches were based on the mid 1970s technologies of ITT, which by the early 1980s was only barely adequate in France and not competitive internationally. Conversely, the other French manufacturer, CIT-Alcatel, which had developed its own distinctive electronic switching technology from the outset, was more successful on export markets than Thomson-CSF. In 1983 it was decided to merge Thomson's telephone switching activities into CIT-Alcatel's.

Nationally responsive subsidiaries are also vulnerable to competition—both domestically and internationally. If these subsidiaries each are substantially smaller than their national competitors, they may face great difficulty in remaining competitive. A senior manager at Brown Boveri described his situation:

> "If we look at the international market as a whole, we have a much bigger share than that of our competitors, but spread over a number of separate national markets, with an average of 20% each. In each market we face a purely national competitor which is bigger in its home market. With the shift to higher turbogenerator unit powers we have to build new plants and acquire heavier equipment. The trouble is that if we make three units a year in each market, Siemens or Alsthom-Atlantique makes twice as many for their national markets alone. So their capacity utilization rate should be better than ours. Our market share in each separate national market being small, our profitability is not sufficient."[12]

This suggests integration. But government control makes integration impossible—in the late 1970s, Brown Boveri started to divest some of its most vulnerable operations; for instance, it sold its French subsidiary to Alsthom-Atlantique and redirected its activities towards segments of the electrical engineering industry less directly controlled by governments.

In sum, nationally responsive subsidiaries are always in a somewhat precarious position, vulnerable both to purely national competitors who can master similar technologies, and to a shift in their industry toward global competition. Some MNCs try to integrate their operations without losing the protection and support of host governments. This usually leads to multifocal strategies.

---

*Some critics suggested that both MNCs were all too happy to divest their operations in France. With heavy investments being made in the telecommunications network in France, employment in their subsidiaries had increased in the early 1970s. Yet the shift from electromechanical to electronic switching technologies implies a considerable drop in labor content per new telephone line. Through the 1970s, the French PTT decreased the proportion of new electromechanical telephone switching units, in favor of electronic ones. Thus, telecommunication equipment manufacturers expected severe overcapacity and redundancies in the late 1970s and the 1980s. In that context, divesting some of their operations could make much sense to MNC managers.

Policies Toward Multifocal Strategies

A multifocal strategy represents, on management's part, an attempt to assess the appropriate trade-off between responsiveness and integration for each decision separately. Since such a trade-off is difficult to reach analytically, it usually becomes the result of an advocacy process within the firm, some executives defending integration, others responsiveness. This creates some ambiguity in the firm's posture. Anticipating the outcome of a political process within the MNC is much more difficult than it is to forecast the conclusions of a substantive comprehensive economic analysis within an integrated MNC. Assessing the consequences of a multifocal strategy is also more difficult than predicting the behavior of autonomous national subsidiaries of a nationally responsive MNC. As a result, MNCs pursuing a multifocal strategy often look "Janus-faced" to host governments. They can look nationally responsive, and some of their managers will talk and act as if they were; yet they may not be, and managers favorable to integration may prevail on particular decisions. Since any new decision may challenge prior ones, agreements with host governments may always be questioned. Indeed, as strategy becomes dissolved into a set of incremental moves over time, it becomes very difficult to maintain consistency in the MNC posture *vis-à-vis* any government. As a result, MNCs following multifocal strategies are less predictable and reliable partners for governments than either integrated or nationally responsive MNCs.

Still, by adopting an internally flexible and negotiable strategic posture, multinational companies make themselves more easily accessible to host governments' influence. Some of the central control over subsidiaries, so critical in multinational integration, is here abandoned, making it easier for subsidiaries to cooperate on specific projects with powerful partners such as government agencies or national companies. Yet these projects are likely to be challenged within the MNC, at one time or another; conversely, because commitments of resources are not likely to be made consistently, and the MNC operations are not likely to be tightly integrated, a multifocal strategy is not likely to make the MNC extremely efficient. High costs of citizenship may thus not be affordable. In short, compared with multinational integration, a multifocal strategy trades off internal efficiency for external flexibility in a continuously variable way. Whereas integration seeks to provide the organization with enough monopoly power to maintain a stable competitive advantage, and provide for financial success, a multifocal strategy provides the flexibility needed for a constantly adjusted coalignment of the firm with the more powerful factors in the environment, and the most critical sources of uncertainty in a much more opportunistic way. Where governments are interested and powerful, a multifocal strategy will be sensitive to the political imperatives they create. Where governments are weak or uninterested, a multifocal strategy will allow integration but not make it the overriding principle of the MNC's organization.

Multinational Strategies, National Policies and Resulting Industry Structures

Where trade-offs are clear, industry structures are simple. Where economic characteristics drive towards integration and government concerns are with economic and social welfare rather than national control, global industries develop. Where national control is a priority, separate national industries survive, usually at a high opportunity cost. Such cost can be seen as the price of control. Such is the case with many high technology industries deemed of strategic value by governments and whose customers are government controlled. There, MNCs can play a role by providing technology and expertise at a lower cost—by avoiding duplication of R & D efforts and harnessing better talent—provided their subsidiaries remain nationally responsive.

Where government control is partial, and government policies more complex, industries often encompass various types of firms: integrated MNCs, nationally responsive ones, MNCs following multifocal strategies and national companies. How is so heterogeneous an industry structure maintained?

First, the potential benefits of integration are not equal for all firms. Obviously, past a certain size, economies of scale and experience are exhausted, and further integration no longer justified against increased transportation costs and the higher risks of producing particular items at a single location to serve the worldwide demand. Such limits to the benefits of integration lead to regional integration strategies, such as carried out by Ford. Few firms reach that critical size in a business, however. By pooling sales volumes from different national markets and specializing plants, larger firms achieve lower costs than can their smaller competitors and reach the most efficient size. The larger firms, therefore, usually strive to serve a globally homogeneous market, from integrated production networks.

Confronted with such a choice by larger firms, smaller firms are looking for ways to differentiate some segments of their market and make the market overall less homogeneous. Beyond conventional approaches to market segmentation they may sometimes capitalize on government concerns for control. Such concern for control may lead to geographic segmentation, even when there is no real basis for such differentiation. Firms are willing to trade off their strategic independence for protection and support by host governments. Privileged access to public markets and public assistance bolster their competitiveness. So long as they ally with one government only they can even maintain their integration and avoid being bogged down into intergovernmental conflicts. In most countries they are integrated—and treated as such—in one country they are nationally responsive. Approaches capitalizing on government-induced market segmentation can succeed only when governments exercise partial control over national markets, but not enough to shelter effectively the whole market from international competition and administer domestic competition.

In these partly controlled markets, firms with the largest overall shares of the world market are likely to find integration more desirable, whereas smaller firms are likely to find multifocal or national responsiveness strategies more suitable, and to enlist host governments' support and subsidies to compete against leading MNCs. In these partly controlled industries integrated firms protect their integration on three grounds. First, they offer options to national customers. Some may buy from integrated MNCs, others from national companies or nationally responsive MNCs according to the users' priorities in procuring a particular type of equipment. The French military could buy some integrated circuits for strategic missiles guidance systems from Texas Instruments, and the bulk of their requirements from Thomson-CSF whenever quality standards were not quite as stringent. They therefore develop allies within the government. Second, their presence increases the bargaining power of host governments. Governments can put pressure on domestic companies to obtain some minimum level of economic, social, or financial performances by threatening to turn to integrated MNCs as suppliers. British Telecom, for instance, was using such a threat to shape up General Electric (UK) and Plessey, suppliers of the domestic "System X" switching systems. Conversely, threats to increase support to national companies or nationally responsive MNCs can be used to lead integrated MNCs to comply with host government demands. Threats to limit or regulate integration are credible to the extent companies following other types of strategies can deliver the same goods. Third, they accept to incur relatively high citizenship costs. How much integrated firms may be willing to give host governments as costs of citizenship in order to maintain strategic integration may vary substantially. A leading integrated firm in a partly government controlled market with no comparable direct competitor may be willing to provide much to host countries. IBM, for instance, reached an implicit agreement with European governments, by providing more than was needed for their minimal level of satisfaction. Conversely, when keen worldwide competition takes place among integrated companies of comparable strength (e.g., Texas Instruments, Motorola, and Intel) the economic imperative becomes much more demanding for each of them, and none may be willing to be accommodating for fear that the others would not match such behavior. In short: the more one integrated firm is subjected to direct competition from other integrated multinationals the less "good citizenship" it will be able or willing to provide host governments, except in exchange for profitable assistance not provided to any other competitors. In these cases bargains with host governments are likely to be clearly and toughly negotiated rather than left implicit and gentlemanly as in the case of IBM. For instance, Ford invested in Spain in 1973 only with the guarantee that terms of the Spanish government's decrees allowing foreign automobile industry investments would discourage other integrated MNCs from following suit.

As a result of the factors described above, a stable mixed industry structure may develop, comprising two broad types of firms:

1. One or several integrated MNC subsidiaries that apply price and service pressures on domestic firm(s), impose economic imperatives on the national supplier(s), and appeal to user-orientated agencies in the government.
2. A privileged "national" supplier—sometimes partly or wholly foreign-owned but not part of an integrated MNC—whose relationships with the state are political and administrative, that provides an alternative to integrated MNCs, a source of bargaining power to the government in its dealings with MNCs and thus, can help impose a political imperative to the MNCs. Such a "national champion" usually appeals more to tutelage-orientated agencies than to user-orientated ones.

In some cases the national champion may be part of a multinational consortium striving to gain some of the benefits of integration without losing responsiveness to host governments. A prominent example of such an approach is provided by the European "Airbus Industrie" group jointly sponsored by several governments (through mainly state-owned aircraft manufacturers) to benefit from a larger market and from integrated manufacturing.

Governments maintain a mixed industry structure by indirectly transferring resources from integrated MNCs to other types of companies. Integrated MNCs contribute citizenship costs and taxes, other companies benefit from protection and support and receive subsidies.

Mixed structure industries, however, are not necessarily static. They tend to evolve toward increased concentration. The stability of mixed structure industries, and the relationships that may develop between firms and host governments, are closely influenced by competition among firms following similar strategies. If there is only one integrated MNC in an industry, and it enjoys such leadership as to make competitors' efforts to integrate and compete on costs a futile exercise, a mixed structure can be quite stable, with relatively little direct government involvement. The lone integrated MNC that finds itself in a secure competitive posture may be willing to incur high citizenship costs to see that its integration is well accepted. It shares with the host governments the benefits from being the only company to follow the most economically efficient strategy. In short, the firm is quite efficient and profitable, with no direct rival (thus only governments to fear), and may see it as its best interest to accept the incurring of heavy costs of citizenship.

Conversely, direct rivalry among several integrated MNCs reduces the willingness of individual firms to incur large costs of citizenship. Such costs, under condition of direct rivalry, may be incurred willingly only as *quid pro quo* for government authorization to make unique profitable moves, that no other company will be allowed to match. Still, it is clear that, should such moves become a norm, they would lock the strategy of integration into a straightjacket of agreements with various countries. The more such agreements, the more the world market is again split by country (with one or another MNC tying its future to this or that country) instead of split regionally or globally between integrated competitors acting relatively free from government intervention. The overall cumulative effect is market fragmentation and the shift of some companies from multinational integration strategies to multifocal strategies to respond to their *de facto* governmental allies. Among integrated MNCs, the relatively weaker are likely to take a shorter-term view and seek active opportunities for explicit alliances with governments, whereas the stronger may take the longer-term view of attempting to be the only remaining integrated MNC in the business. The maintenance of a number of integrated MNCs would assume that they develop a common attitude toward governments, refrain from seeking government guarantees that competitors cannot obtain and from replacing another less accommodating MNC in dealing with governments.*

In summary, one can see two patterns of competition emerging, taking into consideration the structure and behavior of integrated multinational companies. These are described in Table 2.1.

Increasing concentration at the national level is also likely among nonintegrated firms. Governments are likely to encourage the emergence of a single national supplier. Unless clearly separate market segments exist, and each firm can position itself on one such segment, there are few reasons why state assistance would be lavished on several companies rather than on one. In a given country, there may thus remain only two competitors for any market segment: an integrated multinational and a nationally responsive company, either domestic (national champion) or affiliated to a MNC.

Conclusion: Toward a Framework

In sum, in the presence of (1) strong economic and technological pressures toward industry globalization, and toward strategies of integration by MNCs which populate that industry, (2) host governments' desire for control of producers in that industry and (3) different competitive postures among firms, a few simple propositions can be made:

---

*For instance, when IBM decided to withdraw from India, Burroughs—another integrated MNC—was quick to suggest it could make an exception to its operating principles and replace IBM in India, on the Indian government's terms.

TABLE 2.1   *Patterns of International Competition in Mixed Structure Industries*

Pattern 1 One single integrated MNC	Pattern 2 Several integrated MNCs
Willing to incur considerable costs of citizenship. Used as source of economic pressures by host governments on sharing of monopoly economic rent and amounts and form of costs of good citizenship.	Collusive option: adopt the same attitude as direct rivals *vis-à-vis* governments, refrain from seeking nonmatchable moves, defend free trade. Competition option: Integrated MNCs seek nonmatchable moves actively. Weaker firms, among them, become dependent on governments who grant nonmatchable moves. Transition toward pattern 1, with all firms, but one, moving toward administrative coordination or national responsiveness.
Several nationally responsive MNCs, recipients of resource transfers, alternative to integrated MNCs.	Several nationally responsive MNCs recipient of resource transfers, alternatives to integrated MNCs. Likely to be joined, over time, by integrated firms benefiting from nonmatchable moves.
National champions or members of multigovernment-sponsored multinational consortia.	National champions or members of multigovernment-sponsored, multinational consortia.

1. The more extensive government control is over the markets of an industry, the least likely are integration strategies. Government control over markets can be measured by using the percentage of sales from the industry to government-owned purchasers over total industry sales.*
2. The larger the overall market share of a MNC in a free-trade area exposed to international competition, the most likely it is to follow an integration strategy, provided all potential economies of scale and size are not exhausted within the confines of national markets, given existing market shares of the various competitors.
3. Facing the competitive pressures from both large integrated MNCs within a region and low cost importers from outside the region, smaller MNCs and national firms will attempt to differentiate their products and services to escape direct competition. When no economic basis clearly exists for strategic segmentation of the business,

*Recognizing that this is an aggregate measure which specific counterexamples may not always support (e.g., the French state-owned railroads' steadfast refusal to buy French computers).

such companies will try to enlist host government support to create artificial differentiation, usually in the form of non-tariff barriers to trade (domestic preference) or of policies discriminating between integrated and multifocal or non-integrated MNCs (e.g., research subsidies, public purchasing preferences, export assistance, etc.). Alliances among smaller firms from different countries, with complementary skills and market access, are likely to multiply.

4. In industries characterized by moderate levels of government control over markets a multitiered industry structure is likely to emerge. Larger MNCs follow integration strategies, smaller, weaker, ones seek government alliances, which drive them to multifocal and nationally responsive strategies.

The four propositions above can be summarized graphically by hypothesizing the most likely type of strategy an MNC can follow in a business as a function of (1) the extent of government control over markets for that business and (2) the relative market share of the MNC in that business within a given free trade area. The hypothesized relationships are summarized in Fig. 2.1 below.

The following three chapters will analyze in detail the validity of these propositions in three industries at different points on the government control axis: automobiles (where government control over market is low),

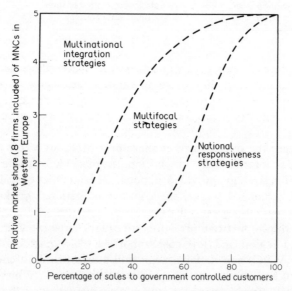

FIG. 2.1.   Customers, market shares and multinational strategies: hypothetical relationships

Note: National responsiveness strategies include that followed by independent national companies in their *home* country.

computers (where it is moderate) and telephone switching (where it is high) (see Fig. 2.2).

In addition, a comparison is made between computers and microelectronics, not because they are closely related industries, but to explore possible differences between industries where there is a single leading integrated MNC (IBM in computers) and industries where there are several integrated MNCs vying for leadership.

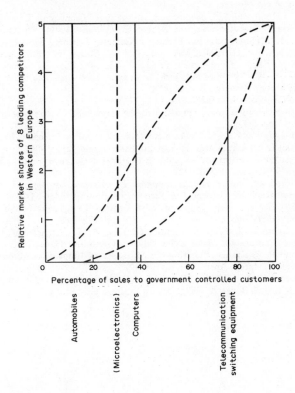

Fig. 2.2.   Customers, market shares and strategies: industries studied in detail

Since the three detailed industry studies were used to develop the framework presented here, they do not qualify for an empirical test. Therefore, in Chapter 6 results from a wider survey of strategies in other industries will be presented to support the validity of the framework. Obviously, in such research there is no possible validation of the results, since a conceptual framework can only be disproved for being unable to explain deviant cases. Surveying additional industries therefore adds only marginally to the validity of the framework in so far as it does not unveil countercases that the framework cannot explain.

56   *Strategic Management in Multinational Companies*

References

1. For a more detailed argument on some of these points, see Y. Doz, "Government Policies and Global Industries", in Michael E. Porter (ed), *Competition in Global Industries*, Boston: Harvard Business School Press, forthcoming 1986.
2. For a summary of the argument see M. Crawford, "The Intellectual Attack Against MNCs", in *Multinational Business*, No. 3, 1977, pp. 10–19.
3. See G. W. Brock, *The U.S. Computer Industry: A Study of Market Power* (Cambridge, Mass: Ballinger, 1975) and Jacques Jublin and Jean-Michel Quatrepoint *French Ordinateurs* (Paris: Alain Moreau, 1976).
4. For the C2I Honeywell Bull cooperation, see my case "Compagnie Internationale Pour l'Informatique" (Harvard Business School Case Study 1979); see also Charles P. Kennedy Jr, "Honeywell in France" (Colgate Darden School Case Study, UVA–BP–234). For GE-SNECMA, see Guss W. Weiss Jr, "The General Electric SNECMA Jet Engine Development Program" (Harvard Business School Case Study, HBSCS No. 9–380–739). See also Jack Baranson, *"Technology and the Multinational"* (Lexington Mass, Lexington Books: 1978).
5. Personal communication to the author.
6. Personal communication from John Stopford, based on unpublished research done at The London Business School.
7. See Steven Gruysinger *et al.*, "Investment Incentives and Performance Requirements" (Washington, D.C.: The World Bank, unpublished monograph 1984)
8. See Y. Doz, "Ford in Spain" (A) and (B). (Harvard Business School Case Studies, HBSCS 4–380–091 and 4–380–092)
9. See Neil Hood and Steve Young, *European Development Strategies of U.S. Owned Manufacturing Companies Located in Scotland* (Edinburgh: Her Majesty's Stationery Office, 1980). See also Neil Hood and Steve Young, "U.S. Investment in Scotland". *Scottish Journal of Political Economy* (Nov. 1976, pp. 279–294).
10. See J. N. Behrman and W. A. Fischer, *Overseas R&D Activities of Transnational Corporations* (Cambridge, Mass: Oelgeschlager, Gunn and Hain, 1980). See also R. Ronstadt and R. J. Kraner, "Getting the Most Out of Innovation Abroad", *Harvard Business Review* (March, April 1982, pp. 94–99).
11. See D. Butler, "IBM in Europe" *Datamation* (October 1978, pp. 103–109).
12. See Y. Doz, "Brown Boveri & Cie" (Harvard Business Case Study, HBSCS 4–378–115).

3

Competition in Global Industries: the Automobile Industry

Three major changes led to the development of automobiles into a global industry. First, the formation of the European Economic Community led to free trade among six continental European countries by 1968, joined by the United Kingdom in 1973 and subsequently by other countries. Life styles had become sufficiently similar among European countries for cars made in one to be sold in number in others. While Italy and France retained a higher proportion of small cars, and Germany, the United Kingdom and Sweden a higher proportion of large cars, the markets were comprised of the same segments in the various countries, albeit of different relative size. International trade within Europe thus increased rapidly, each manufacturer exporting cars mostly to the market segments where its domestic market was largest.

Second, by the late 1960s, after some early unsuccessful efforts to penetrate international markets, Japanese companies engaged in an ambitious export push to become leading producers of high-quality, well-equipped inexpensive vehicles. In the mid-1970s Japan had become the leading car exporter in the world. Major productivity and quality advantages had allowed Japan to take a significant share of the U.S. and European markets.

Third, differences narrowed between the North American market and the European and Japanese ones. The energy crisis of 1973 reversed the U.S. automaker's move toward larger cars. First government regulations on energy conservation led U.S. manufacturers to "down size" their models. Second, real term gasoline price increases in 1978–79 and concern about availability led consumers toward buying smaller cars. Imports (mainly Japanese) benefited from the shift, but U.S. manufacturers introduced smaller European-like cars in the early 1980s. By the late 1970s there was thus an unprecedented convergence of needs for the world's three major markets: the United States, Europe and Japan.[1] As in Europe, though, the relative size of market segments differed with the United States retaining a higher proportion of larger cars.

As a consequence of this convergence, extensive international trade had developed in the industry. Japan, Germany, France, Italy and Sweden were exporting about 50% of their respective car production in the late 1970s. In Europe there was already an extensive interpenetration of national markets since the 1960s (Table 3.1). Altogether West European countries, as a group, exported about 30% of their production to other regions in 1977, a percentage which subsequently decreased in the face of intense competition from Japanese manufacturers. Each national industry, particularly in Europe, has thus become sensitive to shifts in demand and competitiveness among regions of the world and manufacturers. Extensive investments were made in large developing markets with access restrictions such as Brazil, Mexico, Spain and Nigeria.

TABLE 3.1   *Imported Passenger Cars as Percent of Total New Car Registrations*

	1958	1973	1978	1982
West Germany	10.4	25.8	24.5	28
France	1.4	20.9	20.8	31
Italy	4.2	28.0	37.8	42
Britain	2.5	27.4	49.1*	37*

*Including about 12% from Japan, whereas imports from Japan did not exceed 1.8% of the new car market in Germany and 2.4% in France. Japanese imports to Italy were restricted by bilateral trade agreements and were not significant. Imports from countries other than Japan to Europe remained insignificant. Some U.K.-assembled cars also had a high foreign content because of Ford's and General Motors' integration.
Sources: Economist Intelligence Unit, *Motor Business* (various issues), *World Business Weekly*, 2 April 1979, and *SPRU Databank* (1983).

Industry observers expect European market annual growth rates to taper off to about 2% in the 1980s (growth taking place in Southern Europe only) and exports from Europe to decline further as a result of increased local production and Japanese presence in developing countries—leading to a production volume growth of less than 1% per year in Europe. The U.S. market is not expected to grow at an average rate of more than 3% per year and imports (whose share is around 25% in 1983) are expected to capture most of the growth. The Japanese market is also nearing saturation. This slow growth in developed countries during the 1980s is in direct contrast to very rapid growth during the 1960s and early 1970s when markets had often grown at a rate of 10% per year.

Greater difficulties will confront the European automobile industry over the next several years than in the past. Slow growth, decreasing exports from Europe and increasing Japanese exports to Europe mean that productivity gains will lead to employment cuts. Despite higher production volumes in 1977, employment in the industry was already 3.5% lower than in 1973. Significant employment reduction took place in the United Kingdom and later in France. Further cuts of the work force by 60,000 were deemed necessary in France by a government-appointed commission. Although international productivity comparisons are difficult, estimates clearly show that, by world standards, several European manufacturers have lagged behind in productivity. Further, European car manufacturing capacity exceeded potential demand by at least 10%, following significant investments in Spain by GM and Ford. The car industry also exerts a significant influence on the balance of payments, and reduced car exports could durably compromise trade balances in Germany, France and Italy. It is also at the nexus of conflicting national demands for energy conservation, convenient transportation and employment. In the late 1970s employment protection had become the major concern of European governments; in the United States energy conservation has taken priority. More recently the need for employment reduction, given European overcapacity and low productivity, has been recognized, and energy conservation has become less of a preoccupation in the United States. In both cases, though, economic and political demands continued to conflict. Further, increased international competition threatened the survival of national producers. In the late 1970s analysts of the international automobile industry predicted that only a production volume of more than 2 million cars a year, consolidated into a few product lines, might allow independent volume car makers to survive through the 1980s. In 1979 only six car makers were producing more than 2 million units or had the manufacturing capacity to do so.* Still, Europe had thirteen major car makers, Japan five and the United States four. New world competitors are also appearing, particularly producers from Eastern Europe and Korea. Mergers, alliances, or specific collaborative agreements had to develop, if all volume car makers were to survive.

Governments were relatively slow to react to the growth of imports. In Europe the internationalization of the industry in the 1960s was well tolerated because it was relatively balanced among car-producing countries. French car makers exported more and more to Germany, but so did German ones to France, for instance. Japanese imports were targeted first at countries with no national industry to protect, such as Finland, Ireland, Greece, Switzerland and the Benelux countries. Among major European car makers, only British Leyland foundered, and the causes of its decline stemmed partly from Britain's labor relations difficulties, and not just from international competition.

As the Japanese competition strengthened, however, European governments assumed an increasingly active role in restructuring, supporting and

---

*General Motors, Ford, Peugeot, Volkswagen, Toyota and Nissan (to which might possibly be added Fiat and Renault, each with a capacity of about 1.6 million units per year).

protecting their national manufacturers. As free trade limited their options, European governments started to negotiate various "voluntary" restraints to keep the Japanese importers at bay. The United States was facing even more pressure, with a domestic industry ill equipped to respond quickly to the threat from imports, and in 1980 also concluded a restraint agreement with Japan. Governments' actions thus developed along two diverging lines: (1) adapt to the global nature of the automobile industry, and (2) constrain and limit its internationalization.

In this chapter I shall use the automobile industry as a test case of the validity of the framework developed in Chapters 1 and 2 to analyze problems of international industry structures and competition in global industries.

The automobile industry is a prototype of an industry whose structural characteristics have strongly favored multinational integrated operations. The first section of this chapter reviews the structural characteristics and competitive conditions that led to global integration within the automobile industry. In the second section, strategic choices for competitors will be analyzed. In particular, alternatives to multinational integration will be discussed. Data on the product range and manufacturing system of various competitors show the different response of actual companies. In the analysis of strategic alternatives, primary attention will be given to international strategies for free-trade markets rather than the strategic choices of national competitors on their domestic markets or on closed foreign markets. Many of the propositions developed about international competition would apply, however, as well to domestic competition. Host government policies are described in a third section and their effectiveness assessed.

Structural Characteristics of the Automobile Industry: Competitive Imperatives

Integrated operations across borders enable firms to exploit economies of scale. Economies of scale in distribution as well as in production encouraged the evolution to global competition in the automobile industry. Factor costs differences among countries encouraged international trade. Finally, the convergence of product requirements among distinct geographical markets and the adoption of free trade policies by most governments made the internationalization of the industry possible. These structural characteristics are analyzed in this section.

Economies of Scale in Production

Automobile production has for a long time been extremely sensitive to economies of scale. Estimates of the size of the operations needed to exhaust all significant economies of scale are very high: 2 million similar units per year for machining of power train (engine and transmission parts), and 250,000 for final assembly.[2] These figures apply to units of a single type at the various stages of production. Some estimates are lower, however.[3] Substantial cost differences result from economies of scale. In a very detailed study of the body stamping operation, McGee (Table 3.2) suggests that penalties for operating at lower than most efficient scales are significant.[4] The major source of cost increase is the heavy fixed initial investment in dies and tools. McGee's model assumes that some tools are common to several models and shows the effect on unit costs of volume per type and number of types. The model suggests that below a volume of 500,000 units per model per year unit costs increase significantly.

No other car manufacturing operations have been studied so carefully as body stamping, but some sense of the overall impact of economies of scale can be grasped by considering the typical variable cost breakdown of a car and the effect on elements of the variable cost of doubling annual production volumes (Table 3.3).

The data presented above confirm that body stamping is most sensitive to scale, but that manufacturing of mechanical parts is also sensitive to scale. A doubling of annual production rates cuts variable costs by 8.4%, or roughly 5% of the total costs. Low margins in the industry make that difference very important. Net profit margins before taxes usually range from 2% to 5%, and a doubling of model production rates from 250,000 to 500,000 per year, for instance, may achieve a shift from losses to substantial profits.

In the late 1970s most European car models sold fewer than 500,000 units. Yet as model counts are not absolutely clear-cut—some components being common to several models and some others specific to submodels— considering only model assembly volumes may underestimate the extent to which some manufacturers took advantage of economies of scale. Manufacturers do differ considerably in the extent to which they take advantage of economies of scale for major components.

Volkswagen's whole 1977 European product range, for instance, used only two types of manual gearboxes and a single type of automatic transmission. Fiat, however, used six types of manual gearboxes and two automatic ones. Engines and platforms showed comparable differences: few types at Volkswagen, many types at Fiat. Although differences in costs between producing a narrow and a wide range of components may not be large for each item, cumulatively they may result in wide cost differences, other things being equal. One can certainly assume that lower labor cost in Italy made a wide component range more tolerable, or that Volkswagen starting in the 1970s with a whole new product range had more opportunities to design individual components for several models, or even model bodies around existing sets of components. Still, by 1984 Fiat had only

TABLE 3.2 *Hypothetical Die Cost Calculation*

Company	Number of models in company line	Number of unique tools required	Total die costs ($ millions)	Annual sales (million units)	Sales per model (million units)	Two-year die cost per vehicle
A	5	2.8	56	4.0	0.8	$7
B	3	2.1	42	1.5	0.5	$14
C	2	1.6	32	1.0	0.5	$16
D	1	1.0	20	0.1	0.1	$100

Note: This table is based on a detailed study of the manufacturing operations of several major automobile companies. To preserve the confidentiality of the data they provided and to compensate for the situational factor that may affect one or another manufacturer differently, data are presented in a "hypothetical" format borrowing from the experience of several manufacturers.
Source: McGee, "Economics of Size in Auto Body Manufacture", *The Journal of Law and Economics*, Vol. 16, October 1973, p.256.

TABLE 3.3   *Sensitivity of Car Variable Manufacturing Costs to Scale*

Major operations	Cost (as percentage of total variable cost)	Sensitivity to scale*
Engine manufacturing	15%	−15%
Gearboxes	7%	−15%
Axles	10%	−10%
Other mechanical parts	12%	−12%
Body stamping	8%	−30%
Body assembly	10%	−5%
Accessories and seats	11%	Negligible
Final assembly/painting	27%	Negligible

*Average unit percentage cost decrease generated by a doubling of annual production volumes of one model, in the 200,000 to 500,000 units per year range.
Source: Compiled by author from various industry experts' interviews.

three types of engines and five platforms to cover a whole product range. This contributed, among other factors, to Fiat's turnaround in the early 1980s. Other major companies active in Europe fell between Volkswagen and Fiat in terms of the ratios of number of models or number of different major components in the late 1970s, with GM-Europe, Ford and Renault closer to Volkswagen, and all other European companies more similar to Fiat. All, though, were evolving toward greater standardization of parts and subassemblies. A comparable differentiation could be found in Japan where Nissan had more different types of components than Toyota.

As the automobile industry moves through the 1980s, though, the importance of manufacturing economies of scale in shaping its future may well decrease substantially. New more flexible production programming and materials management techniques, often inspired by the practices of Japanese manufacturers, allow substantial reduction in production batches. Reduction in die changing time in body stamping from over 12 hours to less than 1 hour, for example, allow a given press shop to produce a much wider range of panels in smaller series at no cost penalty. Combined product-press innovations (such as General Motor's new "Saturn" method for constructing car bodies) can allow the economical production of vehicles in comparatively small numbers. Overall, automation and computer-assisted manufacturing also contribute to further increased production efficiency at relatively small manufacturing scales.

Economies of Scale in Distribution

As the growth of demand for cars in Europe slowed, and as the customers became more demanding and discriminating, car dealers came to play a very important role in increasing or maintaining the market share of individual brands. To gain dealer loyalty, most manufacturers developed a network of exclusive dealerships which in turn require a broad product range covering all volume market segments. Car makers with a narrow product line are at a disadvantage in attracting and keeping good exclusive dealers.

A minimum market share—often evaluated at about 4% to 5% by industry participants—is also needed to maintain a dense enough distribution and service coverage in a geographical market. Brands with lower shares cannot usually maintain coverage. To have competitive strength in a market—i.e., to be able to exert effective pressures on competitors—a share of 8% to 10% is often deemed necessary.

Frequent product introductions—and therefore short product life cycles—are also a factor in establishing and maintaining competitive strength, as customers' interest for existing models decreases quickly with new competitive product entries. Competitors who can at least rejuvenate the styling of their products often, if not the mechanical components, enjoy a competitive advantage. This encourages manufacturers to introduce the same product in a wide range of geographical markets in quick succession to recover initial costs of engineering and tooling quickly—and be able to shorten the life cycle of their products.

Economies of scale both in production and in distribution impose conflicting requirements. Economies of scale in distribution create pressures for model proliferation and fast replacement, economies of scale in manufacturing call for large volume production of each model over many years. R & D costs also push manufacturers toward large volumes per type. Taken together, they make the minimum size of a competitive volume car manufacturer very high.

Similarity Among Geographical Markets

Converging product specifications among geographical markets accelerated the evolution of the automobile industry toward worldwide competition. U.S. fuel economy regulations led to the development of cars comparable in size and technology to European ones. In the meantime, within Europe the transition from minicar (below 1000 cc) to larger sedans was only slowed by the oil crisis. The 1300 to 2500 cc engine displacement segment consequently emerged as the mainstay of both markets. Product leadership in that segment allowed imports from Europe and Japan to increase their overall share of the U.S. market to over 25%. With comparable products becoming available in the early 1980s, General Motors decided to produce similar cars in the United States and Europe. At the upper end of the market it would produce and sell large cars in North America only, while at the lower end it would rely on captive Japanese exports from its affiliate in Japan, Isuzu, and from Suzuki.

Whereas until Honda's entry in the late 1960s most early Japanese cars had enjoyed only limited appeal in Europe, more modern designs began to gain popularity in the 1970s, so that Japanese imports to Europe increased substantially. In the late 1970s Japanese imports took almost half the U.S. small car market segment. By the early 1980s the 1500 to 2500 cc segment also accounted for the bulk of the Japanese market.[5] From the United States, Europe and Japan, the major line of market demarcation in the medium size segments shifted to differences between developed and developing countries requiring simpler, sturdier, easier to maintain vehicles.

Factor Costs and Productivity Differences

Until the 1970s the lower labor productivity of the European car industry, in relation to the United States, had been more than offset by lower wages. By the mid-1970s labor costs in Europe had almost caught up with U.S. wages, but European productivity still lagged. Japanese productivity had increased faster than Japanese relative wage levels, giving a larger absolute cost advantage to Japanese manufacturers over Europe and the United States. In 1980 this cost advantage was estimated to reach about $1500 per vehicle.[6]

Such cost differences gave an almost unbeatable lead to Japanese manufacturers. Productivity efforts in Europe and the United States could close this gap only partly.[7] Unit margins were so low as to give slight savings on unit variable costs a very large impact on after-tax profits. Although Japanese manufacturers did not price their vehicles aggressively, Europe had become much more vulnerable to lower cost competition.

Free Trade Policies

Since the 1920s, when Ford and General Motors started volume exports to Europe, European markets had been closed behind tariff walls.[8] Protection continued until the implementation of the European Economic Community. In the 1960s the EEC common external tariff was reduced to 17.6% and then decreased to 11% on cars and 9% on parts. Within Europe, trade became completely free and the norms and standards guiding automobile production were unified, at least for major components. A few governments lagged in complete trade liberalization. For instance, Italy imposed a special purchase tax heavily slanted against imported cars and other countries used excise taxes to penalize imports. But on the whole, by the late 1960s, a policy of complete free trade within the EEC and of low, common external tariffs was in effect.[9] Further, in the absence of common EEC investment control policy, MNCs were relatively free to invest in one country or another according to relative factor costs or government incentive, and serve the whole EEC market from whatever location they had chosen. In some cases foreign exchange control regulations were used to limit such mobility of capital. In the late 1970s the surge in Japanese exports was met by increased protection in Europe. Italy and France used regulations to limit Japanese imports to relatively low levels, whereas the United Kingdom and Germany negotiated voluntary trade restraint agreements. The United States at first remained committed to free trade, and then limited Japanese imports to 1.68 million units per year.

In sum, for five main reasons—economies of scale in (1) production and (2) distribution, (3) growing similarity among geographical markets, (4) wide gaps in factor costs and productivity and (5) relative free trade—the automobile industry is characterized by intensifying global competition. The maturing and the slowing growth of the markets in developed countries means that growth for individual manufacturers can come only through penetration of new markets in developing countries—markets usually controlled and regulated by governments—or through taking customers away from other suppliers in mature markets, a difficult and costly process. The growing homogeneity of markets across borders, their finer segmentation between similar customer groups in various countries, and the lesser costs of long distance transportation, make the development of common products for the world market feasible. Once such products are developed, economies of scale often make their production in a single location desirable. Changes in factor costs, particularly in the relationship between wages and productivity, also make the position of Europe more difficult and give a cost advantage to the United States, Japan and newly developing countries. Firms react to these evolutions in different ways.

Firms' Strategies: the Search for Competitiveness

The most obvious strategic response to the changes described above was integration of operations across borders, in search of lower costs and more efficient production to respond to the increasing demands for economic performance. Integration, however, can take different forms according to the starting position of the company and the economic and political constraints on its evolution. Other approaches are the development of new markets, the confinement to small defensible segments and the invasion of poorly served segments.

Integration Strategies

MNCs were the first to feel the pinch of tougher competition, since in each national market they were usually smaller than their national competitors. Yet only MNCs had the advantage of multiple subsidiaries that could be linked into an integrated network. They therefore started by integrating their European operations, then they considered global approaches to increase competitiveness: so-called "world cars" and "efficient module" approaches were the result. Integration of suppliers was another strategy pursued by major car makers.

Europewide integration

The leader of integration was Ford of Europe, created in 1967 to coordinate the activities of Ford of Germany and Ford of Britain. Ford of Europe's basic coordination and integration plan was relatively simple: to specialize the engineering department (mechanical parts in Britain, bodies in Germany), the design departments (exterior in Germany, interior in Britain) and to rationalize production. A common product range of only three basic car lines,* and a van line was developed between 1969 and 1974 to cover most market segments, but with few basic models. Numerous difficulties had to be overcome, and the developing of this initial common product range was late, suffered from cost overruns, and did not meet all market acceptance expectations.[10] By the late 1970s, with the addition of the Fiesta, a very successful small car, the integration pattern of which we analyzed in Chapter 1, Ford succeeded in selling a well-designed, attractive, unique product range covering almost all significant market segments in Europe.

Over the years manufacturing had been rationalized, with most components and parts for any given product made in one location only and assembly distributed among different plants. Much flexibility was achieved in using common components in several models. Ford of Europe also built two new large plants: one in France for mechanical components, the other in Spain for engine manufacture and car assembly.[11] Both France and Spain offered lower labor costs than Germany and better labor productivity than the United Kingdom. Ford had expanded mechanical part manufacture activities in the United Kingdom (such activities are less sensitive to labor disruptions), and body and assembly activities in Germany where the work force was more efficient. In 1979 Ford was further expanding its facilities in the United Kingdom (a new engine plant in South Wales) and Germany (additional assembly capacity at existing plants); it also considered further investments in Southern Europe.

General Motors (GM) followed Ford's lead in the mid-1970s.[12] By the early 1970s, a new management group in Europe recognized that Vauxhall, GM's British subsidiary, was too small to remain viable as an autonomous self-financing unit. General Motors' European management decided to take advantage of its German subsidiary's superior capability and to distribute Opel-designed cars in the United Kingdom under the Vauxhall brand. The Vauxhall cars were very close derivatives of Opel's own

*Not including the Capri model, a moderately sporty coupe.

models, with minor appearance changes, and, in some cases, different engines. Some of these cars were made in Opel's own plants, others in Vauxhall's. Despite a formal corporate commitment to a two-brand strategy, distribution of Vauxhall cars in continental Europe was nominal, with the exception of Belgium. In 1979 Opel also decided to expand capacity in lower cost countries than Germany: Spain for body and assembly work, Austria for engines. General Motors also produced components in France.

"World car" approaches

By the late 1970s General Motors, and to a lesser extent Ford, were moving towards global integration, beyond the rationalization of their European operations. Their so-called "world cars" were new models developed to be manufactured in several continents. Responsibility for the development and engineering of world cars could be allocated to one subsidiary, with the completed design being transferred to other subsidiaries for manufacture, or could be undertaken jointly by several subsidiaries or divisions in different countries. Marketing the world cars on all markets—with adaptation as minor as required by national regulation or consumer taste differences*—can generate large production volumes. Production of specific components can either be carried out independently by each national subsidiary assembling the vehicle, or procured from common sources to take advantage of economies of scale.

Manufacturing patterns for world cars are similar in logic to the Ford Fiesta's integration pattern, except that they can be developed on a global scale. Manufacturers found at least three major benefits in the world cars: the spreading of initial development and engineering costs on a larger total production volume, lower direct unit costs in the production of the most scale-sensitive components (some mechanical parts and body stampings), and fuller utilization of new capacity (minimum capacity increments were smaller in relation to total volume).

Yet many obstacles stood in the way of world cars. Economic considerations alone made full integration unattractive: higher transportation costs often more than offset the gains of further economies of scale for many parts and components. Moreover, complete integration made the whole MNC system extremely vulnerable to local disruptions. A prolonged strike at a single subsidiary, for instance, could paralyze the entire operation. Fully integrated manufacturing thus was not always attractive.

Joint development and engineering tasks were also impeded by differences in regulation of the industry among countries. Safety laws hampered the joint manufacturing of body stampings for European and U.S. cars: the thickness of sheet metals had to be different to meet U.S. and European regulations, thus making common tools and presses impracticable.

* Even within Europe minor differences are needed. For instance, French consumers are used to softer plusher seats than German ones.

A transition to a world car approach is also extremely expensive. The development of world cars is particularly costly: $700 million to $1 billion according to most estimates for design, engineering, tooling and launch costs. Simple calculations show that, given the cost structure of auto manufacture and sales, a cumulative production volume of at least 2 million units of the same model is needed to recover such high fixed initial costs.[13] To some extent, as the first world cars often embody new technologies (at least new to the MNCs developing these world cars), one can expect that future models will not be as expensive to design and engineer. Although world cars represent the logical conclusion of an integration strategy, they may not become the general approach for multinational car manufacturers.

Efficient modules

Short of full integration through world cars, the coordinating of production of components and parts may bring significant savings to MNCs. General Motors, for instance, has developed an "efficient module" concept, i.e., a standard plant size for various components or stages in assembly or operations, running from 300,000 units per year for final assembly to 1 million for casting certain components. Capacity of efficient modules is set at the minimum efficient size for the specific component involved. Capacity utilization for each efficient module involves the coordination of new product development, engineering, product introduction dates, and plant expansions among the various subsidiaries. As a result, capacity utilization can be planned on a global basis and new investments made module by module. The output of each new efficient module can be shared temporarily among areas, in order to find an optimal balance between transportation costs and the costs of underutilization of existing capacity at various locations or of the latest efficient-module-sized capacity increment.

Ford and (later) GM had been the major proponents of integration, but by the late 1970s other companies followed their lead. Volkswagen expanded its operations in Brazil and Mexico and established assembly plants in the United States.[14] Partial integration was achieved among these operations: cars were assembled in the United States from components made in Brazil, Germany, Mexico and the United States. Volkswagen also moved the production of models most exposed to price competition to low wage countries, in particular the global production center for the venerable "Beetle" was transferred to Brazil and large-scale manufacturing was undertaken in Nigeria. New plants in other countries, such as Egypt where labor was abundant and inexpensive, were under consideration.

In France, Peugeot responded to the same competitive pressures as Volkswagen with a series of acquisitions: first Citroën in 1974, and then Chrysler's European operations in 1979. Altogether the new company found itself with no fewer than 45 plants, twice too many, and closed some down, both in France and Great Britain.[15] Peugeot's management decided to rationalize and to integrate industrial activities, without losing the distinct brand identities. With roughly 17.6% of the European market, the new group kept three differentiated brands (renaming the "Chrysler" products "Talbot" and, at first, completely distinct dealer networked. Despite these multiple brands, its European market share fell since 1979. Merging dealerships made the fall even worse. By 1983 Peugeot was back to a market share level predating its acquisition of Chrysler Europe, and was heavily in the red. Still, rationalized components and product ranges, new appealing models, a possible drop of the Talbot brand, and much reduced manning levels give it a chance to resist the world class producers such as Ford, GM and Volkswagen.

Suppliers integration

Integration pressures affected automobile component makers even more, since economies of scale affect components more than assembly. Japan had consolidated early its component industry in a set of specialized suppliers. These suppliers can offer extremely low prices, since they exploit all possible economies of scale. The Japanese automobile manufacturers are thus less vertically integrated than their competitors and derive part of their cost advantages from extremely efficient suppliers. In Europe both national consolidations and multinational integrations take place. Governments have intervened to protect weak national suppliers. For instance, after blocking the acquisition of Ducellier (a major components supplier) by British component maker Lucas, the French have embarked on a national program of consolidation of the industry. The German cartel office also blocked acquisitions by the British firm GKN in Germany. Many German component makers supply the whole German market and export intensively; a notable example is Bosch for fuel injection systems. Whereas governments often took an active role in national consolidations of component makers, multinational integration among component makers often followed car manufacturers' comparable strategies. For instance: ITT was integrating its European car component operations in response to demands by customers such as Ford for lower prices and large volume production.

Quasi-integration Strategies

Short of rationalizing already existing operations into an integrated network (e.g., Ford, General Motors), building such a network (e.g., Volkswagen) or acquiring one through mergers (e.g., Peugeot), other car makers with significant European operations have tried to gain some of the benefits of integration without committing themselves to full integration.

Most national competitors in Europe developed a growing web of agreements and alliances with competitors or suppliers. The most common goal of these alliances is to take advantage of economies of scale, and accessorily to create mutual interests between manufacturers.[16]

Most such alliances involved joint manufacturing, such as the Société Franco-Suédoise de Moteurs producing 2.6 litre engines for Volvo, Renault and Peugeot. Each of these companies taken separately did not have enough volume to justify an efficient engine plant: but together they did. Similarly, some of the Renault 14s engines were made by Peugeot. The small cars assembled by Chrysler in the United States received mechanical components from Volkswagen, Mitsubishi and Peugeot. In the commercial vehicle business, several companies had pooled their interest to develop a common mid-size truck. The agreement was known as "Club 4". Numerous examples of such cooperative agreements could be cited; they all represented efforts by manufacturers to pool their resources and their needs to produce components efficiently.

Some alliances involved product transfers, such as that between Honda and British Leyland (BL). Honda licensed its Ballade car to BL for manufacture by BL for sales in Europe as the Triumph Acclaim. Further joint products are planned. BL, with an ageing model range and few resources to develop a new one, gains a lot from the deal: a new, succcessful model when it is most needed and some insight into Japanese manufacturing methods. To Honda, the BL deal is a way to penetrate the European market without having to set up its own extensive dealer network and circumvent criticism about Japanese imports. Such alliances as that between AMC and Renault, or BL and Honda, can be particularly useful for companies not yet effective in competing globally or too small to maintain a full product range on their own. It overcomes a major barrier to rapid entry by giving them quick access to a new market through an existing dealer network. It also increases their car line production volumes and spreads development costs on larger volumes. Such alliances can also fill gaps in product ranges quickly and at a low cost. Yet because they provide joint volume without joint control they may not allow the same competitive strength as full mergers between companies from various countries would provide.[17]

More ambitious strategies were aimed at exploiting distribution economies of scale. Renault, which had tried several times with only modest success to penetrate the U.S. market on its own, took a major interest in American Motors Corporation (AMC) to distribute Renault cars in the United States and AMC also produces derivatives of Renault models in the United States with a mix of imported and U.S.-made parts and components. Renault, with only 320 dealers in the United States, hoped the agreement with AMC and its 1700 dealers could boost its U.S. sales substantially.[18]

Outright transnational mergers have been few, and met with little success. The most significant was the creation of the Industrial Vehicles Corporation (IVECO), the benefits of which were already mentioned in Chapter 1. Yet after a few years the German minority partner withdrew. The merger of Volvo in Sweden with DAF in The Netherlands met with moderate success; the first joint product (marketed as the Volvo 343) was initially less than successful.[19] Volvo and DAF had very different operating patterns and traditions and the new "343" car line was rushed into production without fully resolving the differences between their respective approaches to manufacturing methods. Following this relatively unsuccessful merger, Volvo's car division started to cooperate more narrowly with Renault, which took a minority interest in Volvo. Typically, most pressures for rationalization and integration were felt by smaller, marginal producers in the global auto industry, those with precious little resources and little time to implement mergers successfully.

The second-tier Japanese companies—small producers in comparison with Toyota and Nissan—had taken an intermediate position between distribution or license production agreements (à la Honda) and full merger with a foreign company. Each of them teamed up with a U.S. multinational. Isuzu (about 43% GM owned) supplied light pick-up trucks and other small vehicles to GM, and distributed GM cars in Japan. With the development of "world cars", Isuzu became more closely integrated into GM's operations. Suzuki became a supplier of minicars to GM. In 1979 Ford had taken a 25% equity interest in Toyo Kogyo with whom it had long standing technical cooperation agreements. Ford distributed Toyo Kogyo's cars in various countries under the Ford brand. Toyo Kogyo's products were also sold independently under the Mazda brand. Finally, Mitsubishi had relied on Chrysler to distribute its cars, under Chrysler's brands, in the United States and other countries. Uncertainties about Chrysler's future prompted Mitsubishi to take control of its own distribution in 1981.

Such quasi-integration strategies as those described in the above examples were expected to continue through the multiplication of interfirm agreements on components. It was expected that vertical integration would decrease, i.e., that volume car makers would buy as many standard components from large volume external suppliers or joint ventures with other car manufacturers as they could, rather than manufacture them.[20]

The major concern of all the quasi-integration strategies was to gain some of the benefits of the integration quickly, at a low cost, while preserving the firm's autonomy, and avoiding the administrative and managerial difficulties and uncertainties involved in full-fledged mergers. Since only national champions survived the waves of national mergers in the 1960s, further mergers would have to be transnational. Managers of car companies baulked at the idea of such mergers because of their political sensitivity,[21] and because the record of transnational mergers in other industries was far from successful.[22] Quasi-integration strategies were seen to offer a way for smaller manufacturers to survive without losing their identity.

Geographical Expansion Strategies

Tariff barriers and, in some cases, extensive regulatory frameworks (with stipulations on local content, ownership, technology fees, profit repatriation and other key aspects) often protect rapidly growing developing countries' markets and shelter the local industry from international competition to encourage its autonomous development. Major international auto makers see several advantages to investing in such markets: it diversifies their earnings base (plant construction revenues and license fees) and puts part of their operations in protected markets.

Protected, low labor cost markets also offer the opportunity to gain unique advantages in global competition. The 1973 Ford investment in Spain, or the 1976 Renault investment in Portugal, or Volkswagen's massive investments in Brazil, were all non-matchable moves, either by law (Spain and Portugal)* or by the mere deterrence created by large investments in a limited market. Beyond a shelter from competition, investing in protected markets offered further advantages:

1. *Component volume*. Most new national car industries start with the assembly of vehicles from "completely-knocked-down" (CKD) part kits supplied by car makers' home plants. Being very labor-intensive, assembly can be conducted in small local plants at no major cost disadvantage. Assembly operations in various developing countries can provide, taken together, the volume needed for efficient part and component production in the home country.
2. *Preemption of growth markets*. Most growth in the auto industry will come from rich developing countries with annual demand growth rates of 10% or more.[23] An early willingness to invest in these countries facilitates a longer-term presence in their markets.
3. *Low cost sources*. If sufficient volume can be reached locally, lower labor costs than in Western Europe or North America could provide manufacturers with a cost advantage. Ford's labor costs in Spain, for instance, were about 35% lower than in Germany.[24] Renault's managers hope low labor costs in Portugal will contribute to restoring cost competitiveness with Japanese competitors.[25] Renault had also

---

* In both Spain and Portugal the regulations governing the automobile industry were amended to make it unattractive, although not legally impossible, for another major car maker to invest into the country. It was expected, however, that by 1982 Spain might become a member of the EEC, a move which would open the Spanish market to importers and put an end to most means of protection for domestic car makers.

used component subcontracting to low cost Eastern European car manufacturers.

4. *Revenues from plant construction and technology transfers.* Both Fiat and Renault turned a weakness into a strength: their expertise in engineering plants efficiently was largely developed in response to difficult labor relations. Labor problems had led both companies to devote a great deal of attention to plant automation and working conditions. This expertise was readily saleable abroad. Fiat's sales of turnkey plants in Russia, Poland and Yugoslavia brought substantial profits and revenues. Renault was also very active in building plants, with contracts in Poland and Yugoslavia for component foundries and turnkey contracts in Algeria.[26]

Despite the advantage described above, only manufacturers already successful in the competitive markets of developed countries can expand into protected markets: only they can offer new models,* provide competence in plant engineering and construction, and guarantee export volumes from the new plants that will at least balance the imports of components. Thus the strategy of geographical expansion is not a potential refuge for weaker producers, but may complement the integration and strategies of already successful manufacturers.

Specialization Strategies

A genuine alternative to integration, however, was offered by the withdrawal to, and the defense of, a narrow, specialized market segment, such as sports cars, luxury cars, recreational vehicles and 4-wheel-drive vehicles. Customers in such segments usually value product differentiation over low prices. Most differentiated market segments are not large enough, however, to warrant penetration by a volume car manufacturer with good profit prospects; thus specialty car manufacturers are relatively immune from competition. Furthermore, perceived product differentiation is usually enhanced by careful image advertising by these specialty suppliers, making it hard, for instance, for Ford or Renault to challenge BMW effectively even if they developed directly competitive products. It is possible thus for several relatively small volume European producers of high-quality, high-performance cars to prosper (e.g., Daimler Benz, BMW, SAAB or Jaguar).

In most markets careful segmentation could identify poorly served needs. For example, there had been a significant unserved demand in the United States for true sports cars styled and engineered between the basic sports cars offered by British Leyland (e.g., Triumph Spitfire) and the

*A major source of dissatisfaction to the Spanish government about the initial investors in Spain (Fiat, Renault, Chrysler, Citroën) was that they transferred to Spain the production of ageing models, already obsolescent in technology and styling in their home markets.

luxury sports cars (e.g., Ferrari). Japanese suppliers took advantage of this gap in the late 1960s and the 1970s with such very successful models as the Nissan (Datsun) 240Z. Japanese suppliers continued to dominate the intermediate sports car segment in the late 1970s. Only in the mid-1980s do U.S. manufacturers respond effectively with competitive models.[27]

Specialization and segmentation strategies could be equated to an extreme form of integration, where all production is concentrated in the home country and foreign markets are served via exports only. Insofar as product differentiation can allow higher prices to offset the diseconomies of serving a small segment, and insofar as concentrated production allows some economies of scale, this is a tenable position. Should the segment become too small, minimum efficiency in production could not be maintained; should it become too big—as the medium luxury car segment in Europe in the early 1980s—competition would come in. Yet, as sources of product differentiation evolve, not all differentiated positions are equally viable in the long run. Volvo built its differentiated position on the promotion of safety in the 1960s, a position no longer defensible by the 1970s when most countries enacted laws requiring all new vehicles to comply with comprehensive safety regulations.

Short of clear-cut specialization strategies, companies could try to differentiate their offerings to follow a distinct approach to the volume market. Volkswagen, in the late 1970s, was positioning itself in an intermediate position, between the volume manufacturers of popular cars (e.g., Ford, Renault, Fiat . . .) and the luxury car makers (e.g., BMW, Daimler Benz) both by its model range and its pricing policies. It adopted a similar positioning in the United States, between Japanese imports and luxury imports. Conversely, Fiat's prices were usually lower than that of some competitors. In Europe, Renault was trying to offer many options to the customers, thanks to more complex manufacturing schemes to generate different models with relatively few different components. To some extent, Renault was emulating the Japanese approach of flexibility in manufacturing.

Flexibility Strategies

In the early 1980s Japanese car producers are succeeding in reconciling strategies of integration and strategies of specialization. The manufacturing processes adopted by Japanese car makers are both flexible and efficient, and economies of scale are therefore much less model-specific than in the West. This allows the Japanese to have a much greater range of models, and to replace models faster, without suffering significant diseconomies of scale. This approach is the opposite of GM's drive toward both product standardization and world cars, as exemplified by the "X" and then the "J" cars. A greater range of models allows fragmentation of the market into smaller segments and to differentiating product ranges and marketing approaches from country to country with more than cosmetic details and pricing. It is also possible for the Japanese producers to forgo some economies of scale, since their cost advantage averages about 20% over U.S. costs.

The causes of the Japanese cost advantage are now well known, and can only be briefly summarized here. Rather than to any specific factor, the advantage can be ascribed to systemic interactions among many different factors. Among these are the quality, training, and responsibility of the work force (which can lead to a quality control approach very different from usual practices in the West and to extremely high product quality), the intimate interaction with geographically close suppliers, the lowering of in-process inventories and the curing of all bottlenecks; precise materials planning processes and creative approaches to machine resetting.[28] These factors, combined, have given a major cost advantage to Japanese competitors. Labor costs and automation contribute less to this cost advantage than is generally believed, which means that integration strategies based on further capacity relocation to developing countries, or on major automation efforts to decrease labor content, would not close the gap. Rather, the advantage is systemic, and the U.S. and European manufacturers are slowly learning to emulate it. Ford of Europe, for instance, launched a major "after Japan" program in 1980–81. To some extent, though, this advantage depends on geographic characteristics of Japan, such as the proximity between part suppliers and car assemblers and the long-term relationships that have evolved between them. It also assumes very different relationships between labor and management than exist in the United States and Western Europe. This explains the reluctance of Japanese producers to invest abroad—where labor characteristics and labor relations may be quite different, and where the system interactions that underly their superiority may be difficult to generate as one or another building block will be lacking. Toyota has no significant overseas manufacturing (if one leaves aside 27 small-scale assembly facilities using CKD kits). It has shown great reluctance to pursue foreign investments (e.g., bowing out lately from a tentative agreement for a large-scale facility in Taiwan), its only major undertaking being a joint venture in California with GM to produce a Toyota-designed joint model. This is widely seen as a test for Toyota and also, should it succeed in replicating some of the conditions achieved in Japan, a challenge for the remainder of the U.S. automobile industry, and a learning ground for GM. Nissan builds pick-up trucks in the United States, but shied away from a major investment in the United Kingdom, building only a small token plant to test U.K. labor conditions and save face, following protracted negotiations with the U.K. government.

The examples of Volvo, Renault, Volkswagen and the Japanese producers suggest choices of strategies are not necessarily a one-time either/or decision. Evolutions can take place from one type of strategy to another over a period of several years. Several strategic moves can also be undertaken simultaneously to improve competitiveness. Volkswagen's example is revealing: integration, move to new countries, and differentiated competitive position in Europe and the United States. Beyond the economic postures of individual firms, the feasibility and relative attractiveness of the various types of strategies for firms competing in global industries were also determined by the policies of the various national governments. In particular one can observe no nationally responsive strategy in the auto industry, beyond the fact that most competitors are responsive to their domestic market, and orient their priorities as a function of these markets' segments, rather than toward worldwide priorities. Otherwise the logic of integration prevails.

National Policies: Facing the Competitive Imperatives

Global industries raise a difficult choice for governments: whether to try to forestall the interdependency created by their economic characteristics, or attempt to benefit from such interdependency. This choice also may look significantly different to countries in which all car manufacturing is carried out by MNC subsidiaries and countries that have their own independent national companies. Further, the choice of a government may evolve over time as its national industry develops. In broad terms, governments can (1) try to limit international interdependency (and the operations of MNCs) and later turn interdependency to their advantage; (2) try to benefit from regulated interdependency and the presence of integrated MNCs; and (3) support their domestic nationally owned industry by helping it to become internationally competitive. Although continued protection, calling for national responsiveness strategies, is conceivable as a policy, no examples were found, for reasons that will become apparent in the discussion below. These national policies in the automobile industry are analyzed below.

Limits to Interdependency

Some countries have set out to become major competitors in a global industry by first closing their national markets to foreign companies (but gaining access to their technology), then by establishing an efficient domestic industry fueled by a rapidly growing domestic market, and finally by assisting this national industry in competing internationally. Japan provides the most striking case of such a growth strategy. In the 1950s all Japanese suppliers were involved in agreements with foreign producers (typically not large, leading multinational companies but second-tier, national firms such as Willys in the United States, Rootes in the United

Kingdom or Renault in France). These foreign producers supplied technology and machinery, and in some cases CKD kits or parts. As technology in the automobile industry was already relatively mature, these second-tier national firms could provide technology comparable to that of major multinationals. In the late 1950s and early 1960s Japan's huge domestic market remained protected by barriers to importers and by the exclusion of foreign direct investment. In the 1960s the Ministry of International Trade and Industry (MITI) encouraged mergers among domestic firms to achieve more efficient production, thereby leading to the consolidation of firms into two major groups, Nissan (who merged with Prince) and Toyota, leaving aside three smaller firms linked to U.S. car makers (Toyo Kogyo to Ford, Isuzu to GM, Mitsubishi to Chrysler), Honda which had not yet significantly expanded from motorcycles to cars, and a few minor producers. Concentration and rapid growth combined with the use of common components across models (within the same firm and across firms) enabled the Japanese industry to achieve very high levels of productivity.[29] Furthermore, model proliferation was then kept to a minimum.[30] The number of plants was also kept quite low, with very large average size. Toyota's production is concentrated in six main plants, three for car assembly, one for commercial vehicle and two for parts manufacture. Similarly, Nissan's production is concentrated at six locations.[31] Until 1980 Toyo Kogyo's production was concentrated in one location at Hiroshima.

The growth of the domestic market was consistently encouraged by the government through policies which facilitated the construction of freeways and highways, despite lack of space and difficult terrain. The rapidly growing economy also fueled the demand for commercial vehicles in the early 1950s, and for passenger cars in the late 1960s. In turn, the growth of the home market made it possible for Japanese manufacturers to become internationally competitive.

One can see from Fig. 3.1 that exports started to grow rapidly when the domestic market started to level off in the early 1970s. Whereas, early on, exports had been a secondary activity; after export experience had been gained in the early 1960s attention was devoted to export markets needs, product quality, and the development of good dealer networks abroad.[32] Exports were also helped by the simplicity and reliability of the vehicles, and the quality of their finish and appointments. In the meantime, the Japanese market remained almost completely protected through a combination of import restrictions and a firm grip by domestic car makers on distribution channels. A notable change in 1971 was the authorization of foreign investors' minority equity position in Japanese companies. This led GM and Chrysler to take an equity interest in Isuzu and Mitsubishi Motors, respectively. Ford followed suit in 1979 by acquiring a 25% equity interest in Toyo Kogyo. The imbalance in trade created by the strategy of

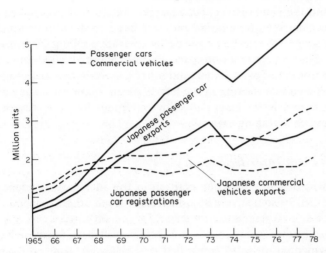

FIG. 3.1   Growth of Japanese car exports and domestic registrations.

domestic protection and export expansion had created numerous tensions, particularly with the United States and the EEC, the two large markets where Japanese penetration was highest.[33] Pressures for tighter protection against Japanese imports increased with the economic difficulties of Europe and the United States.[34]

The situation had reversed itself; other countries now protected their industries against Japanese inroads. In the United States an agreement was reached in 1980, limiting Japanese imports to 1.68 million p.a. for three years. In 1984 the agreement was renewed, with a slightly higher ceiling. Similarly, France, Germany, Italy and the United Kingdom formally or informally limited Japanese imports to levels low enough to prevent Japanese companies from establishing effective distribution and service networks.

Governments have in general tolerated integration in the automobile industry only insofar as no major trade imbalance resulted. The interpenetration of European national markets by European producers was relatively balanced and well accepted, while the development of the Japanese industry was not. Protectionist reactions, therefore, limit the scope for a country to benefit from global integration by maintaining very unbalanced trade in its favor over a long period.

In the 1970s two other countries adopted a strategy similar to that followed earlier by Japan: the Soviet Union and Korea. The Soviet Union, with a huge untapped domestic car market and a shortage of commercial vehicles, acquired automobile technology from Fiat and the technology for commercial vehicles from various truck manufacturers. The Lada car factory and the Kama River truck factory are efficient production centers with a very narrow product line and very large production volumes. Lada was exporting to Western Europe a Fiat derivative selling for considerably less than Fiat's original counterpart. By 1978 about 160,000 cars had been exported from the Soviet Union and other Comecon countries to Western Europe. Korea was starting in the late 1970s to follow the same policies as Japan (and to a lesser extent the Soviet Union) by protecting its home market and encouraging exports.

Benefits from Interdependency

The transition to global competition in the auto industry opened new opportunities for some national industries, but put others in jeopardy. The Australian and Argentinian industries, for instance, were severely threatened. Both countries had mature markets, a well-developed but relatively small fragmented industry controlled by MNCs but isolated from major integration flows. National producers and the autonomous subsidiaries of MNCs were too small to compete effectively in the international market. Stiff barriers to trade could protect the domestic industry but at a high cost to national consumers, yet moving toward freer trade would compromise employment.

Conversely, countries with a large market and abundant labor at comparatively low wages were becoming very attractive to MNCs desiring to develop export bases. For instance, in 1978, according to some local estimates, it was almost 25% cheaper to manufacture a car in Brazil than in Germany or Sweden, other things being equal. Brazil was made even more attractive by government policies such as tax abatements and low interest rate loans to exporters. Cars adapted to the Brazilian market were readily saleable in other developing countries, and ideological and ethnic reasons sometimes made Brazilian exports more acceptable than European, Japanese or U.S. cars in various non-European countries. Ford and Volkswagen, the two largest producers in Brazil, both exported about $200 million worth of cars and components from Brazil in 1978.[35]

Brazil was deriving many benefits from the globalization of the world's auto industry. The Australian government's concern was to ensure the survival of a domestic industry. Until the 1970s the Australian car industry had been protected by local content regulations requiring that 85% of the value of the cars be added locally and by stiff import restrictions. After the 1973 oil crisis, the market shifted to smaller cars and the local subsidiaries of the U.S. MNCs found themselves losing the market share to Japanese imports (authorized by then) and were unable to shift quickly to the "world cars" in integrated multinational production networks, not autonomously in each country. Chrysler, short of cash, and without a multinational network, sold its operations to Mitsubishi.[36] General Motors' subsidiary,

Holden, started negotiation with the Australian government, arguing that it wanted to play a major role in the manufacture of GM's new smaller "world cars" but that such a role was not compatible with the restrictive Australian local content legislation. An agreement was reached in 1979, according to which GM would build a new engine plant in Australia (at a cost of U.S. $210 million) that would export two-thirds of its production. GM would be authorized to import components in excess of the local content requirements and to assemble cars locally mainly from imported components, provided the trade balance was not in deficit. Mitsubishi, after its acquisition of the Chrysler subsidiary in 1979, was negotiating agreements of a similar nature.

Many countries fell somewhere between Brazil and Australia in the mix of benefits they could derive and costs they might incur from the globalization of the industry. Spain, for instance, faced a difficult situation in the early 1970s: it had a substantial local industry, partly foreign owned, well protected, and ineffective. Production was spread between too many manufacturers, each with too many models. Yet it had become clear that with Spain's possible entry into the EEC, protection would have to decrease and the potential international competitiveness of the industry be improved if it were to survive. Spain was also attractive to major car makers, however; it offered both a large national market and low cost labor compared with Northern Europe.[37] This enabled the Spanish government to negotiate successfully to attract Ford in 1973, and then GM in 1979, and to convince Volkswagen to cooperate with SEAT. The aim of the Spanish government, through these various moves, was to provide for a viable industry in 1982, when Spain was expected to join the EEC. Delays in joining the EEC then led to a transitory period during which Spain would progressively relax the regulatory framework and decrease the protection around its car industry. The industry would remain controlled by foreign MNCs; but at least there was every reason to believe it would be efficient and employment would not be compromised when faced with full international competition. It was hoped that by 1986 the industry would need no particular government support to be competitive. In all countries, but perhaps more so in the United States, the benefits of participating in the integrated global industry, rather than isolating one's country from it via protection, were clear. No government, therefore, implemented continued protection as a viable option to ensure the future of its automobile industry.

Support for the National Industry

After World War II, most European governments supported the growth of their national car industry.[38] Trucks were needed for national reconstruction and car ownership became a social goal. Various factors promoted mass car ownership. First, the real price of cars fell substantially, both as productivity increased in the car industry and as real income rose. The real price of gasoline, after taxes, also decreased steadily, at least until 1974. Taxes on cars were kept low, and in most European countries private car transportation was generally indirectly subsidized. Highway construction was also encouraged in most countries, particularly in Germany. Among European countries, only in France and Italy were toll expressways predominant.

Yet there had been significant differences between major European countries. France consistently encouraged the growth of the car industry; in the United Kingdom, following a period of export encouragement after World War II, it was used as a tool for stop–go economic policies in the 1960s and 1970s. Constant changes in credit regulation and purchase taxes created artificial market fluctuations and prevented British manufacturers from establishing a large, stable, profitable home market base. By the late 1960s an overvalued currency also made it increasingly difficult for the British car makers to export. In turn, the lack of stable home market and the difficulties faced abroad did not enable British car makers to renew their model ranges and expand and modernize their plants sufficiently. The British market did not grow, nor did exports; in the mid 1960s Britain had 22% of the world's car exports, a decade later only 6%. But strong unions made a reduction in the size of the industry almost impossible. By 1975 the full consequences of misguided policies were felt: Chrysler-U.K. had to be baled out by the government and British Leyland fully nationalized in the face of mounting losses. Despite public support totalling $2.8 billion, the rationalization of production and the closing of main plants, and successful new models, BL's future remained in doubt in 1981.[39]

Conversely, in France, the government encouraged the steady growth of the industry and its efficiency. In 1945, largely for political reasons, Renault was nationalised by the French state.[40] The state encouraged the growth of Renault in the 1950s, and tolerated its managerial autonomy. This autonomy derived in part from an acknowledgement by senior civil servants of the international nature of the automobile industry, and in part from the skill of Renault's top management in the relationship with the state.[41]

The state's major contribution to Renault was to increase the company's equity to support its heavy investment programs and rapid growth. The state lent money to Peugeot to take over Citröen but, by and large, Peugeot's success was achieved without direct state intervention. Whereas Renault was barely profitable over the years, Peugeot paid hefty income taxes most years until it took over Chrysler's European operations.[42] By now, the automobile industry had become by far the largest exporter among French industrial sectors, and one of the few where employment was substantially increasing. Furthermore, Peugeot was profitable and Renault was not a major drain on the French state budget. As price competition developed, Renault had had no major difficulty in investing abroad (e.g., in Portugal and Latin America) and in negotiating agreements with Eastern European countries to obtain lower cost sources of components.

By the early 1980s, though, the French industry found itself in a difficult position with massive labor redundancies, productivity decreases, and controlled domestic prices. This, combined with a poor timing of new model introductions, led to huge losses at Peugeot and serious deterioration of financial conditions at both Peugeot and Renault. Only in the wake of these losses, and after a policy change towards deflation, did the government finally approve some of the necessary lay-offs.

Conclusion: National Policy Choices

The policy options available to governments varied widely with the starting condition of the national automobile industry: start-up situations, existing foreign-controlled industry, or independent mature domestic industry. The first option—to limit interdependency—fits a start-up situation in which the existing domestic policy decisions over time to use the domestic market to generate high production volumes at internationally competitive conditions.

Japan, for example, had a large, fast-growing domestic market, sufficient to generate high-volume production for a number of different car models. The Soviet Union, by concentrating production on a very few models, could generate volume for each as did Korea with a single model. Low factor costs, at least initially in Japan and Korea, ensured that competitive costs were reached quickly. In the Soviet Union the situation was more complex, with the government subsidizing low price exports through very high domestic prices for the same product.* The car industry was mature enough for technology acquisition to be possible on favorable terms to the buyer. Smaller car manufacturers were willing to release technology, others were willing to set turnkey plants.

Once technology is secured, quality production achieved, and the domestic market is served efficiently through large-scale manufacture, access to foreign sales and service channels becomes the most important remaining barrier. Throughout the 1960s and 1970s the difficulties of smaller European and U.S. suppliers made disgruntled dealers available for new franchises. Japanese exporters franchised many former British Leyland and Vauxhall dealers in continental Europe. Volvo dealers also often took on franchises for smaller Japanese cars. The distribution networks of most major car makers involved two tiers: major distributors,

---

* A Lada was sold by Soviet export agencies for about $2000; the same car in the Soviet Union cost the equivalent of $10,000 or more.

and smaller local service and order-taking points. Among second-tier dealers shifts between franchises were relatively frequent.

Only when Japanese import penetration reached high levels in the United Kingdom did the issue of trade unbalance become critical. Lopsided export strategies such as that followed by Japan led to a revival of protectionism. This constitutes the major limitation to the complete success of such a national industrial policy. Yet assuming the domestic market is finally open to foreign competitors, this strategy, pursued over a relatively long period of time, may lead a fledgling national industry to stable successful position in global industry open to foreign competitors.

Not all countries start from zero, however. Many had already invited multinational manufacturers before the internationalization of the industry. Foreign subsidiaries were usually small, inefficient, autonomous operations. As the cost difference widens between these subsidiaries and efficient integrated operations, a choice is presented to the government: either to prolong and protect the existing operations or to allow integration. Existing operations may be put in jeopardy by shifts to free trade (e.g., Spain's planned entry in the EEC),* or by market changes (e.g., shift to smaller cars in Australia). Regulated integration may thus be the only choices.

Multinational integration may take place largely on the government's terms provided (1) the government retains some control over the market and (2) the country's car and factor markets are attractive to MNCs in their own right. Attractiveness varies with characteristics of the country; Brazil, Portugal or Nigeria are quite attractive; Spain less so; and Argentina or Australia even less so. The most attractive countries may set more demanding conditions, such as large export commitments. This, combined with rivalry among potential MNC investors, may lead to over-investment and to the establishment of one industry much larger than the potential market growth could justify. Major international manufacturers, for instance, had set up in Brazil twice the assembly capacity needed to serve the national market.

Countries with a strong autonomous, domestic, nationally owned industry could bolster its competitiveness through various measures. The experience of France, Germany and the United Kingdom suggests that a combination of direct assistance and encouragement to the car makers, of measures to encourage market growth (usually by subsidizing cars as a means of transportation), and an ability to manage labor relations successfully are required. Germany and France had been able to maintain a leading role in the world automobile industry by fostering domestic market

*Prior to Ford's investment, the Spanish government feared that foreign companies would close their national subsidiaries and serve the Spanish market through imports once the country joined the EEC. GM's closing down of the assembly operations in Denmark and Switzerland in 1970–71 fueled such fear.

growth and helping to maintain at least marginally satisfactory labor relation.[43]* The lack of similar policies in the United Kingdom, to foster a stable growing domestic market, and the inability to maintain good labor relationships and thereby improve productivity were largely responsible for the deteriorating performances of the British industry. Major corporate strategic redirections—such as the evolution of Ford of Europe from autonomous national subsidiaries into an integrated European strategy and coordinated operations—can easily span a decade. A policy of government support to the industry in an openly competitive—France or the United Kingdom after 1960—or in an opening economy—Spain in the 1970s and 1980s—requires much continuity and relatively stable goals and programs. Such continuity could be found in France and Germany, and of course Japan. Support also requires a large and rapidly growing domestic market, as well as government continuity and dedication. The British policy, compared to that of France, or of Spain, lacks continuity and stability.

Conclusion: Competition in a Global Industry

Free trade policies expose the least efficient manufacturers to the strength of global competition. When free trade prevails, government control over foreign investments remains useless. In the absence of a coordinated multinational investment control policy (such as that of the Andean Group) multinationals can serve a market from across its borders through imports. For instance, after seeing its plans to install a factory in France rebuffed by General de Gaulle's government in the 1960s, Ford could serve the French market efficiently from Saarlouis (in Germany, just across the French border). Similarly, in 1978, Ford of Europe concluded that investing in France would not help sales on the French market so much as adapting its car lines better to French customer's needs, by far.† In countries that had retained more extensive means of control than the members of the EEC had, the combination of tight investment regulations with trade regulations, and the existence of a large fast growing domestic market, and of lower cost factors, were major incentives for rapid industry development, either via native firms (Japan) or via multinational companies (Brazil, Spain).

Most structural characteristics of the automobile industry favor inte-

---

*Labor relations at Renault were monitored and influenced closely by the government, and Renault was used often as a pacesetter for wage increases and working conditions improvements. Ability to deal successfully with unions was a major requirement for the head of Volkswagen.

†To block a possible Ford investment in France in 1978, car makers had voiced strong preoccupation about Ford's increased sales in France. Actually, except for "captive" sales to employees and for a vague image of "national" manufacturers, Ford had found these factors not to be critical to higher sales in France compared with product characteristics such as smoother ride and more comfortable seats.

grated MNCs. The product and process technology is widely available, and therefore provides no significant advantages to multinational companies. Scale economies in production, and the need to provide a full range to retain effective distribution, call for integration. There are thus relatively few choices open to companies or governments. Company strategies tend to cluster into *integration strategies* (or quasi-integration when full integration raises untoward political or social issues) or into *specialization strategies* aimed at exploiting particular segments and niches in the market.

As we have seen, policy options for governments are also narrowly constrained by economic imperatives. Smaller, relatively mature, countries (such as Argentina, or Australia) find it extremely costly to maintain a nonintegrated industry (often foreign-owned) producing a full range of products. As a result, they may shift to a policy of regulated trade, and maintain some control over their markets, but let MNCs integrate their national subsidiaries into global production networks (General Motors in Australia). Governments of countries with large and mature markets or with formal commitments to free trade find no alternative but to support the internationalization and integration of their own domestic manufac-turers (e.g., Volkswagen in Germany or Peugeot and Renault in France) in response to economic imperatives. As their foreign market penetration increases, or as they try to increase it, these companies find that they must devote an increasing share of their resources to investments abroad. State-owned enterprises such as Renault or Volkswagen have had to expand more rapidly in new high growth markets rather than serve them through exports from Germany or France.

In the late 1970s it appeared that only major forces external to the industry could possibly reverse its evolution toward global competition and multinational integration. The most likely destabilizing force was further price increases and growing scarcities of gasoline. Fuel shortages could make the market more volatile and make full integration less attractive. In 1979, for instance, Ford of Europe decided to move away from "focused" single model assembly plants to more flexible plants able to assemble a wide mix of models, with production rates for each model shifting on short notice. Yet the logic of increasing multinational integration continued to prevail in the industry. Only already integrated manufacturers, such as Ford, attempted to increase also the flexibility of their manufacturing system to adapt to quick and temporary market shifts.

By the 1980s, however, despite real term gasoline price decreases, the industry may be entering a period of de-integration, based on further shifts in the production process technology from standardization and integration toward flexibility and differentiation. Part of this shift may be attributed to new technologies (e.g., computer-assisted manufacturing and robotics), part to the learning, among major Western manufacturers, of new manu-facturing policies first widely applied by the Japanese industry. Part of the shift may also come from the predominance of more sophisticated customers and from the growing number of families owning several cars in Japan and Europe.

References

1. For historical background data see Mira Wilkins, "Multinational Automobile Enterprises and Regulations; An Historical overview", in William J. Abernathy and Douglas Ginsburg (eds.), *Government, Technology, and the Automobile Industry* (New York: McGraw Hill, 1980).
2. Euroeconomics, "Motor Industry Report", presented at the European Motor Industry Conference, Frankfurt, 1977. Report dated 29 September 1977. See, in particular, Appendix B, pp. 37–40. Figures quoted in the Euroeconomics report were provided by the Bristol University Motor Industry Research Group. The original estimates for the most scale intensive operations, foundry and body stamping were provided by the Ford Motor Company (U.K.) and by D. G. Rhys in *The Motor Industry: An Economic Survey* (London: Butterworths, 1972), respectively.
3. See, for instance, L. J. White, *The Automobile Industry since 1945* (Cambridge, Mass.: Harvard University Press, 1971), for lower estimates.
4. John S. McGee, "Economies of Size in Auto Body Manufacture", *The Journal of Law and Economics*, Vol. 16, October 1973, pp. 239–273.
5. Compiled from various sales statistics of automobile manufacturers, rounded figures.
6. See, for a capsule summary of cost differences, William J. Abernathy, Kim B. Clark and Alan M. Kantrow, "The New Industrial Competition", in *Harvard Business Review*, September–October 1981.
7. Personal communications to the author from several European car manufacturers.
8. For historical surveys of European government policies toward the automobile industry see Louis T. Wells Jr., "Automobiles", in Raymond Vernon (ed.), *Big Business and the State* (Cambridge, Mass.: Harvard University Press, 1974), and Mira Wilkins, "Multinational Automobile Enterprises and Regulation: An Historical overview", in William Abernathy and Douglas Ginsburg (eds.), *Government, Technology, and the Automobile Industry* (New York: McGraw-Hill, 1980).
9. Ibid.
10. See my *Ford Bobcat (A1)* case (available from the Intercollegiate Case Clearing House, Boston, Mass. 4–380–093).
11. See my *Ford Bobcat (A2) and (B)* cases for a detailed description (available from the Intercollegiate Case Clearing House, Boston, Mass. 4–380–099 and 4–380–100).
12. See my *General Motors Overseas Operations—Europe* case for a detailed history of the General Motors rationalization process.
13. "Motoring in the '80s: A Survey", in *The Economist*.
14. See my *Ford Bobcat (D)* case (available from the Intercollegiate Case Clearing House, Boston, Mass. 4–380–102).
15. See Stephen Young and Neil Hood, *Chrysler U.K.: A Corporation in Transition* (New York: Praeger, 1977).
16. Personal communication to the author.
17. See Bruce Kogut. "Strategic Partnerships in the auto industry", Wharton School Working Paper, 1983.
18. See "American Motors' Plan for Survival", in *Fortune*, Vol. 100, No. 1, 16 July 1979, pp. 66–82; also "Renault: Why the French Car Maker Needs the Link Up as Much as AMC", in *Business Week*, 19 June 1978, p. 114.
19. See, for instance, W. M. Steele, "The Volvo Group", mimeographed case study (Cranfield Institute of Technology 1979).
20. For summary data on the components industry's evolutions see "The Multinational Spread of Car Part Manufacture Accelerates", in *Multinational Business*, no. 3, 1976.
21. Renato Mazzolini, *European Transnational Concentration* (New York, McGraw Hill, 1974).

88   *Strategic Management in Multinational Companies*

22. See Milton S. Hochmuth, *Organising the Transnationals* (The Hague: Sitjoff, 1973).
23. Euroeconomics, *High Growth Markets for Automobiles* (Paris: Euroeconomics, 1976, 1977), various volumes by region.
24. See my *Ford Bobcat (A1)* case (ICCH 4–380–093).
25. See Arthur Way and Richard Phillips, *Global Automotive Activity 1977 and Outlook 1978–1979* (London: The Economist Intelligence Unit, 1978).
26. "Renault: Model for a Troubled European Auto Industry", in *Business Week*, 1 September 1975, pp. 36–41.
27. "Japan's Car Makers Drive Up Market", in *The Economicst*, 23 September 1978, p. 88.
28. Among many references good summaries are provided by David Friedman, "Beyond the Age of Ford: The Strategic Basis of the Japanese Success in Automobiles", in J. Zysman and L. Tyson (eds.), *American Industry in International Competition* (Ithaca: Cornell University Press, 1983), U.S. Department of Transportation, *Auto Industry 1980* (Cambridge: DOT Report 10–81–02, March 1981).
29. See, for a summary, Yves Doz and Jean-Pierre Lehmann, "Japanese Business Strategies: Automobiles" (forthcoming).
30. See Owen J. Rhys, *Dependent Industrialization in Latin America* (New York: Praeger, 1977), and National Economic Development Office, *Japan: Its Motor Industry and Markets* (London: Her Majesty's Stationery Office, 1970).
31. "The Rise and Rise of Toyota and Nissan", in *Multinational Business* No. 3, 1975, pp. 28–39.
32. See Masaru Udagawa, "Historical Development of the Japanese Automobile Industry", in P. Friedenson (ed.). *The Internationalization of the Automobile Industry* (forthcoming).
33. See Duncan W. Chandler, *U.S. Japan Automobile Diplomacy: A Study in Economic Confrontation* (Cambridge, Mass.: Ballinger, 1973).
34. See Y. Doz, "Automobiles: Shifts in International Competitiveness", in Milton S. Hochmuth and William H. Davidson, *Reversing America's Industrial Decline: Lessons from our Competitors* (Cambridge, Mass.: Ballinger Press, 1984). See also Robert B. Reich, "Beyond Free Trade", in *Foreign Affairs* Vol. 61, No. 4, Spring 1983, pp. 773–80.
35. "Brazil: Automakers Elbow in on the World Market", in *Business Week*, 30 October, 1978, p. 42.
36. "Chrysler Corp.: Bullish on the Future, but . . .", *Business Week*, 20 November 1978, p. 115; also "Chrysler Blows a Gasket", *The Economist*, 13 May 1978, p. 98.
37. See my *Ford in Spain (A)* case.
38. See Mark Fuller, *Government Intervention in the Automobile Industry* (forthcoming).
39. See Patrick Friedenson, *Histoire des Usines Renault* (Paris: Le Seuil, 1972).
40. See Pierre Naville, J. P. Bardou, Ph. Brachet and C. Levy, *L'Etat Entrepreneur* (Paris: Anthropos, 1971), and also Ph. Brachet, *L'Etat Patron: Théories et Réalité* (Paris: Syros, 1974); and Jean-Pierre Anastassopoulos, "The Strategic Autonomy of Government-controlled Enterprises Operating in a Competitive Economy" (Ph.D. dissertation, Columbia University, New York, 1973).
41. J. P. Anastassopoulos (cited above).
42. See "There is a New No.3 in the World Auto Race", in *Fortune*, 4 December 1978, p. 118.
43. See, for instance, P. Fremontier, *La Forteresse Ouvrière Renault*, (Paris: Fayard, 1971), and "Volkswagen Hops a Rabbit Back to Prosperity", in *Fortune*, 13 August 1979, pp. 120–128.

4

Compromise in Government-controlled Industries: the Telecommunication Equipment Industry

Government-controlled industries present an almost complete contrast to global industries. In global industries, such as the automobile industry discussed in Chapter 3, the limits to government actions are set by competitive conditions, while the opposite is true in government-controlled industries. Government-controlled industries means here those whose products are sold mainly to government agencies or to state-owned customers but not necessarily made by state-owned enterprises. In addition to the military, these include state monopolies, such as PTTs or electrical utilities, railroads, or national airlines.* Instead of a convergence of national markets into a worldwide competitive market, we witness in government-controlled industries the continued predominance of separate, protected and negotiated national markets. International trade among developed countries is low, except for products sold to business and private users, such as private branch exchanges.

Since telecommunication equipment illustrates particularly well the historical predominance of political imperatives in government-controlled industries and their current tensions with competitive demands, we will focus principally on telecommunication equipment in this chapter.[1] The most significant product category is main exchange switching: the central office equipment used to connect lines by reading the digits dialled by a subscriber and finding the adequate "path" through the telecommunications network to reach the desired number. Main exchange switching accounts for over half the capital equipment costs of a telephone network (see Table 4.1).

---

*With the exception of the United States and to a lesser extent of Canada, Switzerland, maybe Britain in the future, and a few other countries, these energy supply and communication activities are run by state-owned corporations or by state agencies.

Because all exchanges of a national network must interface easily, main exchange switching is highly standardized within a country. In almost all markets, except the United States, the major customers are state-owned post and telecommunications authorities which usually operate the entire national telecommunications network.[2]

This chapter first analyzes how government control on markets has modified industry characteristics and structure over time during the international life cycle of a product or technology. Strategic alternatives for firms are analyzed, in the light of the industry's structural characteristics, the evolution of product life cycles and the relative bargaining power of multinational firms and governments. The managerial implications for national government are discussed.

The Historical Dominance of Political Imperatives

National constraints on the telecommunication equipment manufacturers have two main sources: the state-owned customer itself, and the government for which control over markets often provides a privileged conduit to assist in the implementation of broader policies. Constraints from these two main sources are reviewed in turn in this section.

State-owned Customers' Demands on Equipment Manufacturers

Whether they are a separate state corporation or merely a branch of the government's executive structure, national telecommunications authorities

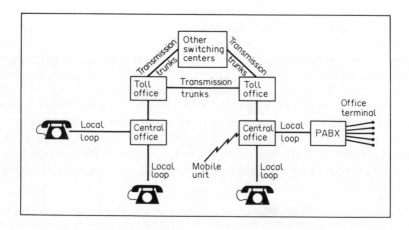

FIGURE 4.1   Simplified sketch of a telephone network

TABLE 4.1 *Characteristics of major product segments: telecommunication equipment industry*

Characteristics	Major telecommunication equipment products				
	Main (central office) exchange switching	Transmission equipment	Private exchange (PABX)	Station equipment (telephone sets)	Cable
Customers	PTT	PTT, military, radio and TV stations	Corporations, hospitals, universities	Usually PTT (leased to users)	PTT
Technology regulation	Specified by customers	Various technologies, flexible specifications, international standards	Free, except PTT interface characteristics approval	PTT-tested, certified	Specified by PTT or transmission equipment manufacturer
Share of capital costs of a telecommunication network	40% to 50%	6% to 10%	n.a.	5% to 8%	5%
Technology	High (clear generations)	Medium, evolving rapidly	Derived from main exchange technology	Low	Low
Major technological change in the 1970s	Stored program control switching; time divided digital coding	Digital coding (pulse code modulation)	Same as main exchange	None	Introduction of optical fibers to replace cables
Economies of scale	High	Low	Medium	High	Low

have usually remained natural monopolies* dependent on the state's financial guarantees and tax exemptions on most of their borrowings. The state also contributes equity increases.

Career paths of senior personnel are often intertwined between government agencies and PTT authorities. It is not uncommon for senior civil servants to be detached to executive positions in telecommunication authorities, and for their engineers or managers to become part of the permanent civil service. Civil service officials and state-owned companies' executives within a country often are in the same professional network due to their common training years at schools such as "Polytechnique" and "Telecom" in France or the national telecommunication engineering school in Sweden.[3]

As a result of their close relations with the state, and of their own revenue generation capabilities, national telecommunications authorities may be entrusted with broader tasks than operating their services, such as leading contributions to employment, trade balances, technological advances, or responsiveness to regional development policies.[4] State-owned enterprises carrying out essential services must also respond to the strategic needs of the state which are often expressed through demands for independent national production to ensure self-reliance. Indeed, from the very beginning of the electrical, railroad, and telecommunication equipment industries, the desire for local national production has been a high priority of the national governments.[5]

State-owned enterprises also have to be responsive to the perceived needs of the public. This puts them in a difficult position since public perceptions of efficiency are often more reactive than comparative and dissatisfaction comes more often from poor performances—breakdowns in essential services—than from comparison of rates or equipment between countries. Consequently, public service industries are highly dependent on the quality of the hardware they purchase to ensure steadily reliable service, and equipment reliability and efficiency are usually more heavily weighted in purchasing decisions than equipment costs. These forces lead PTT authorities to develop relationships with their equipment suppliers in which reliability and control often appear to overwhelm competition: long-term contracts with suppliers are preferred over competitive bidding,

---

*Natural monopolies occur when there would be very strong diseconomies in offering each customer a choice between several suppliers. Natural monopolies most often involve costly dispersed infrastructures that cannot be duplicated. Water, gas or electricity supplies are prime examples. When the infrastructure involves extensive networks, interface difficulties usually call for homogeneous procedures and equipment, leaving little room for equipment purchasing decisions at the provincial or municipal level. Most telecommunication networks are single national entities. Major exceptions are Finland and Colombia. The Italian system has a series of companies, but they coordinate their equipment purchasing decisions. Only value-added networks serving a relatively small number of major corporate customers can be easily operated as separate entity. In the United States long-distance competitors of AT & T still use the same local infrastructure to reach subscribers.

customers control the technology closely, and they demand local production.

Long-term contracts with few suppliers

Unless the equipment is built to the user's own specifications, connecting telecommunication equipment from different manufacturers often involves adaptations to existing equipment or the addition of specific interface equipment or software. Further, relying on a single or a few suppliers minimizes operators' and service training, spare parts inventories, and test equipment needs.[6] The long useful life of main exchange telecommunication equipment is paralleled by slow depreciation (typically 25 to 40 years) and adds further difficulties to changing suppliers.* The main reason to change equipment is technological: newer equipment is easier to operate, less costly, more reliable, and easier to maintain. Finally, extremely tight reliability imperatives† lead PTTs to prefer a few trusted suppliers delivering well-known equipment over a wider range of equipment sources. Trust in equipment reliability, performance capability, spare parts, supplies, installation support, are all more easily confirmed by past experience than by new promises.

Once a supplier has been chosen, he can confidently expect large follow-up contracts over a long period of time. Most such contracts are private, without bidding procedures. Only when they become extremely disgruntled with the performance or with the technology of existing suppliers do customers consider a change of supplier. For instance, in the early 1970s, with all domestic deliveries and new product development programs lagging by at least a year, the British Post Office turned to a Swedish company, LM Ericsson, to supply new switching equipment. Its successor, British Telecom, is using similar threats towards the producers of Britain's new digital switching system, System X, in the 1980s. Except for a few such cases, the predominance of long-term contracts with known manufacturers make it extremely difficult for new manufacturers to break into established national markets. New developing countries with no long standing supplier, or new product lines with no clear-cut trust relationships offer the only opportunity for rapid expansion to equipment manufacturers, but they only provide a small market.

Pressure to control technology

Choice of new products is critical for PTTs which, therefore, want to

---

*Particularly as used-equipment markets are thin, the U.S. Bell system, in particular, had hoped and tried to sell used equipment abroad, without much success.
† Reliability standards for main exchanges are expressed as not more than a total of 2 hours of downtime over a useful life of 40 years.

cooperate with the equipment manufacturing their design. A joint research and development venture (ELLEMTEL) between the PTT and LM Ericsson designs Sweden's new equipment, LM Ericsson representing the interest of international markets, the PTT those of Swedish users. Similarly, the British Post Office led the development of "System X", an electronic exchange system jointly designed by several British telecommunication equipment manufacturerers.* In France, Centre National d'Etude des Télécommunications (CNET) plays a central role in promoting new technologies in cooperation with French companies. France's entry into the digital switching, CIT-Alcatel's E10, was an exchange developed originally at CNET. Some other European PTTs play similar roles.[7]

Developing countries, lacking a domestic manufacturing industry, rely on advice from independent consultants for the selection of suppliers and equipment and often confine their choice to very reputable suppliers whose equipment has already been selected by customers in developed countries. For instance, the Australian choice of LM Ericsson's AXE electronic digital switching system in 1977 was important to LM Ericsson not so much by its order size but because of the great care with which the Australian PTT selected LM Ericsson's equipment through detailed comparative tests with equipment of other suppliers. Although the initial contract was small (4000 lines) and the Australian market not really large—at most 1.5 million lines—the Australian selection did foster other sales for LM Ericsson. The firm used Australia's choice as a reference by which to win larger contracts in countries lacking means to carry out such extensive comparative tests, such as Kuwait, Saudi Arabia and Panama.[8]

National manufacturing

The early multinational spread of technological innovators in telecommunications started in response to requests by customers for local manufacture. At the beginning of the twentieth century, LM Ericsson and Siemens, two European innovators in telephony, already had extensive networks of foreign subsidiaries. Initially, PTT officials saw local manufacture as a way to decrease the risks of relying on distant foreign suppliers for maintenance and follow-up contracts.† The advantages of a knowledge of

* Originally including Standard Telephone and Cables (STC), a subsidiary of International Telegraph and Telephone (ITT), who made significant contributions to the project. In 1982, however, STC withdrew from "System X" development and manufacturing, in agreement with the British Post Office. This left two fully British suppliers, Plessey and General Electric Corp., in charge of "System X". In 1983 Plessey was given lead responsibilities for further development by British Telecom, the telephone operating subsidiary of the British Post Office.

† Also, in the early days of the industry, network operation and equipment manufacturing were often done jointly by MNC subsidiaries, network operation was of even more concern to host governments because of its importance in national emergency situations.

local operating conditions in designing equipment also led customers to favor close cooperation with local manufacturers over dealing with distant suppliers.[9] Further, the public enterprise status of most customers for telecommunication equipment subjects them to economic pressures to create jobs, to cut imports, and to promote national industrialization. Finally importing equipment also exposes PTTs to criticisms of dependence on foreign sources of technology and equipment for the performance of public services.

Direct Government Influence on Suppliers of Equipment

State-owned customers express their demands through the conditions of their purchase of equipment, and governments exercise more direct control on suppliers of equipment. Direct means of control usually involves access to preferential credit, joint ownership, threats to call in new suppliers, the allocation of research and development contracts, and assistance for export sales.

Funding contraints

In most countries government control over sources of credit is extensive enough to allow them to channel funds, under various conditions, to specific sectors and companies. For instance, companies can be provided low-interest rate loans by state savings banks, but qualification for these loans may be decided by a Committee of the Ministry of Finance or by the central bank.

Ownership constraints

To secure national responsiveness, national governments often request an MNC to set up a joint venture with national interest, to manufacture its equipment. Brazil and France demanded that international manufacturers of telecommunication equipment sell part of their equity in national subsidiaries to local interest,[10] and the Austrian state is a joint venture partner in the local telephone equipment manufacturing subsidiary of Siemens.[11]

Invitation of new suppliers

Though such a move is difficult, governments may threaten to call in new suppliers. Spain called in LM Ericsson in the early 1970s to provide a strong alternative to ITT.[12] Similarly, South Africa called in CIT-Alcatel to complement Siemens and replace British suppliers who had no electronic digital switching systems available at that time.[13] Even though it is seldom implemented, calling in new suppliers is a threat customers can brandish to obtain a better bargain from their existing suppliers.

Research and development contracts

The state can use R & D contracts to favor one or another supplier and especially to entice multinational firms to carry out research and development in the country. An example is the large research contracts Germany awarded to several firms—including Philips and ITT affiliates—of the development of optical fiber communication systems.[14]

Export assistance

Many contracts for capital equipment sold to state-owned utilities are negotiated with the assistance of governments. First, they fall within the framework of bilateral trade or assistance agreements, particularly when Eastern European and developing countries are the importers; second, government agencies often are more trusted than private suppliers, as was seen with the British Ministry of Defense being selected as main contractor for the construction of a military telecommunication network in Saudi Arabia.[15] Third, large export sales are often contingent upon the provision of attractive financing that only governments could provide for large contracts. Fourth, top government officials in support can play a key role, as is seen in French equipment sales in the Middle East.[16]

Ownership of the major customers allows governments to play an active role in promoting their own telecommunication equipment industry, either by setting up and encouraging national suppliers or by coaxing MNCs into investing locally, where they can influence their operations. Control over equipment manufacturers vary, however, with the maturity of the market and the position of products in their life cycle. The next section examines how product and market maturity affect the relative bargaining power of MNCs and governments.

Bargaining Power, Market Maturity, Product Technology and the Balance between National Responsiveness and Integration

The MNC bargaining power, in an individual government-controlled business, relative to host governments, varies with both the maturity of the market and the technology involved. The less mature a market and the newer the technology, the greater bargaining power to the MNC. The bargaining power of the MNC is therefore high for new products, where either the technology itself (e.g., optical fibers) is difficult to master or is protected by patents, or where using the product requires difficult and costly competencies (e.g., control software for electronic switching). In new markets, governments increase their bargaining power by pitching several suppliers into direct competition. Conversely, the more mature a product, and the better known and more widespread its technology, the easier independent national production becomes in mature markets either through takeover of MNC subsidiaries or through national companies. Such MNCs are in a comparatively weak position. In a simplified way, the relationship may be portrayed as in Fig. 4.2. We can identify three stages in the interaction between a national customer and multinational suppliers over the life cycle of a product: (1) development of a new market or introduction of a new high technology product in a mature one; (2) transition of a national market to maturity; and (3) the weakening of MNC bargaining power in mature markets for mature products.

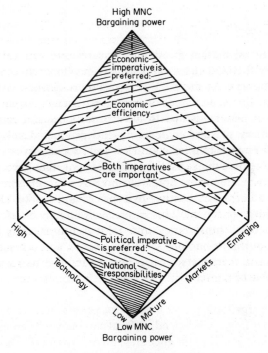

FIG. 4.2   MNC Bargaining Power

Emergence of a product market

Market growth or technological innovations usually create new product markets for which the PTT may invite new suppliers. Such invitations usually take place: (1) during the take-off phase of a market in a rapidly developing country (e.g., Brazil in the 1950s, Saudi Arabia in the 1970s) or

(2) when a new more efficient technology becomes internationally available and is not yet reliably available from domestic suppliers (e.g., digital electronic switching or optical fibers). Several factors may influence which MNC is selected. First, references from well-known reputable users are useful. Second, arrangements that minimize short-term cash outlays and debt carrying charges may be very important to customers whose investment resources are appropriated through the state's budgetary process. (Allegedly, Siemens and Thomson-CSF won the much coveted Egyptian telephone equipment program in 1979, by offering a loan with a $5\frac{1}{2}\%$ interest rate, within a 30–year maturity and a 10–year grace period.)[17] Third, invitation is usually contingent upon a commitment to manufacture locally.[18] The major competitive requirements for success in government-controlled emerging product markets are summarized in Table 4.2, column 1.

Transition to market maturity

As the national market grows and matures and as local production is undertaken by MNCs, closer links usually develop between the PTT and its MNC suppliers. As the PTT becomes more familiar with the technology of the products, and gains operating experience, its engineers usually want products better adapted to local conditions, and request the local MNC subsidiary to start engineering and product development. PTTs may also seek exports to third countries, and propose assistance and export incentives. Further, the subsidiary management may become more independent from headquarters and welcome friendly relationships with the national PTT authority. Control over prices and market shares provides leverage to the government. This way a coalition may develop favoring the evolution of local subsidiaries into joint ventures with local national interests. With the technology widely available, and other manufacturers eager to enter new markets, host governments' threats to call in another supplier in case of non-compliance with their requests for joint ownership become credible.

Although bargaining power decreases, profits may remain high. As a technology matures, an independent local company may enter the market—often with some government encouragement—to provide an alternative to MNCs. Even when it is given a large share of the national market, this local company is likely to remain less efficient than the MNC subsidiaries and to have higher unit costs due to a smaller experience base and a lesser mastery of technology. In most countries, public purchasing laws and regulations limit price discrimination among suppliers or forbid it entirely. The customer is thus likely to set prices high enough for the national supplier to break even, and for the multinationals to achieve windfall profits, particularly when the national supplier finances its rapid growth. In the 1960s

TABLE 4.2 *Evolution of Host-Government Demands in a Government-controlled Market*

1. Emerging product-market	2. Transition to maturity	3. Mature product-market
– *Performance/cost ratios*	– *Local manufacturing*	– Autonomy of local *subsidiary*
– *Up to date technology*	– Adaptation of product *to local condition*	– Better efficiency than national *competitors*
– Reliability, durability of equipment	– Local research and *development activities*	– Responsiveness to national policies *yet*
– *Financing*	– *Exports from subsidiary*	Threat of national-ization and expropriation
– Installation, training *and start-up assistance*	– *Exports from subsidiary*	
– Willingness to set up local manufacturing operations	– Possibility, joint ownership with local interests	
Entry route: Successful tender and new investment	Entry route: Acquisition or joint ventures	Entry route: None profitable, except on emerging segments with unique technology

99

838556

ITT's managers referred to France as the "Golden Cage" because the French PTT were then "growing" CIT-Alcatel. As CIT-Alcatel grew more rapidly than its multinational competitors, but was less cost efficient, prices had to be set very high to sustain its cash flow. Once CIT-Alcatel matured, prices were cut drastically.[19] In Italy, likewise, labor productivity at LM Ericsson's and General Telephone and Electronic's (GTE) subsidiaries was alleged to exceed that of the national company Italtel, although the national company had a much larger market share. State ownership of some local competitors also sometimes encouraged overstaffing and discouraged productivity increases.[20]

Mature markets

The development of local companies that may temporarily provide a price umbrella for MNC subsidiaries may ultimately compromise their position as the market matures. In the long run, local-for-local MNC subsidiaries become self-sufficient and can therefore be operated autonomously. Given enough time, national competitors may become reliable, efficient domestic suppliers and provide a genuine alternative to MNCs. The government may also believe that profits should accrue to national companies only, or that these could achieve larger export volumes than MNC subsidiaries whose exports are regulated by MNC headquarters. As a market matures, therefore, governments become increasingly likely to expropriate multinational companies or, at least to shift market shares in favor of domestic suppliers.

MNC entry conditions parallel the deterioration of their bargaining power as a market matures. Entry into a new product market usually takes place by competitive bidding for large contracts and the subsequent establishment of a manufacturing subsidiary. As the market or the product technology matures, entry becomes extremely difficult, since suppliers are already in place. Entry in a mature market by a MNC usually then involves the acquisition of a faltering national company (Philips' acquisition of Pye TMC in the United Kingdom) or a transfer of ownership among multinationals (LM Ericsson replacing GTE as a partner for Thorn Electric in the United Kingdom). Such acquisitions or transfers of ownership are possible only when the national customer is disgruntled with its existing suppliers and welcomes a new entrant or an injection of fresh technology or managerial talent into an existing supplier. Finally, in mature markets for mature products, entry by a multinational is unlikely; it is both unattractive to the MNC and difficult, as the national market has usually been cornered by national suppliers or well-entrenched multinational subsidiaries.

Conclusion: Technology and the Political Imperatives

In summary, as a national market matures or as new technology becomes more easily available, the bargaining power of the established MNC decreases and market entry becomes increasingly difficult—a pattern rather similar to the historical development of MNCs in other nationally closed markets. Here the technology is the main source of power of the firm—but more than in other sectors governments actively erode the multinational firm's advantage and extract growing advantages from MNC subsidiaries and force them to be increasingly responsive to national requests on issues such as product adaptation, local content, employment, trade balances, location of research and development, and local ownership (Table 4.2).

Monopsony market power makes it possible to ensure that the MNC agree to local production and product adaptation, since it is always possible for the host country to call in other suppliers. The intrinsic technical interface difficulty and the threats by established suppliers to close down and lay off workers limit that threat, however. Our assumption is that, should the technology be low enough, national production would prevail independently of MNCs at least in developed countries. Examples of such situations are provided by the shipbuilding and the small arms industry in which national production prevails. The difficulty of independently mastering the digital electronic switching technology gives MNCs in the telecommunication equipment industry their major advantage over purely national companies. In short, non-integrated multinationals can provide the extent of national responsiveness demanded by governments, and still maintain the technological and export volumes superiority over national companies to be needed by the PTT customer and the host government.

In the early 1980s, however, the position of the MNCs were increasingly threatened. New competitors, enjoying home government support for R & D, with an active domestic market, capable management, and good technology, had entered the world market. Leading new competitors were Northern Telecom and CIT-Alcatel, which had pioneered digital switching technologies. Nippon Electric, with a good system but no domestic market (since Nippon Telegraph and Telephone was not yet introducing digital switches), obtained foreign sales by cutting equipment prices. All three competitors had registered significant orders on markets open to exports and CIT-Alcatel had also engaged into significant technology transfer and technical assistance contracts to various countries.

The traditional industry structure showed much resilience, though. None of these three suppliers broke into major developed countries markets where they had not been present in the past. Only where host countries' PTTs had strong doubts about their traditional suppliers' capabilities to develop digital switching technologies did they occasionally snatch a reequipment order from well-established suppliers. ITT and LM Ericsson lost almost no existing market positions, and companies lagging behind in digital technologies, such as Siemens, GEC or Philips, lost only a few positions. All could promise convincingly to deliver digital switching systems within a reasonable delay. In sum the shift to digital technologies failed to alter significantly the existing industry structures, at least initially.[21]

Yet, at the same time, the structure of the industry seemed bound to become more global. As the bulk of new telephone systems started to use digital technologies, the structure of value added shifted toward microelectronics components (most of which could be purchased from third party suppliers in the merchant or custom-made markets) and toward software development costs recovery. At the same time, considerable resources were still being spent on developing new digital systems by companies such as ITT, Plessey, Siemens, AT & T and others. It was quite unlikely that all those new systems would break even and generate the cash flows necessary to continue the development of further product generations. It was also unclear whether such development could be financially justified, since some experts saw an increasing trend toward standardization and "commoditization" of switching systems. In 1983, already, Philips renounced further autonomous digital switching development and decided to combine its efforts with AT & T's into a common venture, mainly expected to market AT & T's new systems internationally. A few months later Thomson joined forces with the other French supplier CIT-Alcatel. Plessey also bought Stromberg-Carlson, a smaller independent U.S. maker of digital switches. GTE, Italtel and Telettra joined forces to develop a new Italian system, and were later joined by CIT-Alcatel to develop a common large system. Further consolidations or cooperations were expected.

The change to digital technologies was also bound to modify the relationships between MNCs and host countries, since "local manufacture" was increasingly meaningless in a product the price of which is made of purchased components and of amortization of development costs. Contrary to electromechanical systems, which involve labor-intensive tasks, electronic systems do not lend themselves easily to nationally responsive manufacture in multiple locations.

The implication for multinational strategic choices of government control over markets, in industries where technology is the main source of MNC competitive advantage, are discussed below.

Multinational Strategies for Government-controlled Industries

The continued fragmentation of markets into separate government-structured oligopolies has drastically limited the opportunities for integration strategies among telecommunication equipment manufacturers. Trade among developed countries is low[22] and exports are limited to developing countries. Table 4.3 shows usual conditions of access to the world's main exchange switching equipment market. Open markets account for a mere 6.8% of the total, whereas completely closed markets account for 61.4% of the total.

TABLE 4.3 *Conditions of Access to the International Switching Equipment Market (1975-85)*

	Closed	Partly open	Open	Eastern Europe
Percentage of total installed lines, worldwide	75.3%	8.3%	5.0%	11.4%
Annual growth rate (percent) 1975-85 of markets	5.3%	11.3%	8.8%	9.8%
New lines installed each year (percent of total, average 1975-1985)	61.4%	14.5%	6.8%	17.3%

Closed: Dominance of established domestic or MNC subsidiaries suppliers, introduction of new foreign suppliers extremely unlikely.
Partly open: Future orders likely to go to already established suppliers, but some potential for new suppliers willing to invest locally.
Open: May be served by exports initially, to be followed by investments.
Eastern Europe: May be served by licensing and supplying manufacturing equipment.
Source: Arthur D. Little.
Note: Known re-equipment programs of various countries, rates of transition electronic technologies, existing contracts and relationships between suppliers and customers have been taken into account to compute the summary data. Figures are only estimates, however.

Newly internationalizing competitors, therefore, attempted to take away existing markets from established multinational suppliers. CIT-Alcatel, for instance, often tried to woo PTTs into "partnerships", away from their established supplier such as LME, ITT or Siemens. In India, for instance, CIF-Alcatel won a sizeable contract by providing a series of technical cooperation agreements to set up an Indian digital telecommunication equipment industry, backed by government-to-government agreements and guarantees.

Among the well-established competitors, some could match the technology of the new competitors, others could not. LM Ericsson had been able over the years to maintain the competitiveness of its AXE system. ITT, caught off guard by the success of digital switching, backed multiple development efforts in different subsidiaries, and only in 1979 reached a clear commitment for full development of its "System 12" digital system. It promised to be more technologically advanced than any of its competitors, but its introduction had been delayed several times. It was reaching production only in 1983. Early, unsuccessful, efforts in analog switching had delayed Siemens, whose system was only in prototype form in 1983. Plessey and GEC were still working on "System X", the mass production of which had been postponed several times. Siemens and ITT enjoyed a strong presence in numerous markets, but their products lacked the most efficient technologies, at least temporarily. CIT-Alcatel (as well as the U.S. producers Western Electric and General Telephone and Electronics) had advanced technology but lacked established markets; only LM Ericsson had both (Fig. 4.3).[23]

Strategic Alternatives: Technological Leadership vs. National Responsiveness

Differences in the technologies available to them at one point in time and in their market positions led different multinational equipment suppliers to adopt different strategies and to adopt very contrasted positions toward responsiveness, as can be shown in a comparison between LM Ericsson and ITT.

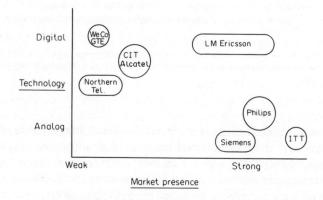

FIG. 4.3   Technology and market presence in the world's telephone switching industry

LM Ericsson, with foreign operations centrally run from Sweden, has introduced many technological innovations. In the 1940s it pioneered the introduction of crossbar switching. In the 1960s LM Ericsson enjoyed a substantial lead in semi-electronic "gateway" exchanges for trunk-lines and international lines. In 1965 its technological leadership permitted LM Ericsson to obtain substantial orders from the U.S Department of Defense for its worldwide communications switching system.[24] By 1976 it had developed a new, versatile all-electronic exchange, the AXE. The AXE was developed entirely in Sweden, with an approach emphasizing flexibility of use through modular design and interchangeable software packages that could be used separately or in combinations so the AXE systems could interface with a variety of electronic or electromechanical switches from other manufacturers.*[25] Over the years the AXE system evolved from analog to digital switching capabilities and remained technologically competitive.

ITT, with a number of large autonomous nationally responsive subsidiaries in major European countries, was somewhat at a disadvantage in developing new technology. Whereas LM Ericsson could centralize R & D in Sweden and cooperate closely with a single PTT—the Swedish one— ITT had to coordinate R & D labs scattered throughout Europe and to consider demands from half a dozen major PTTs. ITT had extensive R & D activities in Belgium, France, Germany and the United Kingdom.

ITT, in contrast to LM Ericsson, had developed several types of electronic exchanges, each tailored to the needs of a major PTT, rather than a single versatile system. ITT had first developed a series of analog electronic switching systems, called Metaconta, in the early 1970s. In the late 1970s its German and Belgian subsidiaries, as well as a U.S. acquisition, had started developing their own digital switches under the broad "System 12" program. In 1979, after some tensions, priority was given to the U.S. development (known as "1240") over the other two. By 1983 the System 1240 was in the final stages of development. Versions were developed to suit different PTTs. A decentralized approach was reflected in the allocation of R & D responsibilities to ITT's various subsidiaries: each national subsidiary was in charge of the detailed development of part of a system for ITT as a whole and was also in charge of the adaptation of the complete system to their local market. This had led major European PTT to wait to adopt ITT's systems, but had made it more difficult to penetrate new markets, or even to keep existing markets, in developing countries. ITT relied principally on long-standing relationships between mature autonomous subsidiaries and mature, technologically knowledgeable, customers. Fragmenting the R & D effort among several subsidiaries contributed to these relationships, but slowed down and made more expensive the development of new systems.

ITT and LM Ericsson also faced national demands for local production differently. LM Ericsson bargained with large developed countries' PTTs

---

*A word on technology is needed here. The key technical difficulty in selling an exchange system internationally is the difference in the equipment with which it needs to interface and in the specific telephone network characteristics in various countries. In electromechanical exchanges, interface difficulties are handled by hardware modifications, in all-electronic exchanges by software adaptations. The difficulty is for the software to have a clear enough operating system structure to be able to adapt certain functions without having to modify all the software for each new customer. A system aimed at diverse export markets must thus have clearly separated software packages and functional units, whereas a system designed for a single PTT authority may have many more integrated software packages and functional units. In the case of the AXE, things were further complicated by LM Ericsson's desire to offer an analog space-divided system (with the least interface problems) susceptible of evolving into a digital time-divided system.

by giving them a part to play in its overall, partly integrated, manufacturing network: AXE processors to Italy in the 1980s, or crossbar relays to France in the 1960s. Generally LM Ericsson minimized the extent of responsiveness needed, and maximized the advantages derived by national subsidiaries from integration, by relying on superior technology and installation competencies to win a large share of straight export sales on the open markets of developing countries. ITT, on the other hand, followed a strategy of national responsiveness. Each of the major national subsidiaries carried out all stages of manufacturing for its domestic customers. Contracts with new customers were negotiated by individual ITT subsidiaries, not the product group headquarters or ITT's regional offices. With comparable equipment being manufactured in several of its national affiliates, exports to developing countries or the responsibility for setting up new plants abroad could be allocated to one or another affiliate according to diplomatic and financial conditions. In the midst of negotiating a major contract with Algeria, for instance, ITT shifted prime negotiation responsibility from its French to its Spanish affiliate when Franco-Algerian relationships soured on immigration issues and on the future of the Spanish Sahara. Spain, aligned with the Algerian position on the Sahara, became a more acceptable negotiation base. With the contract safely secured ITT decided that most exports to Algeria would nevertheless take place from France, to placate French dissatisfaction with low export volumes. Knowledge about the Algerian network also resided within ITT's French subsidiaries. Coordination among the ITT subsidiaries was achieved informally by frequent meetings of their managing directors. Both in ITT and in their own national environment, these executives were quite influential. Their companies had been part of the national industry for a long time. They cooperated extensively with the national PTTs; for example, Standard Telephone and Cables had been partner in the British Post Office's own System X and Standard Elektrik Lorenz in Germany was one of the potential suppliers of fiber optics transmission systems.[26]

Differences in approach to markets were also reflected in preferred ownership patterns: fully-owned subsidiaries for LM Ericsson, partially owned ones for ITT. Yet LM Ericsson also differentiated the role of the boards of subsidiaries and their relationships with Swedish headquarters according to the maturity of their respective product markets. Newly-started manufacturing subsidiaries received much assistance from Sweden and were closely controlled; mature subsidiaries in mature markets (e.g., in Italy) were much more autonomous.[27] ITT, on the other hand, preferred partial ownership, with shares of its subsidiaries traded in local stock exchanges. According to ITT spokesmen, its top management felt that, at least in the telecommunication equipment business, partly owned subsidiaries behaving almost as local companies best answered the need for national responsiveness.

The combination of large production volume in each country and coordinated R & D programs among subsidiaries enables ITT to adapt its equipment extensively to fit the needs of different national customers, without having to build such versatility into the equipment as LM Ericsson. With its already extensive operations in a number of European countries, ITT was in the best position to adopt a national responsiveness strategy. With large national markets, it could hope to reach competitive economies of scale in several countries. In sum, both LM Ericsson and ITT were successful, but increasingly in different countries.

This strategic divergence was probably only temporary, however. Once its System 12 was ready, ITT was poised to undertake a more aggressive market penetration strategy. So was Siemens; but in the meantime new manufacturers had replaced the German firm as major suppliers to many countries.[28] Siemens, therefore, saw the potential sales volume of its new system reduced. Such reduction, in turn, might not allow the company to generate the cash flow necessary to fund the development of new generations of equipment or to recoup its R & D investment in the first generation of digital switching systems. Faced with such a situation of shrinking markets and increasing R & D costs, Philips had sought an alliance with Western Electric, whose switching systems it would now distribute internationally.[29]

The changing cost structure of the telephone switching business also modified the relative benefits of responsiveness and integration. Digitalization cuts manufacturing costs and labor content, but increases R & D costs and software costs. Most components can be bought outside from semiconductor firms. The potential benefits of integration, or the opportunity cost of nonintegration, therefore decrease quite substantially and the key strategic issue shifts to R & D funding. It becomes imperative to generate the cash flow required to recoup past R & D efforts and find new ones, no matter what relationships develop with customers. This is a growing problem, with some suppliers being willing to price close to marginal cost on certain markets rather than incorporate in the price the needed R & D cost coverage and, therefore, drawing all prices down. The growing number of technology transfer agreements also corresponds to this concern of spreading R & D costs over the largest possible volume.

Conclusion

The technological characteristics and the maturity of the product-market mix of a business constrain the strategy followed. *Technological innovators* can usually be more integrated than manufacturers with a lessser technology advantage. This lead is maximized when smaller markets in developing countries are pursued (e.g., LM Ericsson's sales to newly developing countries). An innovator's strategy can also be followed as national markets mature. Frequent introductions of upgraded technologies may preserve the MNCs technology lead. LM Ericsson followed this strategy with various generations of main exchange switching equipment: crossbar switches in the late 1950s, semi-electronic versatile gateway exchanges in the 1960s, all-electronic AXE in the 1970s.

Companies with less advanced technologies, at least at some point in time, but stronger well-established positions in mature markets usually follow a *strategy of national responsiveness.* ITT is the clearest example of such a company.

Newly internationalizing competitors often find themselves being both technology leaders and very nationally responsive. Indeed, they often break into "closed" markets by promising a better deal on both counts: a better technology *and* more control to the local PTT than MNCs deliver or tolerate. CIT-Alcatel, for example, had met success in scattered export sales (e.g., in Africa and the Middle East) and in major technology transfer or cooperation agreements (e.g., India or Finland).[30]

Strategic flexibility is also rewarded in government-controlled industries.

The consequence of these two strategies, national responsiveness and partial integration for economic efficiency in serving new markets, on relationships between headquarters and subsidiaries is contrasted on Fig. 4.4 which summarizes the respective tasks of subsidiaries and headquarters at ITT and LM Ericsson.

The extent of national responsiveness that a given supplier has to provide, or the degree of integration that it can maintain, are likely to vary substantially among markets. Within a business, bargaining power can vary between countries, with generations of equipment, and with the technology lead of individual suppliers. As an example, in the supply of electronic exchanges to Bahrain, a supplier may have much bargaining power, while manufacturing electromechanical exchanges in Brazil may provide no bargaining power at all with the Brazilian government.

The overall success of a manufacturer may thus hinge on its ability to adapt to the various market conditions. Whereas operations in new countries (such as Korea and Iran) were run under close control from GTE's headquarters in the United States, the Italian and Belgian operations were free to be as nationally responsive as they saw fit and to draw on U.S. competencies when needed.[31] LM Ericsson, similarly, let France and Italy be much more autonomous than its other subsidiaries in the early 1970s.

Efforts to provide a varying balance among countries—being responsive where needed, and integrated where possible—usually lead to some multi-

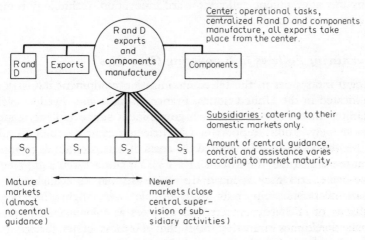

1. National responsiveness in mature markets

Center: administrative tasks
only: planning, budgeting,
resource allocation, plus
coordination of R and D and
export marketing.

Subsidiaries in mature markets:
autonomous operations, full-
fledged companies.

Subsidiaries in new markets:
administered by larger national
subsidiaries.

2. Partial integration for economic efficiency in new markets

Center: operational tasks,
centralized R and D and components
manufacture, all exports take
place from the center.

Subsidiaries: catering to their
domestic markets only.

Amount of central guidance,
control and assistance varies
according to market maturity.

Mature
markets
(almost
no central
guidance)

Newer
markets (close
central super-
vision of sub-
sidiary activities)

FIG. 4.4 Comparisons between two multinational strategies for government-
controlled businesses

focal strategy which allows both the demands conveyed by the subsidiary managers and the needs for worldwide integration to be understood, shared, and traded-off against one another. An alternative by which to avoid some of the difficulties of a multifocal strategy is a two-tier approach in which mature subsidiaries assist subsidiaries in newer markets. Responsiveness in mature national markets is given clear priority, without compromising the penetration of new markets. This is ITT's approach.

In summary, national responsiveness is the most obvious strategy for government-controlled business. Partial moves toward integration are made possible by the time-lag between the leading manufacturer's technology and that of national customers for new products. Yet actual integration is usually too limited in time (e.g., in the introduction of new products) and geography (in penetrating markets in small developing countries) to become the viable long-term strategy. Companies can also develop a posture of national responsiveness in mature markets and of partial integration to serve new markets.

Government Policies

In almost all cases, government policies aim at increasing control over suppliers of equipment. Their ability to achieve such control and the opportunity costs involved vary, however, with the relative bargaining power of the customer. As we have analyzed, the level of technology plays a key role in providing equipment suppliers with a lead over their customers and in limiting the bargaining power of the latter. It is useful, then, to distinguish government policies toward innovation, technology transfers, and equipment imports.

Government Policies in Innovating Countries

Recent innovators in the telecommunication equipment industry have been located in the United States, France, Canada and Sweden. Neither the United States nor the Swedish government supported the manufacturers actively. Public support of LM Ericsson came through ELLEM-TEL, as the Swedish PTT shared the costs of new product development. Yet, at the same time, the Swedish PTT also manufactured equipment for its own use, and thus reduced the domestic market available to LM Ericsson. Political support for overseas sales were slight. The political nonalignment of Sweden and its lack of overseas colonial history favored sales in developing countries.* But the bluntness of its foreign policy pronouncements often hurt them.† In sum, whatever assistance LM Ericsson could draw was more an indirect consequence of (1) the high technological level of the Swedish PTT and their willingness to promote and try new technology, and (2) the nonaligned, noncolonial stance of Sweden's foreign policy.

The U.S. posture was more complex. Domestically, in the 1970s, policies were evolving toward freer competition, to the detriment of American Telegraph & Telephone (AT & T). After its initial development of stored program control switching, and its early re-equipment, AT & T slowed down its technological development. Innovations took place at the fringes of the industry, as was seen in satellite transmissions for which the United States had clearly become the leader through COMSAT and

---

* Sweden had no overseas colonial past, although it had invaded most of its neighbours at some point in history.

† For instance, LM Ericsson's equipment sales in Latin America were sometimes compromised by statements from Sweden's socialist ministers, highly critical of domestic political situations in a number of Latin American countries.

INTELSAT. Such leadership led to substantial U.S. equipment exports and licensing revenues, but AT & T was not the major beneficiary.

Internationally, the United States government was in an ambiguous position. The official U.S. posture favored opening up national markets to international competitive bidding. The U.S. government strongly criticized Nippon Telephone and Telegraph (NTT), for instance, for not soliciting bids from non-Japanese equipment manufacturers and negotiated an end to national preference, in principle. That posture made it difficult for the U.S. government to support explicitly its own manufacturers in export markets. Further, the U.S. government did not support them in the negotiations when U.S. companies were submitting bids to foreign PTTs, lest it weaken the notion of equal treatment among companies. U.S. exporters thus all had equal access to foreign loan guarantees, but could not benefit as much from favorable terms as could European or Japanese suppliers. Altogether, the U.S. manufacturers had not gained strong international positions. They lost major Middle East contracts to European groups; and the one large contract secured by General Telephone and Electronics (GTE) in Iran came to a halt after the Islamic revolution. Some industry observers argued that rapidly developing countries preferred to buy equipment from countries on which they could have more leverage via oil exports, and whose domestic network was operated by a public PTT authority, instead of a private company. Others suggested that legal treatment of commissions to foreign agents had hampered U.S. exports. Newer products, such as LM Ericsson's AXE, were also considered more versatile than U.S. products. AT & T and GTE had developed their equipment primarily for the U.S. domestic market, whereas LM Ericsson and CIT-Alcatel developed theirs with an explicit consideration of its export potential.

France's National Center for Telecommunications Research (CNET) developed digital switches on its own till 1975 with prototypes going into network service in 1972. In 1975 the PTT Ministry entrusted the production and commercialization of digital switching systems to CIT-Alcatel, a major French-owned telecommunications and electronics company affiliated to the Compagnie Générale d'Electricité. the PTT Ministry then signed major supply contracts with CIT–Alcatel and undertook to support export sales actively. This soon established CIT-Alcatel as a major supplier of digital switches, worldwide. Similarly, in its development of digital switches, Northern Telecommunications benefited from a large domestic market and from active support by the Canadian government and the Canadian Bell Company.

Policies for Technological Adaption

Several countries have developed an explicit policy of acquiring, adapting and improving existing technologies to build a national base in their domestic market and to develop exports. As a result these countries were usually closed to foreign telecommunication equipment companies, with the possible exception of the subsidiaries of nationally responsive ITT. The clear cases were Germany, the United Kingdom and Japan. The German government, with a substantial domestic market, supported Siemens' independent course with grants and contracts to develop the EWS-D switching system. Yet ITT's subsidiary SEL was also supplying equipment. In particular, alongside Siemens' own system, it was expected to supply fully digital System 12 switches. Extensive R & D support was provided to German firms, and to nationally responsive MNC subsidiaries. Both ITT's SEL and Philips' Te Ka De were awarded development contracts for fiber optics communication systems. The German government also assisted German companies in developing export markets and financing export contracts.

The multiplicity and the relative weakness of British equipment suppliers led the British Post Office (BPO) to assume an even stronger role in the telecommunication equipment industry. After adopting an intermediate semi-electronic technology (the TXE-4 System) well suited to its requirements but with little potiential abroad, the BPO was leading at great cost the development of the new fully digital System X in cooperation with several British suppliers. It was expected that the system would be superior to that provided by competition and would find a ready market abroad, despite lateness and relatively high cost.[32]

Japan also had developed its own systems with the support of NTT and was selling its equipment abroad. For instance, Nippon Electric Co. won substantial orders in New Zealand in a barter agreement for food products. Such barter agreements were often negotiated under the auspices of Japan's governmental trade agencies.

Many PTTs were willing to subsidize exports on the assumption that exports increased the overall production volume of equipment and thus decreased the prices they had to pay. Most PTTs paid lip service to the need to "internationalize" the market by importing equipment, but none was willing to, except as part of relations between the United States and Japan. Europeans had a vested interest in letting things stand and stayed put. After some negotiating, NTT initially refused to open its bidding procedures to U.S. suppliers for the following six reasons:

1. Foreign bids would result in language difficulties and delays.
2. Reliance on negotiated private contracts with domestic suppliers permit NTT to control R & D in the public interest.
3. Standardized Japanese equipment would make maintenance and repair easier, and ensure a steady supply of spare parts.
4. Foreign firms would be likely to refuse to provide NTT with the type

of detailed proprietary technical information it would seek before awarding contracts.

5. NTT does not have the staff available to inspect and monitor foreign manufacturer's factories.

6. NTT demands for information are so exhaustive that suppliers would choose not to bid.[33]

Protracted negotations led to at least a willingness to consider foreign bids, although the interface problems raise much less of a barrier to international trade with electronic switching than with electromechanical; and despite lip service given to free trade, there is little evidence that barriers to trade are about to crumble. Nevertheless, several trends favor freer trade in the long run. Whereas the PTTs saw the telephone as a social service, they now consider telecommunications as a business tool, and become more concerned with cost effectiveness. Deregulation and privatization of telephone services accelerate this trend. They have also diversified the services offered. Facsimile in France and teletext in the United Kingdom were introduced in late 1970s, and many other services are being planned. Thirdly, technology evolutions make the traditional PTT monopoly less justified unless the PTTs can show that private companies could not provide better services more cheaply. Although the PTT monopoly is not put to question explicitly in Europe (except for the distribution of some attachments on the users' premises), these trends favor the procurement of equipment at the lowest possible cost. Major forces against freer trade are the result of the need to protect domestic employment and national technological autonomy. Some industry observers argue that, given the continuous evolution of electronic technologies (as opposed to the long time which elapsed between former generations of equipment) and the very high development costs of new equipment, few systems will emerge as clear leaders. Consequently, quasi-integration strategies will be needed to cope with future evolutions. Several manufacturers in different countries could join forces in a consortium to jointly develop equipment for the PTTs of the member countries.

In the most logical product candidate for joint efforts, digital switching systems, cooperation is hampered by the fact that various manufacturers' first entries are at very different stages in their life cycle—from CIT-Alcatel's obsolescing E-10 to ITT's just-introduced System 12—and that most attractive collaboration involves complementary product lines or geographical markets, rather than quasi-integration strategies in similar products and adjacent countries.

Technology Transfer Recipients

Several countries with large domestic markets adopted a strategy of import substitution in 1975, when the full impact of oil price increases was felt. Brazil started to restrict imports of telecommunication equipment and took advantage of the selection of electronic switching systems to demand the establishment of joint ventures with local partners.[34] Large potential markets provide bargaining power and both LM Ericsson and ITT complied. Brazil also started developing its own system, with some assistance from Italy.

The policies of countries such as Brazil fit most directly with the usual dynamic models of international trade and investment in the product cycle. Import substitution, given PTT monopsony control, is relatively easy, export promotion is not. Importers usually want their equipment made by the original manufacturer, rather than by potentially less reliable licensees. Costs of the licensee are not likely to be lower than that of multinationals. Thus, short of extremely heavy subsidies, technology transfer recipients find it hard to export. For instance, Brazil did not export much equipment.[35]

A country can develop an indigenous technological capability to evolve from technology transfer recipient to adapter, and even innovator. Let us compare France to Brazil.

Both Brazil and France (1) had a very large domestic market at stake, and (2) were among the first countries to select new electronic equipment. Their contracts were important to LM Ericsson: France was their second foreign customer for AXE (after Finland) and LM Ericsson was the largest crossbar and electromechanical supplier to Brazil. By imposing joint ventures, the Brazilians, who had relatively little domestic capability, ensured the continued transfer of technology from LM Ericsson and ITT to their industry. The French, who already had a technology innovator in time division switching (CIT-Alcatel) and extensive state research teams, faced less of a need to ensure continuous technology transfer. Thomson CSF, the other national supplier beside CIT-Alcatel, acquired technology from LM Ericsson, and then started to develop its own electronic MT 10 and MT 60 systems. These systems were inspired by LM Ericsson's AXE and ITT's Metaconta, but improved upon them. France started to export CIT-Alcatel's time-divided system. Thomson-CSF found some success on competitive international markets only once it started offering its MT systems. It was the competence of CNET and Thomson, and the time division lead of CIT-Alcatel, that enabled the French to export, not the technology transfer from LM Ericsson and ITT.[36] France was moving from a position of technology transfer recipient to that of adapter (with Thomson CSF) and even of innovator (with CIT-Alcatel).

Importers

Most countries, unless their markets are quite small (Panama, Costa

Rica), their capability limited (Kuwait), or their needs urgent (Saudi Arabia), move quickly to attract manufacturing MNC subsidiaries. Some smaller countries, instead of demanding inefficient nationally responsive subsidiaries, prefer to negotiate offsets contracts with the MNCs according to which they produce some simple equipment for the manufacturers' worldwide needs. For instance, Ecuador made connectors for LM Ericsson's worldwide production, and imported complete LM Ericsson exchanges.

In summary, the level of technology is the key determinant of the bargaining power of host governments, and sets limits to their international ambitions. Monopsony power makes import substitution relatively easy. It varies in attractiveness with the size of the domestic market (e.g., Brazil vs. Panama). Export encouragement is a much more difficult undertaking. Although technological and economic forces are undermining the traditional fragmentation of national markets, they have had little impact on government policies and market structures. Freer international trade is paid lip service, but not acted upon.

Conclusion

Host government concerns, and their ability to use market power to influence industry structure, have limited the capability of MNCs to pursue integration strategies, even though the economics of telecommunication equipment development and manufacturing favor such strategies. Only some technology leaders, with a market emphasis away from the most developed countries, have achieved some level of integration. Companies have left national markets as their technological level matured.

Furthermore, government policies have led to overspending in R & D, both by supporting costly domestic developments (e.g., System X in Britain, "Proteo" in Italy, and Thomson's MT system in France) with limited market opportunities. Only the conjunction of a very large domestic market, of a focused R & D effort, and of significant government assistance to exports have led to success, as with CIT-Alcatel.

The shift to digital technologies is so altering the cost of structure of the telephone switching business that the relative advantages of integration and responsiveness are shifting. From an emphasis on cost reduction in a mature electromechanical manufacturing system process, strategic priority of equipment suppliers shifts to the recovery of R & D cost and the capture of a large enough market, at sufficient price conditions, to generate the cash flows the development of the next generation of equipment will need.

This shift has made competitors more willing to engage in trade in technology, either via "partnerships" (such as that now starting in Italy between Italtel and GTE) or via technology transfer agreement (such as the agreement of CIT-Alcatel with Indian partners).

A major concern for employment now animates governments, given the 75% reduction in labor context per telephone line bought by electronic technologies. This increases pressures on MNCs and slows down the adjustment to the new technological conditions. Local manufacture remains important to governments for social reasons, even though the value added and the skills have moved away from manufacturing toward R & D, mainly software on one side and toward the component manufacturers on the other.

Since telecommunication equipment manufacturers are not usually fully vertically integrated in component production, the integration pressures on them are decreasing, and their competitive advantage is increasingly concentrated in technology alone.

The telecommunication equipment, after having been an epitome of a government-controlled industry for decades, is driven by its technology mix closer to the microelectronics and data processing equipment industries analyzed in the next chapter.

References

1. For a background discussion see: (1) "Behind AT & T's Change at the Top", in *Business Week*, 6 November 1978, pp. 114–139; (2) N. Tien Phue and G. Dennery, *L'Economie des Télécommunications* (Paris; Presses Universitaires de France, 1972), pp. 186–225; (3) I. C. Bupp, "Background Note on the Structure of the Telephone Industry" (available from the Intercollegiate Case Clearing House, Boston MA, ICCH No. 9–680–015), and David J. Siepp, "Issues and Options in Telecommunication Competition: A Survey', Program on Information Resources Polices, Cambridge, MA, Harvard University, December 1978, Working Paper W–78–15.
2. See Y. Doz, *Government Control and Multinational Strategic Management* (New York: Prager, 1979), chapter 3.
3. For a detailed discussion of links between the state bureaucracy and the PTT in France see J. P. Anastassopoulos, "The Strategic Autonomy of Government-Controlled Enterprises Operating in a Competitive Economy" (Unpublished Ph.D. dissertation, Columbia University, 1973).
4. There is an emerging body of literature on this point, but little factual evidence. For a summary of research and thinking on the relationship between state-owned enterprises and national government policies see Y. Aharoni and R. Vernon (eds.).
5. See M. Wilkins, *The Maturing of Multinational Enterprises* (Cambridge, MA: Harvard University Press, 1974), for U.S. companies. For Siemens see G. Siemens, *History of the House of Siemens*, vols. 1 and 2 (Freiburg: Karl Alber Verlam, 1957), and for LM Ericsson see *LM Ericsson at 100* (Stockholm, LM Ericsson, 1976).
6. Most PTTs have two to four suppliers and limit the variety of the equipment they are using. See Y. Doz, *Government Control*, table 5–1, p. 107, and Nicolas Jequier, *Les Télécommunications et l'Europe* (Geneva: Centre d'Etudes Industrielles, 1976).
7. For the United Kingdom see *Financial Times*, 18 September 1979. For Germany see Kommission für den Ausbau des Technischen Kommunikationssytems, *Telekommunikationsbeicht* (Bonn: Bundesminster für das Post und Feinmeldewesen 1976). For France see Assemblée Nationale, *Rapport fait au nom de la Commission de Contrôle de la Gestion du Service Public du Téléphone* (Paris: Assemblée Nationale, no. 1971, seconde session ordinaire de 1973–74, annexe au procès verbal de la Seance du 20 Juin 1974). For Italy see "Note on the Italian Distitutional Context (INSEAD Case Study, 1984).
8. Private communication to the author.
9. See reference in note 5.

10. For Brazil see "ITT in Lead, Ericsson out in Brazil Phone Pact Race", in *Electronic News*, August 28 1978, p. 2, and R. Karjion, "Brazil Links Communications with Tomorrow", in *Telecommunications*, April 1979, pp. 73–81. For France see J. Muller, "Government Intervention and the Market for Telecommunications Equipment in France", University of Sussex Working Paper (draft), November 1979. See also R. J. Ragget, "The Power Behind France's Telecom Upsurge", *Telephony*, 24 September 1979, pp. 64–69.
11. See Nicolas Jequier, *Les Télécommunications et l'Europe*.
12. See Y. Doz, *Government Control and Multinational Strategic Management*.
13. See *Financial Times*, Telecommunication Survey, 18 September 1979.
14. Personal communication to the author.
15. See *Financial Times*, 18 September 1979.
16. See "France Elbows in on Worldwide U.S. Phone Sales", *World Business Weekly*, 4 June 1979, pp. 9–10.
17. "Why the U.S. Lost Egypt's Phone Deal", *World Business Weekly*, 8 October 1979, pp. 10–11.
18. "Philips, Ericsson et Bell Assureront l'Equipement Téléphonique de l'Arabie Séoudite", *Le Monde*, 16 December 1977.
19. Assemblée Nationale, *Rapport fait au nom de la Commission de Contrôle de la Gestion du Service Public du Téléphone* (Paris: Assemblée Nationale no 1971, seconde session ordinaire de 1973–74, annexe au procès verbal de la séance du 20 Juin 1974).
20. Personal communications to the author.
21. For details see Y. Doz, "Note on Competition in Digital Switching Systems" (INSEAD mimeographed case study, 1984).
22. For representative data see Y. Doz, *Government Control*, p. 99, National Export Expansion Council, *Markets for Telecommunication Equipment* (Washington: U.S. Dept. of Commerce, 1973), and N. Jequier, *Les Télécommunications et l'Europe*. See also "Market Survey", in *Telephony*, 24 September 1979, p. 111 and U.S. Dept. of Commerce, *Communication Equipment and Systems* (Washington D.C., U.S. Government Printing Office, September 1977).
23. See Y. Doz and C. K. Prahalad, "How MNCs Cope with Host Government Demands", in *Harvard Business Review*, March–April 1980.
24. See LM Ericsson, *Annual Reports* (1965–1966).
25. See Y. Doz, *Government Control*, chapter 7.
26. See "STC, 'Terribly British' and Aiming to Stay That Way", in *World Business Weekly*, 25 June 1979, p. 16.
27. See Y. Doz, *Government Control*, chapter 7.
28. See, *Financial Times*, 28 September 1979.
29. See "Siemens Let $1.8B Egypt Com. Pact", in *Electronic News*, Vol. 25, no. 1255 p. 1.
30. See "Washington's Apathy Lose a $1.8 Billion Deal", in *Business Week*, 27 October 1979, p. 87.
31. See Y. Doz, *Government Control*, chapter 9.
32. See *Financial Times*, 18 September 1979.
33. See *The Economist*, 23 December 1978, p. 72.
34. See "New Brazil Law Clouds Ericsson Bids", in *Electronic News*, 2 August 1978, p. 72.
35. See R. Karjian, "Brazil Links Communication with Tomorrow", in *Telecommunications*, April 1979, pp. 73–81.
36. R. J. Ragget, "The Power Behind France's Telecom Upsurge", *Telephony* 24 September 1979, pp. 64–69.

5

Coexistence in Mixed-structure Industries: Computers and Microelectronics

Mixed-structure industries are characterized by the presence of firms following very different types of strategies: multinational integration, national responsiveness, and multifocal strategies. These industries usually correspond to partial government control over their markets. When mixed-structure industries attract government attention, less than full government control over markets limits government intervention. The coexistence within the same industry of internationally competitive and government-controlled market segments allows a broader range of firms' strategies, requires more complex national industrial policies and raises a difficult trade-off for governments between protecting the nationally responsive suppliers and accepting international integration.

The first section of this chapter reviews the economic and political priorities which condition this trade-off. A second section analyzes various types of national policies that provide at least partial responses to the trade-off. Finally, the third section suggests various multinational business strategies, given the national sectoral policies of host governments. As in the preceding two chapters, the same industries will be used throughout as examples: microelectronics and computers. The two industries must be treated jointly because their technology, markets, and manufacturing processes are closely related. The memory units of computers, for example, are the most advanced mass-produced microelectronics products.

A Difficult Trade-off Between Political and Economic Priorities

Reasons for Government Control

Mixed industries that attract government attention share several characteristics: high technology, strong relationship with national defense, displacement, threats to national industries, control of end-product industries, awareness of future significance in the national economy, and impact on trade balances. These characteristics are analyzed below.

High technology

The difficulty of creating and transferring high technology generally heightens the interest of host governments. Mastering complex technologies on an industrial scale and on a commercially viable basis is often difficult. In microelectronics, for example, difficult process technologies are the key to commercially viable production. The continued presence of experienced specialists on the premises is the only guarantee of reliable production of high-quality circuits. As a result, technology transfers between independent parties are difficult: much of the technology cannot be transferred without transferring the engineers and scientists themselves and often maintaining their links with the original firm.[1] Governments are concerned, therefore, with the difficulty of developing a national industry without drawing specialists from established foreign manufacturers. Though the microelectronics industry may be somewhat of an extreme case, many other high-technology activities are similarly dependent on people, and not easily amenable to contractual forms of technology transfers.[2]

Relationships to national defense

The search for improved performance at almost any cost makes military application the first markets for industrial innovations. The electronics industry again provides a good example.[3] The importance of miniaturization and high reliability of electronic technologies (compared to electromechanical ones) to applications, first in aircraft, then in missiles, which multiplied after World War II, provided a major impetus for the electronics industry and a large initial market for semiconductor and, later, for integrated circuits. This allowed sufficient cost reductions for integrated circuits to become price competitive in many nonmilitary applications. Otherwise, integrated circuits might for long have remained a laboratory curiosity.[4]

The early military significance of high-technology industries creates a dilemma for host governments: the better technologies may be available only from abroad, yet safety of supply demands local production, given the occasional reluctance of home governments to let their companies transfer technologies or deliver high-technology products to foreign customers. For instance, the U.S. government's 1966 embargo on two large control data computers for France's Commissariat à l'Energie Atomique contributed to France's subsequent decision to develop its own computer industry. More recently, the U.S. embargo on pipeline technology to the Soviet Union created similar pressures for the technological autonomy in Europe.

Displacement of national industries

New foreign-controlled industries may have the potential to displace existing national industries. Governments may wish for national companies to adopt the new technology early to avoid the loss of foreign markets to competitors or to provide for an orderly transition of the national market toward the new technology. After displacing the Swiss watch industry, microelectronics threaten process control, calculators, word processing, and other activities where electronic controls and processes are replacing electromechanical ones. Resulting employment cuts may be difficult and painful.[5]

Threats to end-product and system industries

New technologies may put to question traditional boundaries between industries. In electronics, the boundary between component and end-product or systems firms is shifting in favor of component manufacturers. Independent national manufacture of components is difficult since many different types of circuits are needed to protect the independence of diverse national end-product industries, yet national needs only require small numbers of each type. Many types cannot be produced economically in most European countries each with small and diverse needs. Where end-product markets are more concentrated and homogeneous, as in Japan, economical volume production of a narrow range of components is more feasible than in Europe. Japan also concentrated on a global approach to selected mass markets, most prominent among those the random-access memory (RAM) chips for computers.[6] Political considerations add further difficulties. European electronic firms which buy U.S.-made components find their exports to Eastern European countries or South Africa restricted by the United States. This sometimes leads them to undertake inefficient small-volume production of standard components mass-produced cheaply in the United States. Not controlling "core" technologies of electronics weakens such European companies as Philips, Thomson or Siemens, yet they have had little hope of making integrated circuit manufacture profitable.

Entry lags

There is little evidence to suggest great government foresight in identifying potentially significant industrial innovations. Thus, governments often tend to acknowledge the importance of a new industry only when foreign companies have already taken positions. Furthermore, European users often lag behind American and Japanese ones, placing firms with their main market in Europe at an intrinsic disadvantage. Lack of experience in selling new mass market products (such as personal computers) adds to the disadvantage. As a result, European governments' drive for independent high-technology industries often turns into a desperate uphill battle. Rapidly evolving technologies, combined with forbidding economies of scale in R & D and experience in manufacturing, often frustrate government efforts. Major foreign competitors have already captured major leading customers, lowered costs and gained defensible market positions. Yet governments are eager to "redeploy" their industry toward newer sectors of higher growth where they strive for some international competitive advantage. This becomes a major source of tensions between MNCs and the governments of developed countries.

Trade balance

Governments are concerned that free competition in new industries may result in lasting trade deficits—80% of the European integrated circuit market is served by imports from North America and the Far East. This adds to the desire to "redeploy" economies to capture some competitive advantage in high growth industries, and to withdraw from mature lower growth sectors with little potential for exports. The will to guide actively the national economy toward these growth sectors made full dependency upon foreign companies unattractive to many governments unless they had strong influence on company decisions.

The characteristics summarized above suggest strong government intervention to boost the competitiveness of national firms or to harness the capabilities of MNCs toward national priorities. Yet the technological and economic barriers to government intervention are so high as to dampen government desires for intervention.

The Economic Imperative as a Damper to Government Intervention

Several economic characteristics—economies of scale and experience, fast-paced technological evolutions, marketing advantages of existing firms, product similarities across borders, and factor cost and productivity differences among countries—limit the scope for government intervention in the electronics industry.

Economies of scale and experience

Economies of scale in electronic equipment manufacturing generally appear substantial.* Some estimates suggest that total unit costs (that is, manufacturing, sales, maintenance and software) of a firm with 10% of the

---

*In the various lawsuits involving IBM's alleged attempt to monopolize the U.S. general-purpose computer market, economies of scale were hotly debated, and conflicting measurements and interpretations put forward, but their importance was not negated.

U.S. computer market would exceed by almost 20% those of a hypothetical monopolist.[7] An economic comparison of Compagnie Internationale pour l'Informatique and IBM showed that experience effects would confer upon the larger firm a continuous competitive advantage.[8] Honeywell's executives estimated that a 10% share of the world computer market was a threshold to acceptable profitability given the very high front end cost of R & D.[9] Economies of scale and experience are even stronger in the production of integrated circuits. For a given circuit type, unit costs decrease by about 22% each time production experience doubles.[10] Production yield usually improves significantly with experience.[11] In addition, the capital intensity of the semiconductor industry increases rapidly, creating stronger absolute economies of scale. R & D thresholds, capital intensity of production and testing, and economies of experience reinforce each other.

Smaller firms or late entrants thus face extreme difficulties when they try to gain a cost position competitive with that of larger firms. Aspiring competitors must either accept lasting cost disadvantages, or be the first to move into new technologies, a risky gamble.

Fast-paced technological advance

Rapid technological advances as well as falling costs and prices mean that even if a company achieves state-of-the-art technology at one time, it must continue to invest heavily in R & D merely to remain competitive. The larger firms, with the most products based on a given technology, and a larger volume for each product, are in a position to maintain a substantial long-term advantage by sustaining a larger R & D activity over a number of years. Massive and focused commitments of resources over a long period of time are therefore needed for a national champion to gain a stable position in the industry.

In the computer industry, the very high costs of software presented yet another difficulty: short of piggybacking on existing software, the investments were prohibitive. Furthermore, software development remained a complex intellectual activity carried out by skilled, scarce, well-trained, highly paid, individuals. Most European countries had not anticipated the staggering size of software requirements, and the necessary specialists had not been trained in sufficient numbers. As a result, software costs increased substantially over time and software development became a major hurdle for new competitors.

Marketing advantages of established firms and economies of scale in distribution

Early business computer users who were unfamiliar with the equipment relied on better-known suppliers who provided complete systems and extensive service support, such as IBM.[12] This broad base system and service-orientated approach made it more difficult for smaller, more specialized, firms to enter the market successfully.

Eventually, however, as customers became more familiar with computer equipment and applications, and could better analyze the costs and benefits of alternate suppliers, the marketing advantage of large, well-established firms waned. Knowledgeable customers looked for the best deal, or for the most appropriate specialized suppliers. The emergence of plug compatible suppliers who piggybacked on existing software and copied existing equipment, the growth of minicomputers, and the variety of distributed network configurations all contributed to the opening of the data processing equipment industry to a wide range of competitors.[13]

Yet economies of scale in maintenance and service remain very substantial. Network processing leads to more dispersed installations.* Companies with larger market shares can install, service and maintain dispersed equipment at a lower cost than smaller companies, since their field engineers spend more time working on-site and less time travelling and can also answer customer calls at shorter notice.[14] As it converges with the office and telecommunication equipment industries into a broad information technology sector, economies of scope in product range may increasingly affect the computer industry. Some core technologies, such as optical recording, have potential applications throughout the information technology industry, creating economies of scope in R & D. As distribution channels become blurred (with products such as personal computers, "smart" phones, "intelligent" copiers, etc., being sold through multiple channels), advantages may accrue to firms which can leverage multiple distribution channels with a broad product range.

A final difficulty for new companies in the EDP industry is the remaining importance of leasing.[15] It considerably increases the funding requirements of a fast-growing company. Leased equipment often accounted for over half the U.S. industry's shipments, a little less in Europe. Lease-to-sales ratios tended to increase with the speed of technological change, since users were less willing to invest in equipment that could quickly become obsolescent.

Product similarities across borders

International product similarity favors integrated MNCs. In both computers and microelectronics, products are standardized with only relatively minor adaptations to different national standards and local conditions.

---

*Distributed network processing had led to a dispersion of equipment from the large central EDP centers typical of the 1960s to a wide range of interconnected locations, with much less equipment in each individual location.

Software is somewhat more local in nature.[16] Furthermore, in the late 1970s the physical location of the equipment became increasingly spread out as multinational users developed. Teleprocessing, network technology and the low cost of long-distance satellite telecommunication made it feasible—and sometimes more economical—for European users to locate some of their data processing centers in the United States, for example.[17]

Differences in factor costs and productivity

These differences also strongly favor integrated MNCs which can make components in one country, assemble systems in another and sell them in a third. Manufacturing costs being a small part of total costs, EDP equipment was not sensitive to labor cost differences. Most of the other operations (e.g., R & D, software development, application development) involved highly skilled labor, available only in developed countries (except India), with comparable wage levels. Shortages of trained specialists in countries such as Spain, where labor was cheaper on average than in Northern Europe or the United States, minimized salary-level difference among countries.

The situation was quite different in microelectronics: factor costs and productivity differences played a central role in competition. Several stages in the production process must be considered.[18] Crystal growing, the first major stage, is a relatively capital-intensive, scale-intensive operation which a manufacturer typically undertakes in a single or maybe a few locations. It is not sensitive to factor cost differences. Wafer fabrication, the second major stage,* is not labor-intensive either. Third, and most labor-intensive, are bonding, finishing, testing and packaging. In the 1970s these stages were usually undertaken in low labor cost areas, first Mexico and the Caribbean, later Southeast Asia.[19] However, increased automation of these stages started to make "offshore" locations less attractive by the late 1970s.

The five major economic characteristics discussed above—economies of scale and experience, fast technological advances, marketing advantages of established firms, product similarities among national markets, and differences in factor costs and productivity between countries—all favor large, integrated, well-established MNCs over smaller, newer, national firms. Similarity of products for the world's market and differences in factor costs favor integrated MNCs more directly than other firms. Together, they provide the basis for domination of both the microelectronic and computer industries by integrated MNCs.

___

*Once a silicon crystal has been grown, it is cut into thin slices, called wafers, that provide the substrate for integrated circuits. Layers of conducting or isolating substances are then deposited on this surface and selectively removed through etching and chemical treatments to provide the complete circuit structure.

Host Governments' Dilemma

The host governments' dilemma results from the contradiction between the conflicting economic and political characteristics outlined above. Sources of government concern, such as relationships to national defense, displacement of existing industries, threats to end-product industries, and entry lags, call for the development of a broad based independent national capability. Yet the strength of the competitive conditions favoring integrated MNCs makes such an approach self-defeating: very large commitments of resources would have to be made to a variety of new technologies and to small-scale production of a wide range of products, preventing international competitiveness from being achieved for most of them. As a result, trade balances could be improved only via protectionism, at a high cost to the national economy.

Limited national resources would need to be focused on specific product segments for competitiveness on the world market. Such segmentation would imply, though, that only selected national needs be met through local production. Dependence on foreign suppliers would continue for others. Competitiveness would be achieved on a narrow front, but inherent risks of integration would remain.

This conflict between national protection and selective international competition is not easily resolved. Various government agencies fall on different sides; so do national companies. Some strive for blanket protection by the state, others for open competition in market segments in which they are strong. Since no policy is likely to resolve all sources of concern, no dominant solution can emerge. Thus the dilemma may not find a once and for all solution, but merely evolve over time. How various national governments have coped with this dilemma is summarized below.

The Dilemma of National Strategies

To a great extent national sectoral strategies in global industries can be seen as mirror images of multinational business strategies. Government supports to firms competing in selected segments is driven by the same logic as multinational integration strategy: to achieve low-cost production and international competitiveness through high-production volume. Protection of a broad base national industry, like a national responsiveness strategy, aims at a protected national position by responding extremely well to national conditions. Finally, multinational alliances are analog to multifocal strategies. Such alliances attempt to meet economic imperatives without forgoing government control.

126   *Strategic Management in Multinational Companies*

Selective Support of National Companies to Compete Internationally

The logic of this national strategy is clear: to beat the integrated MNCs at their own game. Japan provides a striking illustration of this approach. Japanese firms set out to dominate selected, narrowly defined segments serving selected end products, such as calculators—through the mastery of new significant technologies. In 1972 domestic Japanese producers gained from U.S. exports a 50% share of the domestic market for circuits used in desk-top calculators. Japanese production of such calculators rose from 9.9 million units in 1973 to 15.5 million in 1974 and 32 million in 1975.[20]

The importation of production and test equipment from the United States made rapid volume increases possible. By 1973 desk-top calculators used 80% of the Japanese MOS-LSI* circuit output. Following that fast start, several Japanese companies (Nippon Electric, Hitachi, Toshiba and Mitsubishi) recognized the importance of MOS-LSI computer memories to replace magnetic core memories, and they started development work on such devices. By 1972–73 they started to manufacture 1K and 4K random access memories (RAM).† In the meantime MOS-LSI circuits moved to pocket calculator applications. By 1974 microelectronics had become a priority redeployment sector enjoying extensive government support.

Government and national companies joined forces in 1975 in two parallel efforts: the development of the existing MOS-LSI memories foothold on the world market and the development of new very large-scale integration (VLSI) technologies. The gap between new product introduction by leading U.S firms and Japanese companies had narrowed to the almost simultaneous introduction of 64K RAM in 1979. In 1979 the Japanese suppliers had captured 42% of the U.S. market for 16K RAM, then the largest memories in mass production. By 1982 Japanese suppliers dominated the 64K RAM market with a 70% share. In the longer term, the Japanese are aiming at worldwide leadership for very much larger memories than the 64K RAMs. In 1980 Nippon Electric and Hitachi were already developing 256K memories for 1983 introduction and claimed they would capture more than half of their markets.[21]

The strategy of segmentation and leadership enabled Japanese firms to compete successfully against major MNCs in selected product markets. Experience effects ensured that market share leadership would offer Japanese suppliers lower costs than smaller competitors. In 1984 Germany and The Netherlands started a similar set of policies to sponsor jointly

---

* Metal Oxide Semiconductor Large Scale Integrated Circuits, a high-density type of circuit, particularly well suited to calculator function needs.

† Computer memory capacity is measured in "bits", the standard measurement is noted "K", standing for a capacity of 1024 bits. Each bit is a set of 8 binary units corresponding to a negative or positive charge in a memory cell.

R & D by Philips and Siemens toward a "mega" memory chip of 1024K. They hoped to leapfrog the Japanese.

A similar approach toward the memory market was also attempted by a government-assisted new venture in Britain, called INMOS. By hiring experienced U.S. engineers, scientists and managers, and by carrying out product development and initial production in the United States, INMOS hoped to overcome difficulties of technology transfer and to create the entrepreneurial spirit of a start-up venture.[22] By 1980, however, disputes about the site of the first British factory (the government wanted the factory located in a depressed area) delayed funding and put INMOS's future in jeopardy.[23] INMOS was subsequently acquired by a larger diversified group.

The computer industry had not witnessed such carefully segmented approaches as that of the Japanese or as INMOS's attempt. On the contrary, IBM and the makers of IBM-compatible equipment have increased their lead to the detriment of other manufacturers. Yet in a few cases national companies were attempting to take leadership positions in selected segments through technological innovations. An example is provided by International Computers Limited (ICL), the British national champion. A new architecture, called distributed array processing (DAP), which merges logic and memory on a single circuit board, enabled ICL to build very large computers at very low prices. DAP had been used for scientific research and may still provide ICL with a strong position in large mainframe computers in the 1980s.[24]

The major barriers to the strategy of selective support is the availability of skills and resources. Japanese government support to the development of VLSI alone reached $136 million between 1975 and 1979. A well-managed cooperative research venture succeeded in harnessing the skill of six different companies into a well-coordinated effort, avoiding the wastage of resources and duplication of efforts that often plague government-sponsored cooperative efforts.[25] Total government support to the microelectronics industry was estimated to range between $300 million and $500 million over the same period. This was the only succcessful example of a strategy of acquisition of leadership. INMOS's effort was not so solid. Its resources were much smaller, and industry experts feared that late product introductions, compared to competitors, would prevent the acquisition of a leading position. ICL's DAP is the result of a one-man one million dollar research effort, but its results cannot yet be evaluated. Other European efforts have been too small, scattered and nationally focused to provide for global leadership.

In some cases explicit preference rules were formulated. The "10% rule" in the United Kingdom required state-controlled customers to show foreign offers to be 10% cheaper or guarantee 10% better performance than domestic ICL's in order to be allowed not to buy from ICL. France,

Germany, Japan and the United Kingdom created internal "consulting agencies" to promote the use of EDP equipment in the civil service and to orient public purchases toward favored suppliers. Widespread preference for national suppliers was also exercised informally through ministry of industry channels. In 1979, for instance, an order by partly government-controlled French steel firm SOLMER for a Sperry-Univac system was rescinded in favor of a C2I-HB system.[26]

Protection faced limits, however. First, few countries were capable of developing and manufacturing advanced microcircuits or computers without outside assistance. Second, state-controlled customers not always let themselves be influenced easily in their purchasing decisions. Many European state-owned enterprises remained major customers of IBM. Third, the economic characteristics of the industry made small volume production, sales and service financially untenable. Private customers, who could choose between homegrown products and those supplied by MNCs, often turned to MNCs for lower priced, superior products with better servicing and users' support. Since public sector users provided at most a third of European markets, government influence through market power was limited.

Governments turned to massive subsidies to the national electronic components and computer firms, mainly through R & D assistance. In France, for instance, from 1968 to 1976 the electronic and data processing industries received about $1 billion in public assistance or roughly 15% of the total assistance to all industries during that period.[27] Extensive assistance was also provided to the computer industry in Britain and Germany (Table 5.1).[28]

Protection and Support of a Broad Base National Industry

Most European countries and Japan are following a policy of partial protection. Following the decision to develop an autonomous national computer industry, Japan implemented a wide-ranging protection policy that cut the market share of foreign suppliers substantially. Imported computers accounted for 70% of the Japanese market in 1961, and most locally assembled ones came from the IBM subsidiary. By 1975, however, the share of imported machines had fallen to 15%, and sales by foreign manufacturing subsidiaries to 35%.

A comparison of U.S. and European suppliers' market shares between private and state-controlled computer users in Europe reveals the extent of the preference enjoyed by national suppliers in the public sector of European countries (Table 5.2).

Though the amounts provided by governments were large in absolute terms, IBM's research and development budget ($1200 million per year) or

Table 5.1 Public Assistance to the Computer Industry

	67	68	69	70	71	72	73	74	75	76	77	78	79
1. *Japan* (million yen)													
Computer development						4510	14026	15250	12475	10825			
Peripherals						700	936	1400	900	600			
Computer IC LSI						0	1700	1800	0	3500			
Miscellaneous grants						1137	1529	2150	2182	973			
2. *Germany* (million DM.)													
Computer development		240.6						705.4		140	133	138	143
Research		42					227			44	48	51	52
Education		47						720		94	64.5	57	49
Computer Application		57						558		128	133	144	157
3. *France* (million F.F.)													
Computer development		491.5						910					
Computer Components		91.6						155					
Applications		15.9						165					
Research		117.1						95					
Subsidies to C2I-HB											1200		
4. *United Kingdom* (£ million)													
Subsidies to ICL				13.5		5		40					
Research													
Application								3.38					
Components										10			

Source: G. Nakae, *Market Strategies in the Computer Industry*, DAFSA, *L'Industrie Informatique dans le Monde en 1975* (Paris, DAFA, 1976), and EEC Commission "Report Concerning the Development of the Data Processing Sector in the Community in Relation to the World's Situation" (Brussels: EEC-COM Report No. 76–524, 1976).

129

TABLE 5.2   *Private and Public Sector Computer System Market Shares in Selected European Countries 1971-75*

	Germany		France		United Kingdom		Belgium	
	Total market	Public sector	Total market	Public sector	Total market	Public sector	Total market	Public sector
European suppliers	20%	44%	32%‡	48%‡	36%	59%	25%	64%
U.S. suppliers*	80%	56%	68%	52%	64%	41%	75%	36%

*Including U.S. subsidiaries in Europe.
‡Including C2I-Honeywell Bull as a European supplier.
Note: Figures are not strictly comparable among countries as definitions of public sector markets and of computer systems vary among countries.
Source: Compiled by the author from *Report Concerning the Developments in the Data Processing Sector in the Community in Relation to the World Situation,* COM (76) 524, Vol. III (Brussels: Commission of the European Communities, 1976), various tables and exhibits.

Intel's (the leading U.S. firm in microprocessor technology) capital investment budget ($150 million to $200 million per year) dwarfed government sponsored programs in computers and microelectronics. The forbidding size of resource commitments and the difficulty of segmenting the industries in meaningful ways put government-sponsored efforts in a difficult predicament.

Japan's computer industry illustrates this predicament. In the 1960s the government restricted market access and fully-owned investment by foreign companies. Behind such protection, a burgeoning national industry developed with MITI assistance.[29] The Japanese industry quickly developed computers that were comparable in capability and technology to the IBM 370 series. Yet price declines in the industry, price competition among Japanese suppliers, and the introduction of new products by IBM did not enable the low volume Japanese suppliers to prosper, and only 7.2% of the computers produced in 1979 were exported. Production and sales remained too fragmented to achieve low production costs and to establish effective sales and service organizations abroad. Revaluation of the yen also made exports less competitive despite deep price discounts. Few mainframes had been exported directly, with the exception of exports to Spain, where Fujitsu had set up a 33%-owned joint venture with local interests to manufacture peripherals in exchange for a supply contract from the telecommunication authority.[30] Disappointing results led Japanese manufacturers to retrench, at least temporarily, into a segmented approach to establish strong positions, often as original equipment manufacturers for U.S. firms in some peripherals and in mini and microcomputers.[31] In the longer term, the transition to network processing (where the Japanese are strong) and efforts to master VLSI technologies and new artificial intelligence software may again allow the Japanese to pursue the international market more actively.[32]

Only two independent national companies survived in Western Europe: Siemens in Germany and ICL in the United Kingdom. Government protection sheltered ICL throughout the 1970s and the public sector accounted for about 30% of ICL's sales.

Overall, ICL remained focused on the British market. Some critics argue that the end of preferential purchasing (GATT regulations adopted in 1981 condemn preferential purchasing) might put ICL's future in jeopardy. In 1981 ICL negotiated far-reaching agreements with Fujitsu.

Siemens' position remained precarious too. Financial results improved dramatically between 1975 and 1980, however, from annual losses exceeding $100 million in 1974 and 1975 (on revenues amounting to about $600 million) to break even in 1978–79 (on sales of $1.05 billion).[33] Throughout the 1970s the German government heavily subsidized Siemens' computer R & D for a total contribution of about $475 million to Siemen's total R & D budget of $1.5 billion. Informal preferential purchasing by major government-controlled enterprises also helped Siemens' recovery. Siemens remained largely focused on the German domestic market. Yet Siemens also moved toward a strategy of multinational alliances, first with the Unidata attempt,* later by procuring large computers from Fujitsu.[34] Siemens began marketing Fujitsu computers in 1978, under its own brand. In return for these computers, Siemens applied peripherals to Fujitsu.

Both ICL and Siemens faced a trade-off between market coverage and specialization in some subsegments where their resources and competencies were sufficient to compete internationally; by 1981 neither had found a stable, secure competitive position.

Multinational Alliances

Alliances among national firms are sometimes touted as a panacea: they are expected to provide the critical benefits of multinationality, with none of its disadvantages. By pooling resources and competencies and providing a large multinational market, such multinational alliances overcome difficulties of economies of scale in R & D, manufacturing and marketing, and provide for a broad base capability at a competitive cost. Members of these alliances are not all of the same nature, however, nor are alliances of the same strength. Some involve multinational companies and national ones, others involve a coalition of independent national companies.

Alliances between national and multinational firms

Comparatively weaker competitors, such as Honeywell against IBM, may find alliances with national partners attractive. Governments can welcome partnerships with MNCs, provided these are willing to be responsive to the government's needs and yet can remain internationally competitive. In France, Honeywell is such a company: it provides national responsiveness and a policy of integration that allows it to remain at least marginally competitive. French conditions were attractive to Honeywell. The continuing difficulties faced by C2I had led the French government to accept a scheme initiated by Honeywell Bull's management to merge with C2I. Whereas there was no end in sight to C2I's losses, plans suggested that the new venture could become commercially successful and do without state subsidies after 5 years.[35]

The French government therefore committed itself to support the merger in various ways:

1. The government made available financial assistance to the amount of

---

*Unidata was a joint venture with C2I and Philips which collapsed following the French government's decision to merge C2I in Honeywell-Bull.

FF1.2 billion to the new company, provided in several decreasing installments from 1976 to 1979.

2. The government committed to public sector cash sales to the amount of FF3.8 billion over a 5-year period. Should state orders not reach that amount, the government would grant subsidies equal to 55% of the shortfall. Conversely, if state orders exceeded FF3.8 billion, 55% of the surplus would be deducted from state subsidies.

3. The minicomputer and military activities of C2I were spun off into a new company, including a large plant in Toulouse. Since Honeywell Bull had excess manufacturing capacity on its own, it did not want to take any extra C2I capacity.

The French thus offered Honeywell a privileged access to public sector customers and substantial subsidies. On average, the subsidies could double Honeywell's annual computer research and development budget. Through the French affiliate, Honeywell could also gain access to Eastern European markets that C2I had been cultivating with direct support from the French government.

To the French, Honeywell brought an existing product line, fully competitive with IBM's 370 series. It also brought a strong distribution network in countries where C2I lacked one, and an internationally credible brand name with a strong service organization. Furthermore, Honeywell Bull's top management committed themselves to full independent competitiveness when state subsidies would stop in 1980. The alliance was attractive to both sides.

The alliance between C2I and Honeywell is essentially the coopting of a MNC as a national champion, on the understanding that the MNC will provide extensive economic benefits and national responsiveness through the continued integration of its operations in other countries. Such a strategy is most likely to succeed U.S.-based MNCs which, despite sometimes stringent regulation, seldom face specific U.S. government interventions. A French Ministry of Industry official commented on the cooperation with Honeywell:

For the French government the merger between C2I and Honeywell Bull solved some of the most thorny dilemmas, in particular the one between state support and economic liberalization. The idea was to set very precise objectives for the company and a limited time frame for subsidies necessary to help achieve those objectives and start the company on a growth track. We did not only want some formal legal framework of a viable nature, but also a concrete situation, grounded in an economic strategy that would safeguard our long-run position so long as the French objectives remained reasonable. As Honeywell does not drive for hegemony (in the partnership) and as the French want to reach concrete with a real economic content, we have faced no serious problems.[36]

The combination of relatively clear objectives and flexibility to respond to government demands was achieved through a set of explicit formal cooperation rules between C2I-HB in France and Honeywell Information Systems in the United States.

1. *Reciprocal free cross-licensing*: both C2I-HB and Honeywell Information Systems (HIS) have the right to manufacture freely any item in the joint production line. They can decide to single source certain items provided this serves their respective economic interests.

2. *Research and development*: each partner took responsibility for R & D on a significant homogeneous part of the common product line. The percentage of revenues of each partner devoted to R & D was about the same. C2I-HB remained active in large system and software development work to maintain a consistent technological potential in France. A consultative technical committee was set up to make recommendations on worldwide product strategies, product plans, R & D budgets and product announcements. The technical committee has five members, three appointed by HIS, two C2I-HB.*

3. *Distribution*: each partner was allowed to sell the complete common product range in any country of its choice, the partners decided, however, to allocate export markets among themselves.[37]

Following the election of a Socialist majority in France, the ownership agreements with Honeywell were renegotiated, in 1981–82, but the spirit of the cooperation agreements continued. At least for improvement to existing products, a joint product line was maintained and technology exchanges continued. Honeywell's ownership in C2I-HB was reduced to just below 20%, and the French government resumed substantial financial assistance to C2I-HB in 1982–83.

Despite the advantages of alliances with multinational companies, these are not always preferred, or feasible. First, for some activities, such as military electronics, fear of loss of national control may still prevail in government circles. Second, the number of willing potential multinational partners is often limited.

In the absence of suitable multinational partners, governments often resort to a second type of alliance: that between national firms, none of which is a strong multinational. Such coalitions among quasi-"national champions" are generally of a less comprehensive nature than the partnerships with major multinational corporations. They are often restricted to individual functions (e.g., distribution) or to specific product markets.

Alliances among national companies

Most of the alliances involve cross-distribution of products and sharing of product development and manufacture. For instance, Fujitsu supplied

---

*The appointment procedure stipulates that the company with the largest revenues (among the two partners) can appoint three members, that with the smallest two.

subassemblies for Amdahl computers in the United States and complete systems to Siemens in Germany.

By 1980 the idea of multinational cooperation among national firms was gathering momentum in the European electronics industry. The Commission of the European Economic Communities played a leading role in this effort, drawing stern conclusions on policies of separate national support. A 1980 Commission report on the computer industry concluded:

The different national aid programs have fostered competing national enterprises, while leaving key long-term needs unmet. Europe has neither the continental market of America, nor the common strategy of Japan.

More aggressive competition from IBM starting in 1978–80 gave a sense of urgency to the Commission's conclusions. The heads of several European computer manufacturers echoed the Commission's suggestions for some form of cooperation.[38]

In the face of a very uncertain situation, and in the absence of complete control over market access, governments have been hedging their bets. First, officials were generally not prepared to take extreme actions to reduce IBM's leadership in the computer industry, or that of Texas Instruments or INTEL in the microelectronics industry. The benefits provided by these leading companies outweighed the disadvantages of their integration, so long as their leadership could be prevented from becoming dominance. Both in terms of new products and technologies and in terms of economic and social performance these leading companies made outstanding contributions. They also set the difficult standards of technical and economic excellence their competitors had to face. Over the 1970s, IBM's position in the European market had been remarkably stable, as witnesses a constant market share. National policies avoided a clear choice. Some companies would follow economic imperatives, others political imperatives. By supporting the economically weaker companies, governments could maintain some balance in markets, and prevent leadership from evolving into dominance. This directly contributed to maintain the mixed-structure industries in Europe. The three types of national strategies—selective international competition in narrowly chosen product-markets, protection and support of broad base national industries, and multinational alliances—do not exclude leaving an important role to integrated MNCs. Shifts from one national strategy to another are also possible over time. Developing a national industry of any type requires initial protection, otherwise incentives to invest private capital into the new industry would not exist.

In some cases serving the national needs provides the production volume to achieve international competitiveness, for instance with circuits for desktop calculators in Japan. Once the national industry thrives in its national market it may become an attractive partner in a multinational

TABLE 5.3 *National Policies*

Government tools	Selective competition	Broad base protection	Multinational alliance
1. *Market access control*	Important to establish domestic base and provide early volume to decrease costs. Early sales may be subsidized. Unneeded later on.	Provides only possible market and underlies choice of this policy. (e.g., problems with the French military buying TI's circuits rather than SESCO-SEM's).	Contrary to the purposes of the alliance, but useful to bring in MNC partner or collective protection (e.g., the EEG limiting US imports.
2. *Subsidies and grants*	Required to provide resources needed to acquire commanding positions in selected segments: R & D assistance, investment grants, employment/training subsidies. Should disappear after a few years if policy successful.	Unescapable unless full market control is achieved, and only higher priced or less performant equipment is made available (e.g., SESCOSEM pre-1978).	Should be minimal, except at start-up phase. Similar to selective competition approach. May be necessary to bring in valuable partners (e.g., C2I-Honeywell).
3. *Fiscal incentives*	Possible: tax rebates, accelerated depreciation, capitalized R & D, etc.	Same as for selective competition, but less critical if more direct means of protection are available.	Same as for selective competition.
4. *Export assistance*	Very important, particularly to controlled markets (e.g., Soviet Union).	Possible, but success may only take place where major companies are forbidden to participate (e.g., microelectronics manufacturing equipment sales to Polaroid).	Very important. May be needed to bring valuable partners.
5. *Pricing policies, financing policies.*	Higher domestic prices and high debt leverage to provide cash flows to expand abroad. Domestic prices to be lowered later on.	Prices set to ensure viability of firm, higher than international prices.	Should apply pressure to align prices with those of integrated MNCs.

136

alliance, or attempt to gain international competitiveness in selected product markets. Policies may then shift from protection to support. In European countries, where international trade agreements exclude formal protection, a wide array of tools are used simultaneously and differences among strategies may not be extremely clear cut. Table 5.3 summarizes the correspondence between major categories of policy tools and the national strategies being followed.

Multinational Business Strategies

MNC strategies in the data processing equipment and microelectronics industries clustered into multinational integration and multifocal approaches. The largest multinational firms followed strategies of multinational integration, the smallest ones multifocal strategies. A closer look at these strategies, as they were implemented by multinationals in both industries, provides a fuller explanation of these choices.

Multinational Integration

Leading firms in both EDP and microelectronics industries, namely IBM and Texas Instruments, were integrated, but in somewhat different manners. Pressures to lower production costs were considerably more intense in the microelectronics industry than in the computer industry. Historically, IBM had been able to establish a leading differentiated position; price competition did not predominate but service was a major competitive factor. Computer prices had remained relatively high, lessening the pressure for integration to squeeze costs. Further, IBM had no competitor of comparable size and, until the 1970s, customers were not extremely price sensitive.[39] Until the intrusion of plug-compatible manufacturers (PCM)—who undercut IBM prices with copies of IBM's products, using IBM's software—price had not been a critical competitive factor. IBM then cut some prices and accelerated the development and introduction of new products.

In microelectronics, price competition was the name of the game. Leading companies used to cut prices very early in the life of a product to expand primary demand; capture it, and ride down the experience curve faster than other competitors. Therefore, they set prices very low in order to generate large volumes and decrease costs.[40] Similar products were made by several competitors. Prices, delivery schedules and quality led customers to one supplier or another, not service.* The industry, however, was more segmented than the computer industry: different technologies

---

*There remained only a small segment of the market where customers looked for special purpose circuits not commercially available and had them designed and custom built to their specification. There, service was the main competitive variable, rather than price.

and different functions had different leading competitors and different market structures. The segmented nature of the industry, the intensity of experience effects and price competition, and the importance of manufacturing costs, made clear leadership of the whole industry by one company impossible.[41]

These differences in competitive variables, opportunities for segmentation, and cost structures have led to dissimilar patterns of integration between the EDP and microelectronics industries.

In semiconductors integration took place by stages in the manufacturing process: capital intensive, knowledge intensive activities in the home countries, labor intensive activities in developing countries.[42]

In computers, on the other hand, manufacturing integration took place among developed countries. IBM had developed a Europewide integrated manufacturing network. Purchased parts were generally procured from countries where IBM had no manufacturing facilities (e.g., Belgium and Finland). Two sources existed for each product: one in the United States, one abroad.* Benefits drawn from economies of scale were deemed to offset transportation costs, logistical complexity and managerial difficulty on a regional basis, but not on a worldwide basis.[43]

Following in IBM's tracks, Honeywell had developed a global integration pattern by 1974. Manufacturing was shared between U.S. plants and subsidiaries in Britain, France, Italy and Germany. The partnership with C2I-HB complicated this process. At the initiative of the French government, C2I-Honeywell-Bull took advantage of Honeywell's mainframe range in 1978, which so far had been supplied from the United States and a European factory in Scotland. C2I-Honeywell-Bull's management argued that their manufacturing cost in France was substantially lower than the transfer prices charged by Honeywell, thus the move was not only politically expedient but also economically sensible.[44] It was generally expected that the partnership with C2I-HB would to some extent reduce Honeywell's integration.

Other companies manufactured primarily in one country: Burroughs had pulled back most manufacturing operations from Europe to the United States, Digital Equipment had built only one large plant outside of North America, in Ireland. Control Data did some manufacturing in Europe, and had several OEM contracts with European companies. ICL and Siemens kept the bulk of their manufacturing operations in their home country. Among the smaller computer manufacturers only NCR had extensive manufacturing operations in Europe, inherited from its cash register activities.

Smaller, newer U.S. computer companies were not much interested in

---

*Following the split of international operations into two geographical companies (one for Europe-Middle East-Africa, the other for the Americas and the Far East) the company was in the process of shifting to triple sourcing for some equipment.

building major plants in Europe. They made mostly smaller office systems and minicomputers, products in which European governments had not yet evinced much interest.

None of the major U.S. semiconductor firms had foreign operations prior to the development of the semiconductor industry: all were new firms. Though well-established electrical equipment firms such as RCA, General Electric or Westinghouse had an early lead in semiconductors, they were all quickly eclipsed by new firms such as Texas Instruments, Motorola, Fairchild, National Semiconductors, and others. In Europe the major electrical firms such as N. V. Philips, Siemens, Thomson, General Electric Company (GEC) also took an early leadership, but no new European semiconductor firms emerged to compete with them. Differences in the availability of venture capital, mobility of scientists, military programs, and development of the computer industry explain this major discrepancy in the structure of the semiconductor industry between Europe and the United States.[45]

Texas Instruments, among others, was quick to see the void in the European industry. In the late 1950s TI moved to Europe. In the absence of a homegrown computer industry, the military represented the only large customer for the types of products offered by TI. Aware of the military's concerns for local production, TI set up subsidiaries in several European countries, with engineering, circuit design, manufacturing and marketing functions. By the 1970s, concerns for the safety of supply could be answered by the development of national licensees (e.g., SESCOSEM) and the bulk of the market had shifted to private customers who cared little about location of manufacture and based their decisions on price. TI responded by integrating its European operations and transferring the most labor-intensive activities to the Far East. This served the company well till the late 1970s.

By then, the European governments had become fully aware of the overall importance of microelectronics to their economy. New large government-controlled markets also developed: telecommunication equipment in particular. Though TI continued to be quite successful in military sales, it was not very well positioned toward these new markets. By 1978, with the appointment of a key TI corporate officer to head European semiconductor operations, the pendulum was swinging back to more responsiveness to host government concerns.[46]

TI's major competitors from the 1960s, Motorola and Fairchild were in a difficult predicament. They were attacked from three sides: TI, government sponsored ventures in Europe which were taking away part of their markets, and rapidly growing more narrowly focused more innovative firms in the United States and Japan, National Semiconductors and Intel (created by Fairchild defectors) in particular. In time, both Fairchild and Motorola moved away from a strategy of integration in Europe. Motorola engaged into partnership with Thomson-CSF.[47] Fairchild was bought by Schlumberger in the United States.*

The structure of the two industries, computer and microelectronics, was thus becoming increasingly similar. IBM and TI remained major integrated leading multinationals. Both strived to be "good citizens" and to maintain as much responsiveness as was compatible with integration. The relative lack of price pressure on IBM made this easier than it was for TI, which was exposed to much more intense price competition. In the computer industry, NCR was integrated, but remained a much smaller company than IBM or TI, and was active in a segment of the industry which drew little government attention.

A second tier, in the industry structure, was constituted by partnerships between U.S. multinationals and European firms. In the computer industry C2I-Honeywell-Bull was a prime example. In microelectronics Motorola's and Fairchild's alliances with European companies typified this approach.[48] There was also a single major European multinational supplier: N.V. Philips. Some of the more recently prominent U.S. semiconductor companies, with no strong international presence, joined in such alliances in order to obtain, quickly and inexpensively, a foothold in Europe. National Semiconductor, for instance, teamed up with Saint Gobain-Pont à Mousson (SGPM)—a very large diversified French group. SGPM was trying to redeploy its own activities from mature businesses where it held a leading position in Europe (e.g., steel tubes or flat glass) to fast growing high technology industries, such as microelectronics.[49] National firms, with only limited foreign operations, constituted a third tier in the structure of both industries. We have already discussed the dilemma of competitiveness vs. market coverage they sometimes create for their home governments. Strategies of alliances were often seen as a way to escape this dilemma, but these did not always fulfill their promises.

Patterns of competition in the semiconductor and computer industries fitted those hypothesized in Chapter 2 (Table 2.2). IBM was more willing than any semiconductor firm to accommodate host government requests and provide citizenship costs. In both industries the weaker multinational companies were drawn into alliances with a specific government or into moves toward multifocal strategies.

Multifocal Strategy and Multinational Alliance

As we have argued in Chapter 2, multifocal strategies offer the potential to maintain some of the benefits of integration, while quenching the host government's desire for control, a tightrope that N.V. Philip's microelec-

---

* Schlumberger is a French-American firm, active in oil exploration services, pumps, meters and electronic test equipment, in particular. Observers did not expect the firm to serve as conduit of French government influence on Fairchild's operations.

tronics business had learned to walk. It had in the main integrated its semiconductor activities, specializing plants in each country into specific product lines and technologies. However, the allocation of production to various countries did not always match their governments' desires. Allocations could sometimes be made in response to government's requests, as in the case of VLSI consumer product development in Germany. In 1976 the German ministry of Science and Technology showed concern about delays in very large scale integration (VLSI) technologies. The desire to protect the competitiveness of end-product industries was at the basis of this concern. Many new consumer products, such as teletext or video recording, and new features for existing products such as digital tuning, remote control or displays, can be made cheaper with VLSI circuits. The German electronics industry was dominated by two diversified firms: Siemens for capital goods, Philips for consumer goods. Philips, whose managers were considering a VLSI research program on their own, decided to initiate it in Germany rather than in the Dutch central services, so as to match the German Government's interest. According to a key manager in Philips' German subsidiary:

We receive substantial subsidies, about 50 million Deutschmarks per year. We acted in a very straightforward way, explaining to the ministry officials that in order to make a success of VLSI we would have to cooperate internationally within the Philips group, but would do it with the full knowledge of the government. We took officials from the Ministry of Science and Technology on a tour of our operations throughout Europe, to show them our technical foundations. The tour was a breakthrough; the ministry officials got a feeling for the problems we had as a multinational, and a sense that some of their problems could only be solved by Philips acting as a multinational. We are transparently open in terms of how we spend their funds, and where; this contributes to building up trust. Philips could not commit themselves to such a large research program only for a purely Germany strategy; we have to find a balance between the German government national strategy and the Philips' multinational one. The officials now understand that the logic of our business is different from theirs, and see our need to find a balance between the goals of the one and the other.[50]

For professional circuits, however, the German government turned to Siemens, rather than to a foreign firm. With applications largely in the telecommunications and military systems fields, reliance on a foreign multinational was not feasible.

Philip's approach provided for large enough production volumes, and low enough unit costs, to compete on unprotected segments with companies such as TI or INTEL. Yet, short of an agreement among European governments to share production, they had no particular reason to support Philips any more than other companies, unless they could change the allocation of production responsibility within the company in their favor, which several tried to do. These pressures led to great tensions within the organization, and to more strenuous relationships with governments.

Matters were further complicated by a relative lack of clarity in the way Philips managed operations. Within the firm, manufacturing and marketing were theoretically decoupled; each subsidiary manufactured part of the electronic components line for all other subsidiaries, procured complementary products from other subsidiaries and sold the full line to its national customers. Overall profits to the national subsidiary, however, were higher for products both manufactured and sold locally. They were also easier to sell: customer engineers could interact directly with the engineers who designed and manufactured the products they bought. This was not so when a product was sourced from another subsidiary: technical questions and special requests, as well as orders, were routed through product group headquarters in Holland to the relevant subsidiary, a cumbersome process. To facilitate their task, and to increase their margins, sales operations had a tendency to emphasize special applications, and partly differentiated products, precisely those where the interface between customer's and vendor's technical personnel is important. There were few incentives for managers in national subsidiaries to improve substantially this process: microelectronics were not seen by them as a major profitable business, and thus did not deserve much attention.

The difficulty of the situation was reflected in the comments of a senior Philips executive in charge of the microelectronics business at headquarters:

> Over the last few years we have been trying to cut the microelectronics organization within our National Organizations.* Manufacturing would thus be more closely guided from the center, and development projects would be allocated by the center to the National Organizations. The commercial activities would remain much more independent.
>
> The parochialness of the European environment is a very fundamental weakness in our industry—but it remains true that Philips is the only European company with a chance to be successful in this industry. We need to assess very carefully our limited strength, and define and set our priorities both for strategy and structure. Also our administrative system is too complicated, cumbersome, and inaccurate for this industry.
>
> The whole purpose of this rationalization move is to limit our cost weakness. That is the rule of the game that the U.S. companies force us to follow: they are totally and centrally managed for success in integrated circuits. At the same time, we should be able to use our knowledge of the European end-users and of the IC marketplace to be more successful than they are, commercially.[51]

This shows some of the difficulties of a multifocal strategy: Philips tried to compete with the major electronics firms at their own game, while relying on its diversified end-product activities and European origin to hope to surpass them in responsiveness to national market and government conditions.

National Responsiveness

The structure of the industry, and the limits to the extent of government intervention, made strategies of national responsiveness unattractive to MNCs. Only weak national companies found reliance on the state rewarding: C21 in 1969–74 and ICL throughout the 1970s.

---

*The name Philips gives to the national subsidiaries.

Being responsive to national concerns remained important to MNCs in the computer and microelectronics industries, but that was achieved through incurring high costs of citizenship, as I discussed in Chapter 2. Mr. Jacques Maisonrouge, Chairman of IBM World Trade commented:

While recognizing that our principal role is economic and that our contribution to a given economy is modulated both by the scope of our activities and the host country's particular requirements, we try to look at our total responsibility to the country. That is to say, we try to go beyond a minimum level of accountability by contributing more to the community than pure business requirements would dictate. . . . [52]

The relative weakness of IBM's competitors had enabled the firm to take a long-term view of relationships with host governments, and consistently to devote resources to their betterment. IBM was using the efficiency of its operations and their high profitability to justify its existence (the high amounts paid in taxes and the quality of the products provided) and to generate resources. To IBM managers, this approach represented good business judgement, not merely high ethical standards: in the long run, the support of host governments was absolutely needed to maintain IBM's competitive edge. At various times, following the lead of the U.S. Federal Government, the EEC Commission had set out to review the activities of IBM in Europe, and to initiate antitrust action. At best, it had received lukewarm support from member states, and no concrete action has resulted.

Conclusion

The blending of strong economic and political imperatives in some industries leads to a broad range of firm's strategies. Though the coexistence of widely different firms remains based on a precarious balance between political and economic imperatives, it serves the host governments well enough for them to help actively to maintain the balance. Mixed-structure industries combine features of both worldwide and government-controlled industries. They raise the most difficult dilemmas between economic and political imperatives, but also offer the best opportunities for cooperation between MNCs and governments with growing government involvement in the economy, more sophisticated industrial policies and the eruption in the international order of countries whose complete national markets are closely government controlled, such as Japan, Brazil or Mexico, where mixed-structure industries are likely to increase in number and significance.

References

1. See C. Layton, *Ten Innovations* (London: George Allen & Unwin 1972). Also E. Braun and S. MacDonald, *Revolution in Miniature: The History and Impact of Semiconductor Electronics* (London: Cambridge University Press, 1978).
2. See T. A. Allen, *The Flow of Technology* (Cambridge: MIT Press, 1977).

144   *Strategic Management in Multinational Companies*

Industry" (Working Paper CPA77-5, Center for Policy Alternatives, Massachusetts Institute of Technology, 30 June 1977).

4. See R. H. Meikes, "The Role of An American Multinational in Europe" (Address to the Semicon/Europe Conference, Zurich, 1975).

5. See Communautés Européennes, Parlement Européen, "Rapport sur la Proposition de la Commission relative à un règlement concernant les actions communautaires dans le domaine de la technologie microélectronique" (EEC: Brussels, 27 April 1981).

6. France is an example of a country with a very diverse end-product market. See P. Schaeffer, "L'Informatique n'est plus un support pour l'Industrie Française des Circuits Intégrés", *Le Monde*, 22 September 1977, p. 32. For Japan, see W. H. Davidson, *The Amazing Race* (New York: John Wiley & Sons, 1984); see also M. Borrus, J. Millstein and J. Zysman, "Trade and Development in the Semiconductor Industry: Japanese Challenge and American Response", in Zysman and Tyson (eds.), *American Industry in International Competition* (Ithaca: Cornell University Press, 1983).

7. G. W. Brock, *The U.S. Computer Industry* (Cambridge, Mass: Ballinger, 1975).

8. See P. Gadoneix, *"Le Plan Calcul"*, unpublished doctoral thesis, Harvard Graduate School of Business Administration, 1975.

9. Quoted in J. Jublin and J. M. Quatrepoint, *French Ordinateurs* (Paris: Alain Moreau, 1975).

10. See Boston Consulting Group, *Perspectives on Experience* (Boston: Boston Consulting Group, 1968).

11. See Federal Trade Commission, *The Semiconductor Industry* (Unpublished Report, January 1977), chapter 2.

12. See "International Business Machines: Can the Europeans Ever Compete", *Multinational Business*.

13. See G. W. Brock, *The U.S. Computer Industry*. Also K. D. Fishman, *The Computer Establishment* (New York: Harper & Row, 1981).

14. The point was argued in vain in suits against IBM. See *Memorex* vs. *IBM*, and *Telex* vs. *IBM*.

15. See P. Gadoneix, *Le Plan Calcul*.

16. See Y. Doz and Sylvain Carnot, *Cap-Gemini-Sogeti* case (Available in French from Centrale des Cas, Chambre de Commerce et d'Industrie de Paris).

17. Personal communications from major users.

18. For concise summary data on manufacturing see, W. G. Oldham, "The Fabrication of Microelectronic Circuits", in *Scientific American*.

19. Y. Chang, "The Transfer of Technology: the Economics of Offshore Assembly in the Case of the Semiconductor Industry" (New York: United Nations Institute for Training and Research, 1971).

20. See *Industrial Review of Japan, 1976*. See also M. Borrus, J. Millstein and J. Zysman, *International Competition in Advanced Industrial Sectors: Trade and Development in the Semiconductor Industry* (Washington, U.S. Government Printing Office, 1982).

21. I. Mackintosh, *Microelectronics in the 80s* (Luton: Mackintosh, 1979), and also "The Micro War Heats Up", in *Forbes*, 26 November 1979, pp. 49–58, and "Japan's Strategy for the 1980s", in *Business Week*, 14 December, pp. 40–44. Also "Chips Wars: The Japanese Threat", in *Business Week*, 23 May 1983, pp. 50–64. For a detailed history of the Japanese effort see W. Ouchi, *The M-Form Society* (Reading, Mass: Addison Wesley, 1984), chapter 5.

22. See "Britain's Late Start in Semiconductors", in *Business Week*, 28 August 1978, p. 31, "Silicon Island", in *Forbes*, 13 November 1978, pp. 70–76, "Government Responds to the Challenge in Micro-electronics", in *Trade and Industry*, 8 December 1978, National Economic Development Office, "Report 07, Electronic Components" (November 1978, mimeo).

23. See "The Funding of INMOS: Public or Private", *World Business Weekly*, 21 January 1980, p. 64.

24. See "The Game has Changed in Big Computers", in *Fortune*, 21 January 1982, pp. 82–90.

25. See "The Japanese Challenge in Semiconductors", in *Business Week*, 11 July 1977, pp.

72–76, *Electronic News*, 24 April 1978, p. 68, and "Japan's Strategy for the 1980s", in *Business Week*, 14 December 1981, pp. 40–44.

26. See "Sperry Asks French Firm for $1.2M for Cancelled Pact", in *Electronic News*, 16 April 1979, p. 16.

27. For a summary see H. Hannoun, "Rapport sur l'aide publique à l'Industrie" (Paris: Ministère de l'Industrie, mimeo, 1979).

28. See EEC Commission, "Report Concerning the Development of the Data Processing Sector in the Community in Relation to the World Situation" (Brussels: EEC-COM, report 76–524, 1976). See also C. A. Michalet and M. Delapierre, "Impact of Multinational Enterprises on National Scientific and Technical Capacities: Computer and Data Processing Industries" (Paris: OECD, 1977).

29. See "MITI Works Out 3-pt Plan for Computer-Data Industry", in *Japan Economic Journal*, 22 August 1978. See also E. K. Yasaki, "Japan's Computer Industry", in *Datamation*, September 1976, pp. 91–102, and Bro Utall, "Exports Won't Come Easy for Japan's Computer Industry", in *Fortune*, 9 October 1978, p. 140.

30. See "Japan's Computer Challenge", in *Financial Times*, 21 July 1976, p. 33, and "Japan Prepares to Battle IBM in Electronics", 30 October 1975, pp. 65–66.

31. See Bro Uttal, *Exports Won't Come Easy for Japan's Computer Industry*, and S. T. McClellan, *The Coming Computer Industry Shake Out* (New York: John Wiley and Sons, 1984).

32. See "Japan's Strategy for the 1980s", in *Business Week*, 14 December 1981, p. 66. See also E. A. Feigenbaum and P. McCorduck, *The Fifth Generation* (Reading, Mass: Addison Wesley, 1983), chapter 7.

33. See my case, *Compagnie Internationale pour l'Informatique—Honeywell Bull* (forthcoming).

34. See J. Jublin and J. M. Quatrepoint, *French ordinateurs*, op. cit.

35. See my case, *Compagnie International pour l'Informatique* (Harvard Business School Case Study, available from the Intercollegiate Case Clearing House, Boston, ICCH).

36. Personal communication to the author.

37. See *Compagnie Internationale pour l'Informatique Honeywell Bull.*

38. Quoted in "L'Informatique Européenne en Morceaux", in *Le Nouvel Economiste*, 4 February 1980, pp. 52–53.

39. See Y. S. Hu, *The Impact of U.S. Investment in Europe* (New York: Praeger, 1974).

40. See F. Bucy, *Vectors Worldwide leadership* (Dallas: Texas Instruments, 1974).

41. See "Texas Instruments Shows U.S. Business How to Survive in the 1980s", *Business Week*, 18 September 1979 pp. 66–76, and see "The Microprocessor Champ Gambles on Another Leap Forward", *Business Week*, 4 April 1980, pp. 93–103; and "Innovative Intel", in *The Economist*, 16 June 1979, pp. 93–95.

42. See Y. Chang, "The Transfer of Technology: "The Economics of Offshore Assembly in the Case of Semiconductor Industry" (New York: United Nations Institute for Training and Research, 1971).

43. See my "IBM Profile" case (forthcoming).

44. See *Compagnie Internationale pour l'Informatique Honeywell Bull.*

45. See J. E. Tilton, *The International Diffusion of Technology: The Case of Semiconductors* (Washington: The Brookings Institute, 1971), and W. F. Finnan, "The International Transfer of Semiconductor Technology through U.S. Based Firms" (Washington, D.C., Unpublished National Bureau of Economic Research Working Paper, October 1975).

46. Personal communication to the author.

47. See "Le plan composants est complété avec un léger retard", in *Le Monde*, 13 Juillet, 1978, p. 29.

48. See "France's Electronic Strategy: The Americans Know Best", in *The Economist*, 18 November 1978, p. 119 and "Motorola Investit l'Europe" in *Le Nouvel Economiste*, 13 November 1979, p. 72.

49. "France's Glass Maker Bids for an Electronic Future", in *The Economist*, 17 November 1979, p. 81.

50. Personal communication to the author.

51. Personal communication to the author.

52. See A. Pantages, "IBM Abroad", *Datamation*, December 1972, pp. 54–57.

6

The Spread of Global Competition

By comparing competition in global industries, in government-controlled industries, and in mixed-structure industries, a more concrete meaning has been given to the general propositions developed in Chapters 1 and 2. I have shown that, given high economic and competitive pressures for integration, the type of strategy a multinational firm adopts depends both on the host government's interventions in its industry and on the position of the firm *vis-à-vis* its competitors. The central proposition is that the policies of a country toward an industry and the competitive position of a multinational firm in that industry interact to make certain types of strategy more or less attractive to the MNC for managing its operations in that country. In the case of Western European countries, the higher the extent of government control over an industry's markets and the weaker the competitive posture of a multinational firm in that industry, the less likely the firm is to pursue an integration strategy, and the more likely it is to seek alliances with host governments, and to be responsive to their policies and desire for control. By using more general data on eight more industries, this chapter tests the generality of this proposition. Industries were selected for this study because they are internationally competitive and their economic characteristics suggest that integration strategies would be prevalent. Individual industries were selected from those meeting the above conditions in order to cover a wide spectrum of government control over their markets. Government-control measured by the share of market accounted for by government-controlled customers in Western Europe varies from zero in agricultural tractors to 100% in aerospace defense systems (Table 6.1).

Within the selected industries the strategies and competitive postures of the largest firms were examined in some depth using a mix of public data sources and field interviews.

Multinational companies—or businesses within diversified multinational companies—were identified as pursuing one of three types of strategies: integration, multifocal, national responsiveness. In addition, major European competitors operating primarily from their own countries were considered as national companies. Assigning a strategic type to each

TABLE 6.1 *The Sample of Industries and the Extent of Government Control (percentage)*

Industry	Average approximate extent of government control over markets
Color television tubes	0
Agricultural tractors	close to 0
Automobiles	2
Trucks	12
Microelectronics	20+
Computers	30
Aero engines	45
Civilian airframes	50
Drugs	60
Telecommunication equipment	68
Electricity-generation equipment	90
Military aircraft	100

Note: The extent of government control over markets is measured by the share of market accounted for by government-controlled customers in Western Europe, measured in percentage form. Government-controlled customers are defined as government agencies, local administrations, state-owned enterprises and public authorities.

Source: Compiled by author.

business was based on several criteria. First, the extent of intersubsidiary cross-shipments was a proxy for integration. Businesses with high levels of such cross-shipments are integrated, businesses with low levels are not. Cases like Ford or Brown Boveri were clear; it was not, however, possible to determine a well-justified cut-off point that could apply easily across industries.

It was therefore decided to rely on two other elements: (1) the recent evolution of cross-shipments and (2) the opinions, understanding, and rationale of executives within the firm. Firms where cross-shipments have been increasing, and where management was committed to specialization of plants across borders, were considered as pursuing a strategy of integration. When, however, the managers interviewed saw tight limits to integration and stressed an overriding need to benefit from host government support, despite some level of integration, the strategy was identified as multifocal. Before labeling a business as multifocal, detailed data were obtained on this business through interviews, secondary sources, and company documents. Whilst the decision to label a business as multifocal was admittedly judgmental, it was based on specific information on the business and on the strategic logic developed by its managers.[1]

The first section of this chapter is a summary analysis of the sample of forty-two businesses in the industries studied. It also addresses the issue of performance, although the difficulties of developing a meaningful test of performance limit its conclusions. (The only meaningful way to address the issue of performance is to question whether, other things being equal, a firm would have been "better off" had it followed another strategy.) The second section draws managerial implications of the analyses made thus far; and the third section draws implications for industrial policies by host governments.

Industry Structures, Strategies and Firm Performance

Industry Structures Compared: A Summary

A systematic comparison of market shares and types of strategies of companies in the eleven industries studied here shows very clear patterns: the larger the market share of a company within an industry, the more likely it is to be integrated. The more extensive government control over market, the less likely integration strategies become. The relationships are not linear though. These patterns are presented in summary form in Fig. 6.1 below. Along the abscissa of Fig. 6.1 industries are arranged according to the average percentage of their sales going to government-controlled customers, i.e., government agencies, local administrations, public authorities and state-owned enterprises. Percentages run from about zero for standard color television tubes to about 100% for military aircraft. Within Europe there is surprisingly little variation for a given industry in the percentages sold to government-controlled customers in different countries.

Within an industry there are significant variations from product line to product line. Data disaggregation by product line and a detailed study of strategic, structural and administrative differences in the way individual firms managed various product lines in the telecommunication and electrical equipment industries suggest even stronger and clearer relationship than the one described above.[2] Unfortunately, not all firms in the sample made a detailed study of their management processes product line by product line possible. Disaggregated data—using narrower product lines instead of industry aggregates—thus remain fragmentary. Such difficulties made it necessary to delete data on a twelfth industry, ethical drugs, since it was impossible to select a clear level of aggregation between the whole industry and specific product lines.*

---

*What remains clear, however, is that most drug companies had to adopt some form of multifocal strategy, and that the market share of most major multinational companies was high in the particular product lines in which they competed. Relative market shares of the drug manufacturers, product by product, were commonly in the 2 to 4 range, as defined in Fig. 6.1.

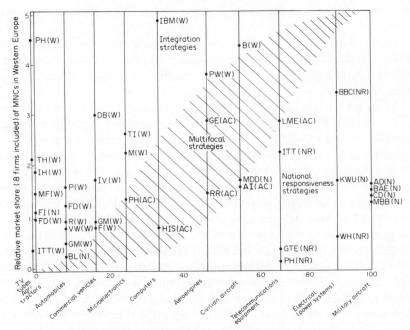

Industries ranked by percentage of sales to government – controlled customers

FIGURE 6.1   Customers, Market Shares, and Multinational Strategies

Legend:

1. *Types of Strategies* are indicated next to company initials:

W: Worldwide (or regional) integration;

AC: MultiFocal

NR: National responsiveness;

N: National company;

2. *Company names* are represented by initials:

P	= Peugeot S.A.;
FD	= Ford of Europe;
R	= Renault;
VW	= Volkswagen;
GM	= General Motors;
BL	= British Leyland;

DB	= Daimler Benz;
IV	= IVECO;
F	= Ford;
TI	= Texas Instruments;
TH	= Thomson-CSF;
AD	= Avions Dassault;
GD	= General Dynamics;
M =	Motorola;
PH	= Philips;
IBM	= International;
HIS	= Honeywell Information;
LME	= LM Ericsson;
MF =	Massey Ferguson;
PW	= Pratt & Whitney;
GE	= General Electric;
BAE	= British Aerospace;

ITT	= International Telegraph & Telephone;
GTE	= General Telephone & Electronics;
BBC	= Brown Boveri;
KWU	= Kraftwerk Union;
WH	= Westinghouse;
FI	= Fiat;
B	= Boeing;
AI	= Airbus Industries;
IH	= International Harvester;
RR	= Rolls Royce;
MBB	= Messerschmitt Bolkow Blohm;
MDD	= McDonnell Douglas.

Within an industry, firms are ranked by their market share relative to that of the eight largest firms in the industry in western Europe (in terms of sales, not necessarily manufacturing). A ranking of "1" would mean that the firm's share was just equal to the average share of each of the first eight firms. A ranking of "3", such as Daimler Benz's in trucks, means that the firm's share was three times larger than the average share of the largest eight firms. With that definition, a monopolist would rank "8", but since no market share was found to rank more than "5", Fig. 6.1 has been truncated.

Each dot on the figure represents one firm, identified by its initials and characterized by its strategy in the industry: (1) multinational integration, (2) multifocal strategy, (3) national responsiveness or (4) national companies.

In industries where free trade prevails, economies of scale and experience are high, and product differentiation along global segments possible, competitors were found to follow a multinational integration strategy. The penalties of following another strategy may be such as to deter companies from competing except as integrated MNCs. Even state-owned enterprises such as Renault and Volkswagen in the automobile industry were found to follow integration strategies actively. Though their adoption of integration strategies had been delayed somewhat by their overriding concern for the protection of domestic employment, the strength of globalization forces in the automobile industry had led both firms to develop global manufacturing and distribution capabilities quickly. Similarly, in the color TV tube industry, major European manufacturers Philips and Thomson-CSF were integrating their European tube and set manufacturing operations to face Japanese price competition. The major agricutural tractor manufacturers had for long been integrated. Retrenchment to a national position was usually ineffective and meaningless, unless complemented by active government protection. In 1980 the issue of protection for the automobile industry was raised both in the United States and Great Britain, whose industries had not only lost many of their export markets, but also found it increasingly difficult to defend their home markets against competition from Japanese and continental European imports.

In industries in which economic forces lead to integration, but in which governments also take a keen interest and partly control markets (though free trade formally prevails), mixed structures develop. In the microelectronics and computer industries many national competitors survive besides the few multinational ones plotted in Fig. 6.1. Examples are International Computers Ltd., Siemens, or Hitachi in computers, Thomson-CSF, Siemens, Plessey, Nippon Electric or General Electric Co. in microelectronics. Multinationals adopt various strategies, the largest companies opting for integration, the others for other strategies. In some cases a firm may ally with a single government, as Honeywell did with the French, and maintain integration in other countries. More often, however, simultaneous alliances with several different governments require complex multifocal strategies, as with Philips' semiconductor business. Philips' management had to be concerned both with how to compete with integrated companies organized to succeed in semiconductors, such as Texas Instruments, and with how to negotiate with several European governments key aspects of Philips' strategy, such as the location of R & D, the types of products made in each country and the levels of employment. As we discussed in Chapter 5, it was often difficult to enlist the support of governments and align their approaches with the requirements of a competitive strategy. Smaller national manufacturers often banded together to develop specific products or to exchange components so that they could offset some of the disadvantages of small scale. Such alliances among national producers were particularly widespread in the airframe industry, in which almost all new European aircraft programs were undertaken as such cooperative ventures in the late 1970s. Some led to permanent multifocal corporate forms—such as Airbus Industries—others remained discrete integrated programs jointly run by several national companies.

Finally, in industries where markets are state-controlled, almost all multinational competitors found a nationally responsive approach necessary. The only major exception to national responsiveness was LM Ericsson. As we discussed in Chapter 4, a strong technology orientation, successful introduction of new products ahead of competition, and a concentration of new activities in developing countries where technology guaranteed much bargaining power, enabled LM Ericsson partly to integrate its operations.

Patterns suggested by Fig. 6.1 can only represent the overall priorities of individual companies, however. They are supported, albeit casually, by large sample studies of MNC manufacturing interdependency patterns, however.[3] The figure was built from data on operations in Western Europe, and assumes that, in a given industry, restriction to trade is the same in all countries. The homogeneity of trade conditions imposed by the EEC regulations explains the similarities in industry structures throughout Europe. Restrictions to trade were imposed more or less similarly by all large European countries, through the purchasing power of government-controlled customers.* More far-reaching differences among countries would have been found by considering other regions of the world. Latin American counterparts to the EEC have lacked success, and wide differences exist in the policies of African and Asian countries. Any individual company will have deviant subsidiaries in various parts of the world, because within a given industry trade restrictions and governments' demands vary between countries. Nationally responsive MNCs are likely to prefer separate, protected national markets in any industry, while integrated MNCs are more easily active in countries giving priority to free trade. MNCs therefore run their operations in various regions of the world quite differently, for instance operations in a business being integrated in

*Though negotiations were taking place in both GATT and EEC bodies for the liberalization of trade goods sold to government-controlled customers, managers in most of the companies studied in the course of the research expressed deep scepticism on their outcome, and did not seriously consider the possibility of fuller free trade. On the contrary, many were concerned about growing threats of renewed protectionism.

Europe and nationally responsive in Latin America. With even more difficulty, Singapore may be an export platform and Malaysia a closed market, even though the countries are adjacent. Attempts at uniformity therefore usually fail. As an example, IVECO integrated its European activities and then tried to move in the same direction in Latin America, and faced severe problems before moving again toward more national responsiveness. Some companies may adopt multiple strategies in the same business, where integration strategies prevail in Western Europe, North American and some Asian export platforms, and national responsiveness strategies in the rest of the world.

The very clarity of the patterns shown in Fig. 6.1 does not necessarily imply, however, that we can recommend specific strategies to individual firms on their basis. The issue of how specific patterns relate to firms' performance and of what normative implications can be derived from this analysis is addressed below.

Firms' Performance and Choice of Strategy

The relationship of strategic choice to performance is difficult to address fully. First, performance is difficult to define and measure: even if we take a restrictive measure, such as ROI, it is not clear that all firms should be measured in the same way (financial performance is seldom a goal for a state-owned national champion), nor that such measurement can be made for each firm and comparable data obtained for their international operations. (Swiss annual reports, for instance, are often opaque, and even U.S. firms only recently started to report results by geography and by business segment.) Second, and even more serious, performance levels for a firm are meaningful only in relation to what they would be had the firm chosen another strategy, other things being equal. Meeting this test with actual firms is impossible.

Despite these difficulties, some generalizations may be ventured, however. Overall, integrated firms do better than their competitors in each industry, and better than nonintegrated firms over all. Managers in firms which integrated expected improved efficiency and cost decreases for specific product lines and components. The full impact of integration, as we mentioned in Chapter 2, however, may become visible only after a number of years, and may never be fully disentangled from other evolutions.

Large nationally responsive companies in government-controlled industries, such as Brown Boveri and ITT, were more profitable than their national rivals, though less profitable than integrated MNCs in general. Firms following multifocal strategies were usually low performers, but since multifocal strategies are often adopted by weaker MNCs in partly government-controlled markets, their mere survival and ability to gain assistance from host governments is a testimony of success.

More revealing were the cases of misfits, that is, of companies which did not adopt the strategies we would have predicted. Chrysler, for instance, was slow to integrate its European operations. Internal conflicts and active union involvement in Britain made the integration of Rootes around the hub constituted by SIMCA in France slow and difficult.[4] The integration of Chrysler's Spanish subsidiary, Barreiros, proceeded somewhat better but was also slow. From the collapse of its British operations in 1975, through the takeover of Chrysler's whole European operations by Peugeot in 1979, to Peugeot's subsequent difficulties, it is clear that Chrysler's operation would have greatly benefited from integration. British Leyland was another misfit: it had sold off most of its foreign operations to raise cash, but proved unable even to integrate its domestic operations in Britain successfully.[5] Lack of early integration of GM's European operations, of Philips' TV tube activities, and of Brown Boveri's small motor business all cost these companies dearly.[6]

The unsuccessful attempt of Westinghouse to integrate its European operations in the early 1970s in a government-controlled business illustrates a converse misfit: eagerness to integrate in face of mounting host government interest in the industry. By the late 1970s Westinghouse had shifted back to a strategy of national responsiveness. Massey Ferguson similarly faced great difficulties in trying to penetrate developing countries' markets as an integrated MNC.[7]

The evidence on the profit impact of strategic choices sketched above remains quite fragmentary, but it is suggestive of the critical importance of these strategic choices: we are not trying here to measure minute differences in profitability but to determine the condition for survival and success of firms in internationally competitive industries. Crude as it is, the evidence suggests that, by considering the economic and political characteristics of an industry, the competitive position of a firm within it, and the policies of various host governments, it is possible to determine analytically which type of broad strategy is best suited to the firm.

Implications for MNC Management

The analyses conducted so far have several important managerial implications. First, it is important to recognize the basic differences among industries in globalization and localization forces. These forces make one strategy more attractive than another. Second, within an industry in which governments evince interest it is important to consider simultaneously the competitive position of the firm and the policies of host governments. The competitive strength of the firm *vis-à-vis* its competitors and its bargaining power *vis-à-vis* host government interact in offering strategic opportunities and creating threats. Careful assessment of the competitive strength of the firm and of its bargaining power *vis-à-vis* governments is therefore required. This assessment needs to be made at a detailed level to be meaningful: within an industry different product lines may be affected differently by economic and political imperatives; in other words, careful strategic segmentation is needed. Finally, strategic fine tuning may have diminishing returns: at some point the administrative and managerial complexity created by increasingly differentiated strategies outweigh the benefits of finer strategic segmentation.

Globalization vs. *Localization*

Economic imperatives affect different industries to varying degrees. In some industries, the combination of very high economies of scale and experience, forbidding research and development expenditures, product differentiation and intensive marketing tasks makes integration desirable. High-technology industries, where achieving market penetration is important, and maturing industries where low-cost positions become critical, are affected most.

In high-technology industries rapid market penetration may lead MNCs to prefer exporting from well-known production bases rather than set up nationally autonomous subsidiaries. This is particularly true of U.S. companies, where entirely new companies are often created to exploit major technological innovations. Major examples are Digital Equipment in minicomputers and Intel in microelectronics. Both companies gained large shares of the world market mainly through exports from the United States. Plants were located abroad not to serve local markets, but to exploit lower factor costs. As we argued in Chapter 1, integration may provide the way for European operations of multinationals to remain competitive in maturing industries threatened by competition from newly industrialized countries.

In other industries, economic characteristics make the pay-offs of integration insufficient to justify the loss of national responsiveness, or governments' sufficiently value national responsiveness over economic performance in these industries to make integration impossible, as we emphasized in Chapters 4 and 5.

Full recognition of these differences is critical to the success of the firm. The success of many Japanese firms in global industries can be largely attributed to their early adoption of a global perspective. The contrast between Sony or Matsushita and Zenith, in their approach to the world's television set market, is striking. In 1972 Zenith's president commented:

We have always had our hands full with U.S. demand and we have always tended to stick with what appeared to be the biggest payoff and what we knew how to do best. For example, an additional two market-share points in the Los Angeles area alone represents more sales volume than there is in most foreign markets. Also, we did not feel we could compete with the local companies in those markets unless we were willing to sacrifice some of our margins, and we were unwilling to do that. We are basically a U.S. company, and likely to stay that way.[8]

In contrast, as early as 1953, Sony's approach was to become an international company; provided they could develop unique products in their areas of expertise and capitalize on their policies they could even become "the strongest company in the world", according to Akio Morita, Sony's chairman.[9] Zenith's management saw the United States market as the limit to their ambition, Japanese TV companies saw rapid growth and dominance of their own market as a mere precondition and springboard for dominance of the TV industry worldwide. Many parallels can be drawn from motorcycles, cars and ball bearings, to semiconductor memories and cameras.[10]

Successful response to globalization also requires the willingness and the ability to make long-term commitments. Concern with short-term profitability is unlikely to allow bold integration moves, the payoffs of which may be spread over decades whereas the costs are incurred in the short run. Concern for short-term profitability is likely to lead to orderly withdrawal from activities, countries and businesses exposed to intense competition. In the long run, however, the overall competitive position of the firm is eroded. Japanese competition in the international motorcycle market, traditionally dominated by the British, started with smaller machines which had a large market in Japan. British manufacturers retreated to the market segments for larger machines, which remained highly profitable. After a few years, large-volume production of small motorcycles enabled the Japanese to cut their manufacturing costs sufficiently, and improve their production methods, to move against the British with higher quality, less expensive motorcycles than the British could make. As the Japanese moved up market over time, the British companies shrank till they could no longer mount any effective countermove against the Japanese.[11] Integration moves require major commitments of resources, and the longer they are delayed the less available large resources may become. Past a certain point, a deteriorating international competitiveness becomes irretrievable.

Leading globalization through early integration may have tremendous pay-offs in many industries. Integration may take competitors off guard, unable to respond fast enough, and erode their position. Financial, managerial and technical barriers to integration may sufficiently delay their responses to enable the first firm to integrate to take a permanent market leadership. Ford's early integration of European operations propelled it to a leading position in the European automobile industry in the 1970s. Ford's leadership, however, was compromised in the late 1970s when shortages of resources forced difficult trade-offs between sustaining a leading position in Europe through continued reinvestments, and using cash flows from Europe to support ailing U.S. domestic operations.[12] Lack of reinvestment over time is another threat. Though integration provided a one-time improvement, it is not by itself a guarantee of long-term success unless the benefits it provides are systematically exploited.

Integration is no panacea, however. First, as we discussed, economic conditions may make it unattractive in some industries, as several U.S. food companies learned the hard way.[13] Second, host governments may thwart integration plans. Besides the European Common Market, there are few industries and few countries in which MNCs are free to integrate. Integration has to be negotiated, as Ford did in Spain in 1972, or as General Motors was doing in Australia and Brazil in 1979. Explicit long-term commitments to their host countries limit the strategic freedom of integrated MNCs. In many countries and industries integration is downright impossible, no matter what the economic pay-offs might be.

Assuming integration has been possible, it is also critical to ensure that it does not result in a complete loss of responsiveness to national demands. The bits and pieces of an integration strategy have to remain acceptable to the involved host governments. Ensuring the effective representation of national perspectives in managing integrated multinational operations is thus important. This involves both ensuring that top management remains sensitive to national differences, and giving a voice to national subsidiary managers in the determination of patterns of integration.

Conversely, even when the operations cannot be integrated creating a capability to explore effectively possible partial integration opportunities is important. A nationally responsive company has little capability to consider integration opportunities unless counterweight is provided to the national focus of subsidiary managers. Worldwide corporate product planning stuffs may provide such counterweight.

In fact, except at both ends of the spectrum of industries we considered, complete freedom to integrate or overwhelming need for national responsiveness, the choice of strategy is seldom raised as a straightforward alternative between adopting a set strategy and not participating in the market. Specific choices of strategy, for a business in a country depend both on the competitive strength of the firm and on its bargaining power with host governments.

Competitive Strength and Bargaining Power

The appropriate response of a MNC to government interventions may vary with its competitive posture. As we hypothesized in Chapter 1, and documented for some industries in succeeding chapters, the bargaining power of a MNC over a host government also is an important consideration. Beyond adapting to economic and political conditions in an industry (e.g., by integrating European consumer product operations and providing for nationally responsive telecommunication equipment subsidiaries), companies can try to use economic conditions to gain political freedom, or vice versa. Texas Instruments' establishment of a fully-owned subsidiary in Japan provides an example of the first situation: the company used its competitive strength to bargain for less control than usual by the Japanese. In the late 1950s the Japanese government solicited participation by leading U.S. semiconductor firms in the development of a domestic semiconductor industry. As a condition for American entry into the Japanese market, the government required that joint ventures be established with Japanese partners who would have a leading managerial role. TI was unwilling to enter a joint venture, for fear that the technological lead it then had over its competitors be lost by transferring technology to Japanese partners. After protracted, and at times heated, negotiations, TI reached an agreement with the Japanese government to set up a wholly owned subsidiary in Japan to supply the domestic electronic industry with high-technology components and circuits. TI was able to resist Japanese demands for a joint venture because of its superior technology for which the Japanese industry could find no easy alternative. In other words, TI used its competitive strength to maintain integration and be less nationally responsive than some of its competitors who engaged in joint ventures in Japan. TI was bargaining with the government from a position of competitive strength.[14]

Conversely, as we reported in Chapter 5, Honeywell, faced with tough competition in the computer industry, found it convenient to cooperate with the French and gain access to new resources and new markets. A more extreme case of bargaining from a position of competitive weakness was Chrysler's 1975 threats to close down its British subsidiary. Chrysler's weak position gave it significant leverage with the British government which had more to lose—both economically and politically—by letting Chrysler close its plants in the United Kingdom than by subsidizing them.[15]

In deciding what strategy to adopt for a particular business in a host country, it is therefore critical to assess the interaction between competitive strength and bargaining power. Larger companies with the better technologies can use the potential benefits of integration to justify its adoption to host governments. An integration strategy may not be desirable if its economic benefits are offset by citizenship costs or if it does not provide market leadership or low-cost positions (e.g., if there are already larger integrated MNCs active in the same business). If a government is unwilling to reward national responsiveness, a lop-sided approach to integration and national responsiveness is possible: responsiveness to one country, integration in others. It was clear to Honeywell's management that an alliance with the French could provide a way to compete successfully against IBM and eliminate one national champion without altering its position in other European countries. These were not interested in cooperating with Honeywell, anyhow.

As we discussed in Chapter 2, the advantages of any type of strategy vary much with the existing patterns of competition among MNCs. When there is a wide gap between a leading integrated MNC and its competitors, alliances with host governments may be more attractive for all companies but the leader than when several companies of relatively equal strength compete for industry leadership. In the latter situation each company may want to preserve its strategic freedom so long as industry leadership is not established. Their managers, however, may be tempted into agreements with host countries which provide for the establishment of a unique privileged position in serving their market. This is particularly true for countries which manage, at least temporarily, to benefit from asymmetrical trade conditions. Ford for example, drew benefits from the EEC's liberal policy toward car imports from Spain and from Spain's own ban on car imports. Ford could serve the EEC's markets from Spain and still be secure that no other MNC would compete with it in Spain. The advantage was only transitory, however: Spain's eventual entry into the EEC as a full member will require full reciprocity of trading conditions and expose manufacturers established in Spain to competition by imports from other EEC members. These conditions were particularly attractive to Ford, because they provided the company with a head start in penetrating the Spanish market without much constraining its strategic freedom once Spain became a regular EEC member. Negotiating unique privileged access with host governments usually restricts a firm's strategic freedom more durably than Ford's entry into Spain, however. The cumulative impact of such moves may be to dissolve integration strategies into difficult alliances with multiple governments leading, in turn, to multifocal strategies. Given the managerial difficulties they create, multifocal strategies need to be carefully considered. Careful strategic segmentation may help circumscribe the need for multifocal strategies.

Beyond the cumulative erosion of the firm's strategic freedom, agreements with governments sometimes expose the firm to political instability. In 1975, when Honeywell was negotiating with the French, its subsidiary was a target for "nationalization" by the French Left's Union, whose victory in the election was a serious possibility. Actual electoral success in 1981 triggered renewed negotiations with Honeywell. In 1973, when Ford committed to operations in Spain, the transition from Franco's dictatorship to a liberal monarchy faced many obstacles. The key to success here is (1) that the long-term interest of the MNC and of the country be aligned, as they were in both cases, and (2) that the agreements be spelled out in sufficient detail to satisfy both partners.

Strategic Segmentation

Meaningful analyses of strategic choices are dependent upon a strategically significant definition of a business. Careful segmentation is needed, since different segments of the same market may not be affected similarly by political imperatives, nor share similar economic characteristics. At a gross level, segments of an industry may differ substantially; for instance, private branch telecommunication switching and main exchange public switching. At a more minute level, in such complex purchasing processes as that for medical electronic equipment, the political imperative may vary quite substantially according to the relative weight of doctors vs. hospital administrators, since doctors may be less concerned by the nationality of the suppliers in the purchasing decision.

The appropriate trade-off between integration and responsiveness in a business also varies over time, with shifts in underlying technological conditions (e.g., the diseconomies of small scale may decrease with the introduction of new robotics and computer-based flexible manufacturing centres), in governmental policies (e.g., more LDCs looking for active participation in globally integrated industries rather than self-development), in market evolutions and in competitive developments.

Strategic Clarity vs. *Administrative Complexity*

Ideally, MNC managers would like to see the differences analyzed above—between industries, between firms and countries within an industry, and between market segments within an industry and over time—reflected by differences in the management processes for different businesses and different subsidiaries within the firm. Yet, finer differentiation has administrative costs: it makes the management of the firm increasingly complex as strategies are more and more diverse.

MNCs, therefore, face the usual tensions in any social system between maximizing the current steady-state efficiency of output and maintaining the effectiveness of the system in responding to diverse and changing external circumstances. In the MNCs studied, top management had to pay attention to both short-term efficiency and longer-term effectiveness. Integration could not be pursued relentlessly, in any multinational business, without also maintaining an awareness of the limits to integration and, therefore creating mechanisms within the organization to ensure that needs for responsiveness were not ignored or suppressed. Conversely, nationally responsiveness companies could gain by developing a selective capability to integrate certain of their activities.

These issues will be addressed in detail in the following three chapters, where the managerial and organizational requirements of each broad strategy (integration, responsiveness, and multifocal) are analyzed. Each chapter starts with an analysis of the required managerial tasks and then analyzes the managerial and organizational capabilities (and how to create them) needed to perform those tasks successfully, drawing on illustrations from the individual companies studied in the research.

Implications for Industrial Policies

The deep differences between industries, and between the competitive postures and strategies of different firms in the same industry, have strong implications for host governments trying to devise and implement consistent industrial policies. It is important for government to understand both the characteristics of the industry structures they try to affect, and the differences in the efficacy of various means of intervention into these structures.

International Industry Structures: A Host Government Perspective

Industry structures are not homogeneous. International markets differ in the extent and dimensions of possible segmentation. The characteristics of customer demands and the nature of the products offered affect the dimensions of differentiation among customer groups, from similar groups existing in various countries to each national market having its own needs and tastes. Since the extent and dimensions of differentiation within industries largely determine their potential for internationalization, these differences are important to host governments. The nature of the products—for example their bulk to value-added ratio—also limit or encourage the internationalization of their production and distribution. Different segments of an industry, or different product lines, may be affected to very different extents by internationalization forces.

Differences between competitors also contribute to industry structure heterogeneity. As we pointed out in Chapter 2, various types of national and multinational firms compete in the same industry, providing a mixed structure. As we stressed in Chapters 1 and 2, multinational firms following different types of strategies are likely to respond to the same host government policies in widely different ways, and their responses are not equally predictable to government officials. More factors outside the purview of the host government are usually taken into consideration by managers of integrated MNCs in decisions affecting one country, than are considered by managers of nationally responsive MNCs. Government officials thus find it more difficult to predict their responses. The behavior of companies following multifocal strategies is often even more difficult to predict, since their decision-making processes are more political than national. Whereas the integrated MNC reaches strategic decisions through economic analysis, the multifocal one resorts to an internal advocacy process whose results are often difficult to predict.

Such variety of possible responses is a source of advantage to host governments. First, on its own, it minimizes the possibility of active or tacit collusion among international firms in an industry: their interests and competitive postures are disparate enough to make agreement on industry structure among firms difficult. Second, the different logics of firms participating in an industry can be used by governments. In some cases, such as with state-owned enterprises, governments can determine directly the logic of some industry participants. In other cases, where a cosy relationship prevails between a government and private national champions, the government can exercise much influence and use these firms actively in competing against multinationals. We have already seen in Chapter 3 that British Leyland's state ownership could deter some of its multinational competitors from aggressive competition in the United Kingdom. It is also possible for host governments to play nationally responsive MNCs off against integrated ones, and vice versa, as we analyzed in Chapter 5. An alliance with a weaker multinational may offer the state both a way out for a faltering national champion and a leverage point to extract citizenship costs from integrated MNCs.

Governments can also consider whether to promote competition among relatively similar companies or to encourage the emergence of a single company following a given type of strategy. We have suggested in Chapter 4 that a dominant integrated MNC in an industry might more easily accept high cost of citizenship than would direct competitors locked in rivalry for industry leadership.

The extent, dimension, and origin of heterogeneity in an international industry, both in the markets and in the firms serving them, provide enabling conditions and a limit to the types of industrial policies host governments can realistically contemplate.

It is important to recognize that companies do not compete in an undifferentiated way; they follow identifiable strategies that are not similar. They have different reasons for participating in the industry and visibly different logics about how they compete. Their mix of skills and resources, as well as the strategies they follow and the way in which they are managed, make them more or less susceptible to one type of government intervention or another. Faced with the same demands from a host country, one multinational company may opt out and another gladly jump in. To a large extent these differences in behavior are predictable; they correspond to different tradeoffs between economic and political imperatives. The same proposals by host governments may improve the competitive position of weaker firms, and cause deterioration in that of stronger. It is doubtful whether IBM would accept the same terms as Honeywell or Sperry Rand from a host government.

Selecting which firms to negotiate with, and for what, thus becomes a critical element of industrial policy in international industries. Unfortunately it is relatively difficult to carry out such an analysis in the abstract, but the argument presented in Chapter 4 and the analyses of industry structures developed in Chapters 5, 6 and 7 provide a basic framework to analyze international industries.

This analysis will not be repeated here; we can merely stress the importance of an understanding of the internationalization forces and of the costs of maintaining national control. The development of technology plays an important role in the evolution of industry structures: new technologies usually require larger scale, more capital-intensive production to achieve efficient size; therefore, they increase the pressures for internationalization of an industry and for the integration of multinational companies active within that industry. As we have seen with the European governments' concerns with microelectronics, technological change can also shift the boundaries between industries, or put an industry into a different value-added structure. Technological developments can also bring together industries where the balance between economic and political imperatives has traditionally been different. The teletext and data access systems now being promoted by European PTTs represent a merger between telephones and television sets, and might eventually lead either to a system where the PTTs would rent TV sets to consumers, thus putting the whole TV set industry under direct government influence, or to a system where the consumers could freely purchase all kinds of equipment to be plugged into telephone links, thus decreasing government control over a whole range of telecommunications equipment.

Bargaining Power of Host Governments

The ability of a host government to implement an industrial policy successfully in an international industry depends on its bargaining power *vis-à-vis* MNCs, as well as on the opportunities for leverage provided by industry heterogeneity. The bargaining power of a host government depends primarily on the attractiveness of its markets and of its production factors, and on the government's ability to regulate multinational companies' access to the market.

The market size and growth prospects in an industry are major bargaining points. Major car manufacturers moved into Brazil on the assumption the Brazilian automobile market would rapidly become one of the largest in the world. Brazil, generally, as a large rapidly developing country, found it relatively easy to attract major MNCs and to regulate their operations. Countries with smaller markets, and slower growth potentials, have much less bargaining power.

The availability and cost of labor and energy are another major source of bargaining power. Developing countries in which dedicated work forces were paid relatively low wages found attracting and controlling multinational companies relatively easy. Cheap sources of energy were also major advantages in certain industries such as petrochemical or aluminium.

The exercise of bargaining power, however, demands that government regulate foreign trade and investments. As we stressed in the discussion of the automobile industry, once EEC members had relinquished control over foreign trades they could but outbid each other with subsidies to attract MNC investments. Conversely, governments which kept control of trade, such as Spain, could engage in direct negotiations with MNCs. EEC members retained control on some industries by controlling their markets as we discussed in Chapter 4. There is no escape, however, from the fact that an active sectoral industrial policy in worldwide industries assumes some degree of mercantilism. Foreign trade is welcomed, but also controlled. Until the late 1970s, the internationalization of the automobile industry had been well accepted by most governments, primarily because it was accomplished through the relatively balanced interpenetration of national markets. European companies exported to the United States, but U.S. companies invested in Europe, and within Europe the existence of the major national champions such as Volkswagen, Fiat, Renault or British Leyland was not put in jeopardy: they lost some domestic market shares, but gained export volumes. The emergence of clear winners (Japan) and losers (Britain and, perhaps, the United States) in the late 1970s put to question the continuation of free trade in the automobile industry. The major difficulty for governments is that, whereas the benefits of internationalization accrue to a broad indiscriminate group over a long period of time, the costs of the adjustments that implies fall quickly on a well-defined smaller group. With employment protection the key concern, adjustments are difficult. Adjustments are also difficult because they often require the government to designate winners and losers: not all firms can survive, and subsidies spread equally may only prolong the survival of an uncompetitive national industry.

Negotiating with MNCs

As we have mentioned in Chapter 3, and will develop in further chapters, differences in the strategy of multinational companies are reflected in their organization and management processes. These management structures and processes constrain the strategic flexibility of firms. Though diverse approaches tailored to the economic conditions and bargaining power of each country may be desirable, they would excessively complicate the firm's management process, and therefore may not be adopted by management. The relative uniformity of approaches among countries used by an MNC implies that it will be well equipped to handle certain types of government demands, while others would involve major departures from its usual *modus operandi*. The firm's top management may thus reject such demands and opt out lest they should complicate top management's task to compromise the integrity of the firm's management process.

An understanding of these issues may be precious to host government officials in negotiating with MNCs. Again, the same host government demand may trigger very different reactions from seemingly comparable

164   *Strategic Management in Multinational Companies*

MNCs. These issues go beyond the usual cost/benefit analysis and concern for financial aspects: a firm may very well shy away from a financially attractive proposition that would increase the complexity of its managerial task. Some diversified companies such as International Telephone and Telegraph have attempted to develop a capability to deal with the diversity of host government demands by grouping their business according to the nature of demands typically made upon them by host governments. Other companies develop categories of countries according to the extent of host government control, and manage their local operations with varying degrees of headquarters involvement.

It is also important, therefore, for host government officials to understand how the firms with which they negotiate are managed and how the managers of these firms approach the trade-offs between strategic flexibility (and therefore complexity) and managerial simplicity.

References

1. For a discussion of issues of market and business definition, see M. E. Porter, *Competitive Strategy* (New York: The Free Press, 1980), and D. F. Abell, *Defining the Business* (Englewood Cliffs: Prentice Hall, 1980).
2. See Y. Doz, *Government Control and Multinational Strategic Management* (New York: Praeger, 1979).
3. See P. D. Buckley and R. I. Pearce, "Overseas Production and Exporting by the World's Largest Enterprises: A Study in Sourcing Policy" (University of Reading Discussion Papers in International Investment and Business Studies No. 37, September 1977), and S. Young and N. Hood, *Dynamic Aspects of U.S. Multinational Operations in Europe* (Farnborough: Saxon House, 1980).
4. See N. Hood and S. Young, *Chrysler U.K.: A Corporation in Transition* (New York: Praeger, 1976). Information was also provided by private communications to the author.
5. See Lord Ryder, *British Leyland: The Next Decade* (London: Her Majesty's Stationery's Office, 1975).
6. For Brown Boveri, see Y. Doz, *Brown Boveri & Cie* (available from Intercollegiate Case Clearing House, Boston). Philips attributed its lackluster 1979 financial performance largely to problems in the color TV business, see Philips, *Annual Report*, 1979. Personal communications to the author also evidenced that difficulties of integration in TV tube manufacturing were the root cause of the difficulty.
7. See P. F. Mathias, "The Role of the Logistics System in Strategic Change: The Case of the Multinational Corporation" (unpublished doctoral dissertation, Harvard Graduate School of Business, 1979).
8. See Neal Bhadkamkar, *The U.S. Television Set Market 1970–1979* (Harvard Business School Case Study, available from the Intercollegiate Case Clearing House, Boston, ICCH No. 1–380–181).
9. Quoted in Nick Lynes, *The Sony Vision* (New York: Crown Publishers, 1976), p. 61.
10. See Central Policy Review Staff and The Boston Consulting Group, *The Future of the British Motorcycle Industry* (London: Her Majesty's Stationery Office, 1975). For automobiles, "The Rise of Toyota and Nissan: The Ingredients of Success", in *Multinational Business*, No. 3 (1975), pp. 28–39. For ball bearings see "A Low Profit Boom for Makers of Bearings", in *Business Week*, 15 October 1979, pp. 160–166. For semiconductors see "Japanese Semiconductor Makers are Close to Competing Equally with U.S. Manufacturers", in *Industrial Review of Japan, 1976* and also "The Japanese Challenge in Semiconductors", in *Business Week* 11 July 1977, pp. 72–74.

11. See Central Policy Review Staff and The Boston Consulting Group, *The Future of the British Motorcycle Industry* (London: Her Majesty's Stationery Office, 197).

12. See M. S. Salter and M. Fuller, *Ford Motor Company* (cases available from the Intercollegiate Case Clearing House, Boston

13. See C. A. Bartlett, "Multinational Structural Evolution. The Changing Decision Environment in International Divisions" (unpublished doctoral dissertation, Harvard Graduate School of Business Administration, 1979).

14. The example is drawn from Y. Doz and C. K. Prahalad, "How MNCs Cope with Host Government Intervention", *Harvard Business Review*, March–April 1980, pp. 149–157.

15. See N. Hood and S. Young, *Chrysler U.K.: A Corporation in Transition* (New York: Praeger, 1976).

7

Managing an
Integrated Multinational Business

The success of multinational integration strategies is predicated on two related sets of assumptions: (1) that integration provides the MNC with a competitive advantage over its competitors and, (2) that the organization can successfully trade-off with host governments some of the proceeds of its competitive advantage—either via citizenship costs or the opportunity cost of a less than economically optimal network—against the continued licence to operate as an integrated MNC.

This chapter analyzes the organizational and managerial conditions that allow the above assumptions to be true. First, it reviews the managerial tasks implied by integration strategies. Second, it describes approaches that allow the MNC to gain a competitive advantage from the integration of its operations. Then it analyzes the conditions that allow a successful compromise to be reached with host governments and with local unions. Finally, it analyzes the management of relationships between headquarters and subsidiaries within the integrated multinational.

Integration Strategies: the Managerial Tasks

For integration strategies to succeed they need to yield competitive advantages, mainly in terms of costs and margins, through efficiency of the manufacturing and logistics networks. As was discussed in Chapters 3 and 5, economies of scale and economies of location often underly integration strategies. A first task of management, therefore, is to manage the manufacturing network efficiently. This, in the main, involves three critical tasks.

(1) Creating and maintaining an efficient manufacturing system, both in its mix of locations and in the types of process technologies being used. This involves not only the firm's own plants but its suppliers and subcontractors, as well.

(2) Programming production efficiently to exploit economies of throughput.

(3) Managing logistics effectively to minimize transportation and inventory costs.

Too exclusive a focus on manufacturing and logistics efficiency—and therefore on costs—might be counterproductive, though. To maintain good market access and high margins, the integrated MNC needs to remain sensitive to market differences in such aspects as customers' needs and tastes, distribution channels, usual commercial practices, and so forth. Combining integration in manufacturing—and therefore low cost—and responsiveness in marketing—and therefore high margins—is one of the most rewarding challenges to multinational management. Marketing and distribution are often less integrated than manufacturing, and more autonomy is left to subsidiary management in making critical decisions. Continued successful market presence may require accommodating to integration strategies. Competitors may also adopt widely different pricing and distribution policies, for instance, even in contiguous national markets, and even when they are global companies selling uniform products worldwide. Responses in specific national markets may have to be based on local idiosyncracies *and*, at the same time, on a broader multimarket set of competitive interactions. The issue, therefore, is not simply one of integrating manufacturing and decentralizing marketing but of maintaining a balance between a centrally managed strategy based on cost reduction and global competitive interactions and a series of national marketing strategies adjusted to specific national conditions.

The success of integration strategies also requires viable compromises to be reached with host governments on the sharing of the economic rent derived from integration and on the acceptable opportunity cost of a suboptimal network for the MNC. One most difficult issue for managers is to decide when national developments, somewhere in the network, warrant headquarters consideration and, possibly, a realignment of operations with systemwide consequences. This implies that government concerns are identified early and demands assessed accurately. Constraints on integration, and the amount and mix of costs of citizenship, have to be assessed realistically, to achieve a fruitful relation with host governments without letting them gain excessive influence on the MNC. Similar issues are important in relationships with local workforces and national unions. Again, the issue is not one of centralized rigidity vs. decentralized flexibility, but of a variable trade-off between economic optimization and political compromise in dealing with host governments. The content of the centrally determined strategy ought to reflect the aggregation of national constraints, compromises and priorities. These are usually first identified and best assessed by local subsidiary managers. A second key task of top management, therefore, is to ensure an effective representation of host country parties and interests in key headquarters decisions. The incorporation of host countries concerns may, in turn, create new managerial tasks. For instance, national governments may insist on R & D being performed in their countries. Meeting such demand may considerably complicate the R

& D management task for the MNC. The managerial cost of complex network configurations must also be taken into account.

In sum, once we move from the broad realm of strategy to the nitty-gritty of organizational issues, the trade-off between integration and responsiveness reappears, even within the relative clarity of an integration strategy. Although integration may be preferred, compromises still have to be reached, and trade-offs between priorities set. This first assumes visibility to performance and clarity to data, so that the information and criteria needed to assess choices both in the perspective of the overall network and in that of individual subsidiaries are available. Second, the responsiveness views, although obviously not dominant, must not be silenced either. Top management must structure communication channels and decision processes to ensure that subsidiary perspectives and head-quarter priorities are effectively traded off.

The remainder of this chapter analyzes how these tasks were performed by management in the MNCs studied in the research, in particular Ford, IBM and Texas Instruments.

Managing and Developing the Integrated Network Effectively

Manufacturing efficiency usually is the driving force behind integration, as in the Ford and IVECO examples described in Chapter 1. Yet, as was discussed above, government demands for R & D activities to be located in their country may drive abroad the location of R & D efforts the MNC would have much more happily performed in its home country. Finally, distribution and marketing networks raise more complex responsiveness vs. integration trade-offs. The management of these three key functions is analyzed, in turn, in this section.

Manufacturing and Logistics Management

The central operational task in integrated MNCs is manufacturing management and production programming. Companies with complex integrated manufacturing networks usually entrust the programming of each plant to a central real-time inventory management and logistics system that keeps production in balance and checks inconsistencies in the schedules of integrated plants. Inputs to the system are usually made via monthly meetings between plant managers, headquarter manufacturing staff experts and managers from marketing and sales operations. The time horizon of the system varies with manufacturing and marketing lead times. At IBM, for instance, the manufacturing program was firmly set for a period of six months, with options extending to eighteen months. The six-month schedule was updated monthly. At Ford of Europe, particularly following the "After Japan"* efforts to reduce inventories in the early 1980s, more short-term flexibility was introduced in the manufacturing network.

Ford's production planning process had functioned very much like IBM's, with the needs of the various European sales subsidiaries being consolidated monthly into a production program covering the following six months. A programming and distribution office, reporting to the marketing staff, set up a tentative production program and shipments plan according to location of plants and countries of sales. The final manufacturing program was updated in a series of meetings with production experts reporting to the vice president for manufacturing. The program was then broken down into major components through a computerized process and delivery orders were submitted to Ford's plants and to outside suppliers on a fortnightly basis.

The number of closely integrated plants included in the network was often limited to avoid excessive complexity and vulnerability. IBM, for example, maintained two largely independent manufacturing networks, one in the United States, the other in Europe, and was developing a third in the Far East. Similarly, Ford of Europe was largely independent, industrially, from the Ford's U.S. operations. Texas Instruments, on the other hand, with fewer foreign plants, ran centrally a worldwide manufacturing network. European plants were programmed and monitored directly from Dallas headquarters. Dual sourcing (with at least two plants making the same components) was still widely preferred for safety of supply reasons.

Flexibility of supply and efficiency of manufacturing operations were traded-off carefully in most integrated MNCs. Integrated MNCs also followed closely developments in flexible manufacturing systems and robotics, which offered opportunities to alleviate this trade-off.

Decisions concerning the expansion or contraction of the integrated network are more difficult than its smooth day-to-day operation. First, manufacturing location and resource allocation choices can be made only in light of their effect on the integrated system as a whole and, therefore, can hardly be left to local management. Second, conflicting priorities often preside over such choices: for instance, system efficiency (e.g., choice of low cost locations) vs. host government acceptability (e.g., balance of payment neutrality) usually come into play in the selection of new manufacturing sites. Other parties, such as national unions, also affect such decisions, German trade unions, for instance, extracted from GM massive investment commitments in Germany against their support to GM's investments in Spain. Third, transnational investment decisions are essentially risky and uncertain: assumptions about wage and exchange rate

---

*Following detailed studies of Japanese car makers' manufacturing techniques by Ford executives a series of coordinated efforts to improve productivity were undertaken at Ford. They were known collectively as the "After Japan" program.

levels—which often discriminate between locations—are difficult, and even carefully analyzed decisions run significant risks as Volkswagen discovered dearly when the dollar rose dramatically after Volkswagen had invested in the United States, eliminating the central justification for the investment.

For all these reasons, centralized investment decision making prevails in integrated MNCs. Central staffs (or regional ones in the case of Ford of Europe or of IBM-Europe-Middle East-Africa) prepare decisions, involving several functions. Typically, beside manufacturing and plant engineering specialists, purchasing, finance, government affairs and marketing staffs also participate in the analysis of investment options. Specific choices are then made by top management. Some companies, such as Ford, also seek government subsidies actively, although their management argues that government incentives alone would never determine an investment decision. Despite the appearance of centralization, the preparation of choices being delegated to regional managers, and often involving close interaction with host government officials, top management often but ratifies commitments already made at lower levels. Although the evidence is too scanty to be conclusive, a detailed study of Ford's, and GM's investment in Spain, as well as other data on foreign investment decision processes in big firms, suggest that view.[1] The task, then, for top management is to create the appropriate context for managers who prepare their decisions to work in the best interest of the integrated MNC.[2] This aspect will be dealt with later in this chapter.

Top management also makes divestment decisions, and these are rarely recommended by lower levels.[3] Integrated MNCs usually face few major divestment decisions, however, since major divestments are often made when the integrated network is first set up: marginal subsidiaries or peripheral product lines may be dropped during the rationalization process.[4] In fact, integration is often seen by MNC executives as an alternative to divestment. Complete integrated networks may sometimes be divested, such as Union Carbide's sale of its European petrochemical operations to British Petroleum, but such divestments are very few. Studies of divestment patterns with multinationals have suggested that most divested operations were not part of an integrated network.[5] Conversely, a study of 440 divestments shows that a high level of integration (measured by the ratio of intra network sales of the subsidiaries to their total sales) decreases the probability of divestment.[6]

Research and Development Management

If the economics of global manufacturing often provide the incentive for integration, the internationalization of R & D is often one of the unwanted consequences. In developed countries, the location of R & D in host countries is often part of the implicit or explicit exchange of value with host governments. Mature integrated MNCs such as IBM therefore often find themselves carrying out R & D in many different countries, and managing such R & D centrally.

Although some integrated companies eschew the central management of research and development, arguing that multiple technologies and products ought to be explored, and that central management of research would so reduce research creativity and productivity as to be self-defeating, most MNCs carry out basic research in their home country only, and tightly manage from the centre what applied research efforts are carried out abroad.[7]

This, however, has not always been the case. Mature MNCs, which grew in protected countries, often carried out applied research and product development separately in various countries, in particular when their products also differed between countries. GM's German subsidiary, Opel, designed and developed its own cars and did research on new technologies earlier than its parent company. Integration usually makes the continuation of such separate efforts unwarranted and their costs more apparent. The issue then becomes to single out one design or one product for cooperative development and worldwide introduction. First attempts at moving from diversity to focused development are usually traumatic for the organization as exemplified in the genesis of IBM's 360 series (its first computer for worldwide markets) in the 1960s or in the more recent development by ITT Europe of the U.S.-originated "1240" digital switching system over competing European designs.[8]

To avoid the recurrence of such difficulties, integrated MNCs have usually developed procedures to coordinate product development among subsidiaries. IBM provided a prototypical illustration of such procedures.

At IBM product development is carried out in a number of centers, three located in Europe (United Kingdom, Germany and France), and one in Japan. Categories of products and technologies are assigned to development centers on a permanent basis, printers to the German center, semiconductor logic units to the French, and so forth. Specific product development decisions are made centrally, and work is farmed out to the various development centers.

Centers can be responsible for "mission" or "control". "Mission" involves the worldwide coordination of the early development of a new product. "Control" encompasses all development stages to product introduction: achievement of product specifications, detailed product development, and production start-up. "Mission" and "control" responsibilities are centrally allocated, but successive generations of like equipment (e.g., disk memories) are usually developed by the same center. The head of each center reports formally to the managing director of the corresponding national company, but has global responsibility for all products and related processes developed by the center.

Several information channels to corporate management allow IBM's regional units to influence product development. Regional market planners consolidate national market needs conveyed by marketing executives and service engineers into new product requirements. Regional units also influence the development process: evaluations submitted by national subsidiaries are consolidated into regional positions considered in every product review and prior to each announcement decision.* Much of this influence is exercised at a relatively low level through product managers, but in case of serious disagreement an operating unit could reject a product strategy or decide not to market some products. Conversely, in some cases, products may be developed for a specific geographic market only (e.g., the 3750 PABX in Europe) or adapted to peculiar characteristics of national markets (e.g., different credit card transaction and cheque coding systems requiring different bank terminals in the United Kingdom and France).

Many other integrated MNCs developed technology management approaches similar to that of IBM. For instance, both Ford and General Motors organized their product design and engineering activities on a worldwide scale in response to the staggering costs of developing new cars and the convergence of market requirements among regions of the world. Ford conceived the Fiesta in the United States as a potential world car in the early 1970s and then assigned responsibility for its development to Ford of Europe. Subsequent Ford products, such as the 1980 Escort, were jointly designed and engineered as "world cars" by several regional units. Following Ford's lead, General Motors established multinational project centers to design and engineer new cars. Once global products and technologies are developed, national development units often tailor them to national needs and local mores, when needed. Tensions are inescapable in managing these product adaptation units: too much national product differentiation compromises the benefits of integration, too little jeopardizes the penetration of national markets. Further, once set up, these units tend to grow into independent development centers and challenge the central management of technology.[9]

Further difficulties are faced with acquired units abroad. Philips, for instance, found it difficult initially to integrate R & D at Signetics (a U.S. semiconductor firm which it acquired from Corning Glass in 1975) with that of its own integrated semiconductor R & D operations. Similarly, Ciba Geigy's European and North American pharmaceutical research and development operations were long left unintegrated.[10] Concerns about loss of research creativity and worries about "not-invented-here" reactions

---

*The development of specific products at IBM is submitted to a series of "product reviews" (also called "phase reviews") where executives not involved in developing the new product evaluate the development program and may decide to stop or redirect it. The final review takes place just before "announcement", i.e., the notification to customers that a new product will soon be introduced and may now be ordered for early delivery.

have led corporate managers to move only gingerly toward R & D integration.

Finally, when markets are known to top management only through acquired subsidiaries, it is relatively easy for subsidiary management to over-emphasize the need for product differentiation to meet local market needs. Although this argument could hardly be sustained either at Ciba Geigy or at Signetics—both electronic components and drugs being global products—it could slow down integration or obfuscate the need for integration.

Marketing Management: Balancing Local Needs and Headquarters Demands

Even when products are global—such as pharmaceuticals—their marketing may still require customized approaches with the result that marketing is usually the least integrated major function since distribution channels, advertising media and messages, and other elements of an appropriate marketing mix can differ extensively among countries. Developing good relationships with distributors, selecting and motivating new ones, shedding some, are all personalized tasks that can only be performed by local managers who know the territory very well. Only when specialized selling tasks are little affected by national differences and when contracts are relatively few, can full integration of marketing make sense. For instance, aircraft manufacturers have specialized mobile sales teams rather than a permanent network of marketing subsidiaries. In such cases the complexity of the marketing task would not permit a multinational company to maintain the needed depth of competence in the field. Computers represent an intermediate position between centralized marketing and sales and autonomous national marketing. "Industry competency centers" (one for each major client industry) assist IBM's national field sales and marketing organizations, which can draw on them to support their own personnel in negotiating contracts with major customers.[11]

In summary, managing and developing the integrated MNC network efficiently for a business involves a series of focused trade-offs:

— Improving the productivity of the manufacturing network, vs. enhancing its acceptability to host governments; when to optimize vs. when to compromise.
— Integrating R & D management (and avoiding duplications but, maybe, also stifling creativity) or letting various R & D centers develop freely competing designs and ideas (but forgoing the benefits of integration).
— Developing uniform marketing approaches for "world products" or adapting approaches to multiple national conditions.

The danger, in an integrated MNC, is that managers will feel so strongly for global competitive strategies that these trade-offs will not even be raised. Integration priorities may dwarf the need to be sensitive to national differences. A critical requirement to address these tradeoffs, therefore, is the effective representation of national perspectives in management decision processes.

Effective Representation of Host Country Partners: Government and Labor

Integrated MNCs must remain acceptable to host governments. Host government demands have to be faced centrally since integration prevents their disjointed consideration by autonomous subsidiaries. National subsidiaries, therefore, have to provide a link between host government and MNC headquarters. They also have to provide a link with national trade unions.

These links have to ensure the effective representation of host country government and trade union interests at headquarters. Though integration remains the primary orientation, there is a need to represent effectively a national orientation against it. The purpose of this section is to analyze means for integrated MNCs to maintain a capability to incorporate national perspectives.

Host Government Representation

Demands by host government may determine integration patterns. Yet these demands often lack clarity. Integrated MNCs may strive for the clarification of such demands in order to facilitate their central consideration but miss the opportunity of influencing their original definition and subsequent clarification unless MNC executives are closely involved with government officials. Early involvement with government is difficult for integrated MNCs. Government officials demand "responsible interlocutors", i.e., managers with clout within the company and the ability to make key decisions. They are not willing to take advice from powerless subsidiary executives nor to make them privy to their own evolving concerns and policies-in-the-making. This leaves integrated MNCs at a disadvantage: their managers can hardly learn about important policy issues early enough to influence their resolution. Since integration usually conflicts with joint ventures, partners are seldom available as sources of information and influence.

To overcome this difficulty, some integrated MNCs have appointed senior local personalities in a type of ambassadorial function. In the late 1960s Westinghouse appointed Louis Armand Vice President for European Operations. Armand was a former head of the French national railroad, a member of the French Academy, and had held several senior civil service positions. In a more formal way, Ford created a European Advisory Council composed of European personalities. The Spanish Minister of Industry who had negotiated with Ford in 1972–73, Sr. Lopez de Letona, was asked to be a member of the Council, once he was no longer part of the Spanish government. Most other members had similar government backgrounds. Many other companies have developed similar arrangements.

Whilst both senior local ambassadors and advisory councils may play a key role in the early identification of sociopolitical trends and potential changes, and may have access to critical information more easily than subsidiary managers, their actual usefulness to the MNCs remains questionable. It is difficult to integrate their inputs into the management process, and they may lose credibility in their own country. French officials frowned upon Louis Armand's association with Westinghouse, and saw corporate line executives as the only viable interlocutors. Henry Ford II himself negotiated the new investment of Ford of Europe with heads of governments. Similarly, the 1975 negotiations between the French and Honeywell on the merger of C2I and Honeywell Bull made good progress only after Honeywell's president was involved.[12]

Among integrated MNCs, IBM had been more successful than most others in building local credibility. The creation of IBM Europe-Middle East-Africa, as a full-fledged operating unit reporting directly to the corporate level, and the personality and the skills of its head, Jacques Maisonrouge, as well as his nationality, account for part of this success. IBM's good citizenship policies certainly played a determinant role. Finally, IBM's flexibility was somewhat greater than that of other companies: It was willing to develop country-specific products or extensively adapted ones, and to maintain some nonintegrated operations working directly for host governments (for instance, a military division in France). Finally, many of the senior managers of IBM and most of the national subsidiary heads had long been well-regarded local nationals. The credibility they enjoyed both in their national environment and within IBM gave them influence.

Labor Relations

Integrated multinationals raise a difficult issue for national labor organizations. Union leaders would prefer a world without integrated MNCs, an environment easier to influence, where corporations would have fewer options.[13] A complex debate has been raging for years about the effect of investments abroad on employment in the home countries of MNCs.[14] Tentative findings suggest that domestic employment may benefit from direct foreign investment.[15] In host countries, the issue is that of mobility:

MNCs may invest less and even close their facilities in the country if unit labor costs increase relative to other locations or if labor unrest becomes widespread. This sets the stage for a complex three-way conflict between MNCs, host governments and national unions. In some cases the MNC and the host government may cooperate to maintain peaceful labor relations. In other cases, the MNCs and the unions join forces to jeopardize the policy of host governments. In some countries, labor and government cooperate to harness the MNCs. Integrated MNCs are not in a powerful position to face such situations. Despite union fears, they cannot so easily shift production from one country to the next: the movable factory is not a practical approach. Integrated MNCs remain vulnerable to disruptions in one country which may bring their production network to a standstill. Potential costs and damages of local labor conflicts are thus very high. Furthermore, unions have sometimes considered joint multinational actions to gain increased leverage on multinational corporations. In some cases (e.g., AKZO) joint actions have been at least partly successful.[16] Despite much publicity given to such instances, the national focus of most unions and their disparate attitudes and structures limit their potential for joint actions.[17] German unions want to influence management and participate in formulating industrial policies, whereas French or U.S. unions keep their distance from management. In France, for instance, unions have developed along political and religious lines, in the United Kingdom along trade demarcations, and in Germany along industrial sectors.

Government involvement in industrial relations varies immensely. In Spain, unions were run by the government. In France, the government remains the traditional arbitrator. Conditions are set in national covenants and disputes settled by specialized courts. The French also use state-owned enterprises, such as Renault, as pace-setters for industrial relations.[18] In the United Kingdom the structure for labor relations is much more fragmented, almost to the shop floor level, and the public administration is less involved in labor disputes.

The mechanisms for labor representation also vary widely, with codetermination taking hold in Germany and Scandinavian countries, but collective bargaining remaining predominant elsewhere.[19]

These differences between countries in the attitudes and organizations of the unions, and the role of the government, make coordinated multinational moves toward individual MNCs ineffective.

Even within a country, agreement may be difficult. Foreign investments affect various categories of workers differently, e.g., favor semiskilled workers, but leave others unaffected or worse off. Such differences in impact make the determination of a union position difficult.

Responses by integrated MNCs to such diversity are typically twofold. First, the MNCs own employees are made prime recipients of citizenship costs. Second, responsibility for labor relations is left to the national subsidiaries. Both responses should minimize the risk of confrontation with national unions. As we described in Chapter 2, IBM had generous employee benefit policies that took into account the personal needs of its employees on such issues as education or maternity leaves. Integrated MNCs also often paid higher wages than other companies in the same industry. These generous policies had permitted IBM to remain nonunionized in Europe. This also built loyalty toward the company within its personnel. In some other cases MNCs were among the few companies able to maintain house unions rather than accept national ones. Chrysler's subsidiary in France, Simca, had been such a case prior to the acquisition of Chrysler Europe by Peugeot. The company seldom had a strike, and was by far Chrysler's most productive foreign subsidiary.

Second, negotiating with unions has been left to the exclusive responsibility of the national subsidiaries, with, at the most, headquarters involvement in an advisory role.[20] Only when settling labor disputes involves complex trade offs with other involved parties does top management assume a leading role. In the fall 1978 strike in Britain, for instance, Ford was caught between unions and government. By claiming a large wage increase, the unions had made Ford into a test case to challenge the Labor government's wage guidelines. Ford's willingness to compromise led to a direct conflict with the government's wage control policy. The government threatened Ford with various sanctions, and decided to curtail public orders for Ford vehicles. Such government intervention led Ford's top management to follow the strike closely, but such attention was exceptional.

Codetermination creates an even more serious problem to integrated MNCs than being host to conflicts between unions and governments. Codetermination may eventually give to its employers the power to set the strategy of a subsidiary. Integration strategies may thus become difficult to implement, since their usefulness to each and every subsidiary would have to be demonstrated.[21]

With codetermination spreading to a number of countries, integrated MNCs may have to justify each trade-off between subsidiaries to unions in the various countries—a very constraining exercise. In the long run, codetermination may force MNCs to revert from integration strategies to selective agreements among strategically autonomous subsidiaries, i.e., alliances not very different in nature from those that were described in Chapter 5 as quasi-integration strategies. Such an evolution would make the development of the means for subsidiary managers to exert an influence on multinational strategy formulation without jeopardizing integration all the more important.

Structuring Headquarter Subsidiary Relationships

Even in the integrated MNC, therefore, subsidiary managers play a more critical role than the sometimes monolithic appearance of integrated MNCs would lead outside observers to believe. Subsidiary managers have key responsibilities in organizing government relations—although they may not be themselves the most visible actors—and in managing labor relations—determining a substantial part of total costs and dealing with one of the major sources of vulnerability of the integrated MNC. An effective representation of host country perspectives at headquarters, that sets realistic but not excessive constraints and integration strategies, ultimately rests with the willing and thoughtful participation of subsidiary managers in key decision processes.

The number of subsidiaries, and often different businesses in the diversified MNC, make it impossible, however, to let subsidiary managers independently put their points forward to top management. They must be given means to exercise influence without compromising the integration of the business. This implies some quality to decision making processes, otherwise, in a complex network of choices and issues, performance and data can all quickly become blurred. Clear operating goals must be given to the various parts of the network, and measurement and incentives must support them. This section analyzes how clarity and focus can be built into the relationships between subsidiaries and headquarters. The section starts with requirements in individual management systems and concludes with a discussion of overall management structures.

Management is likely to reach different trade-offs between economically optimized and politically compromised patterns of integration for different functions. Research may not be integrated; product development may be integrated at a worldwide level; manufacturing at a regional level; and marketing integrated in certain aspects (e.g., pricing policies) but not others (e.g., advertising or product positioning). Interdependencies across variously integrated functions may create major difficulties, unless carefully managed.

Subsidiaries are also closely interdependent, be it only through extensive cross-shipments of components, subassemblies, and end-products.

Related business is also interdependent: a component business, for instance, may transfer part of its production internally to one or another end-product group or subsidiary, and sell the rest to third parties.

In these interdependencies, any subunit of the MNC can create several difficulties. First, transactions and their effects must be made visible so that subunit goals can be set, results measured, and performances evaluated. Confusion can quickly result from intense interdependencies that have no such visibility. Second, measurement standards must be set; and, third, performance measured against them. In other words, subunits need to be isolated, and separately measured, for several purposes. Yet they also need to be brought together. Subsidiary managers must have a strong enough voice, and variously integrated functions or businesses need to cooperate, when the locus of decision making in these functions varies between headquarters and subsidiary management.

Fostering Clarity in the Organization: Building Visibility to Subunit Performance

Clarity of accounting is a prerequisite for the successful management of integrated multinational businesses. Yet transfers of goods, services and payments confuse accounting at the national level. Pricing such transfers realistically is often difficult, for lack of a clear market price to provide a yardstick. In such cases, accounting formulae (e.g., standard costs plus a fixed mark-up) may be advisable. When outside price references exist, negotiated transfer prices may be applicable. Host governments' suspicions of manipulation of transfer prices further complicates the issues: specific transfer pricing arrangements may have to be justified from a number of different perspectives, including those of several governments. Erratic short-term fluctuations in exchange rates and interest rates add to the difficulties of accurate accounting. Many MNCs now set their own inter-subsidiary exchange rates and internal capital interest rates for a given period, typically six months or a year. These rates are revised at the end of each period.

Whatever the characteristics of the accounting system, it has to address two issues: (1) how to make visible the consequences of local actions on the whole system, and (2) how to ensure that unwanted strategic biases are considered. The example of Ford of Europe illustrates the first issue. When it integrated its European operations, Ford of Europe faced the problem of how to run its sales subsidiaries. Prior to integration, subsidiaries merely bought cars from Ford of Britain or Ford of Germany, at some "export price" set by the manufacturing company. The performance of subsidiaries was measured by their net profit. Yet there was no way to ensure that their actions served the interest of the corporation as a whole (for instance by pushing the most profitable products of Ford of Britain or Ford of Germany), or of those whose unit contribution was most sensitive to volume changes (i.e., products whose output could be increased without cutting that of others). Following integration in 1967, a complex accounting system was set up to track the marginal profitability of a car to Ford of Europe as a whole.

A key manager commented upon the beneficial aspects of providing clarity:

Our accounting system now allocates a share of the corporate (Ford of Europe) operating profits to the various national subsidiaries. This is accompanied by an annual business plan for each company. Before this accounting allocation system was implemented the Managing Directors of the sales companies had no idea of the overall profitability of what they were doing. Now, the impact of their actions on corporate profits can be measured, and they are evaluated on what they generate for the corporation as a whole. This plays an important role in shifting the focus of our sales companies from that of internal agents to that of real businesses, run by general managers, and playing their part in the whole corporation. This has been a tremendous eyeopener and has led to much more aggressive pricing and market strategies now that these can be related to the corporation as a whole.[22]

The ability to measure concretely the contribution of marginal unit sales of specific models in individual countries provided the necessary information for subsidiary managers to become active contributors to a consistent European strategy.

Visibility of subsidiary contribution to the whole, in addition to visibility of subsidiaries as stand-alone units, also allowed decisions to be supported and trade-offs made on the basis of detailed analyses of their likely consequences, rather than on hunches or judgments. Judgments were not eliminated, of course, but led to where they really matter: real uncertainties and risks, rather than accounting fuzziness.

Consistency between acccounting practices and desired strategic directions is also important. Let us take one example. A major multinational electronic equipment company transferred components at cost to its end-product subsidiaries. The subsidiaries responded to the availability of inexpensive components by using more components than their competitors to perform a given function. As a result of this over-engineering, the quality of their products gained a market share for them, and the end-product divisions were profitable. Such transfers at cost were defended by the argument that larger end-product market shares brought the components manufacturing division enough added volume to cut its unit costs drastically. Much lower average unit costs made third party component sales possible, and very profitable, and the component availability also sold to third parties. Whether to sell new proprietary components to third parties (which competed with the company on end-product markets) or restrict their use to the company's own end-product divisions (and still transfer them at cost) was a constant bone of contention. It was decided as a corporate policy to allow third parties sales only 18 months after the introduction of new components in the firm's own products.

The result was somewhat paradoxical: since they alone were receiving the first production batches of new components, at a high unit cost, the end-product divisions slowed down innovation, or sold their new products at a high price. After eighteen months they had seldom established strong market positions for their new products. In fast-evolving markets, where component technologies paced end-product innovation, the company steadily lost its leading positions.

Although the transfer pricing and third party sales policies were clear, and at first sight made sense, they ultimately undermined the firm's objective of maintaining high market shares. Clarity of accounting in the integrated MNC is therefore not an ideal objective *per se*, whatever clarity is achieved ought to provide visibility with regard to performance, and affect the measurement of subunit performance in ways that are consistent with the overall corporate strategy, without introducing bias in the action of subunit managers.

In the context of an integration strategy, clarity of accounting is but the prerequisite for the measurement of subunit performance. Clarity of measurement allows top management to evaluate progress and to assess the results of key choices. It is also a basis for any incentive policy to support the firm's strategy.

We can use IBM's attempt to set up a measurement system for its subunits as a model of the measurement system developed by integrated MNCs. Agreed-upon plans serve as a yardstick for measurement of results along a set of predetermined criteria: strategic direction, functional strategies, year-to-year growth and plan-to-plan comparison of results. More detailed analyses of results are carried out within each of these broad categories. For instance, strategic direction includes both financial and operating aspects. As a link between planning and measurement, the same data are used by all staff groups for plan review and for measurement of actual performance against plans. Consistency is thus maintained between staff and unit inputs and over time, between the planning, budgeting, measurement, and evaluation processes. Furthermore, all operating units are measured using similarly defined data, so that their performance can be compared. Thirteen elements of performance (e.g., cost and revenue mix, business volume, manpower, etc.) are analyzed monthly by corporate staff. Revenues, not earnings, business volumes and manpower are reviewed regularly by a Corporate Managing Committee (CMC) composed of IBM's top three executives. Substantial deviation on other measurements are reported on an exception basis, after analysis by staffs. Finally, some parameters are defined in the budgets as high and low boundaries, and any deviation from within the boundaries triggers detailed study.[11]

IBM's measurement system mixes financial dimensions, (e.g., cost and profit), as well as substantive criteria (e.g., manpower). Interdependencies within the integrated network usually defy the simplicity of profit centers or centralization vs decentralization approaches, and the complexity of the resulting management task often calls for a mix of substantive and financial measurement to ensure clarity and a sufficient degree of comprehensiveness. Full recognition of interdependencies in measurement is the only way to provide for fair personal incentives.

In order to provide for clarity, personal accountability has to match the extent of control of individual managers on various functions. A senior manager in one integrated MNC commented:

A country manager is broadly responsible for all that happens in his country. His profit and loss statement includes everything. Yet, if something goes sour, corporate staffs go back to the various plans and budgets and trace the source of current problems. It remains up to the country manager to identify and signal problems and do his best to solve them, but he is not blamed for the problems themselves, unless they originate within his organization. Poor understanding of national customers, or misallocation of sales personnel are examples of things he would be blamed for, not cost overruns in a lab which happens to be located in his country.[23]

The approach described above enabled the company to assign responsibility for performance more precisely than a financial performance-based approach could have allowed. Compensation may also be tied to overall corporate or business performance, worldwide, or within the integrated region, rather than to specific subunit results. Managers' evaluations may also use inputs from business managers, functional managers and national managers.

For instance, recognizing the effects of integration, TI based rewards for its managers in Europe on market growth and penetration results (marketing oriented yardsticks); only in the United States was there a complete profit and loss statement by business. Research and development budgets spent in Europe and Japan were charged to the product group, not to the local management.

Integrated MNCs also usually stress long-term rewards through promotion for contribution to the corporation. The following comments are typical:

We are a very inbred company. By the time they get into making significant managerial decisions, our people have developed their own information channels, their own informal network of buddies and personal relationships. They have also internalized a number of procedures and share the general corporate attitude. People know implicitly just what can be done and what can't be done within the company culture.[24]

In the course of their career, managers of integrated MNCs often alternate between jobs in national subsidiaries and headquarters, and between line and staff responsibilities, so managers of significant subunits do not have a parochial view. This makes them less likely to promote the interests of their own subunit over those of the integrated network as a whole. Subsidiary managers did not develop long-term commitments to local operations, and yet they felt responsible for their performance within the context of the integrated network.

The major danger of such an approach is that managers lose touch with the national environment and culture of the countries in which they operate, a criticism often levelled at executives of U.S. multinationals. Some companies, such as IBM, did not rely on third country nationals in subsidiaries, but rotated local national managers to regional and corporate headquarters so that they could become responsive to the needs for integration and yet remain attuned to the subtleties of operating in their own country.

Clarity of accounting, clarity of measurement, and clarity of evaluation and rewards are required conditions which allow the objective consideration of national constraints within the dominant perspective of integration. They allow what compromises need to be made, and what arrangements to reach with host governments, to be decided on the basis of facts and analyses rather than impressions or hunches. They allow the subsidiary manager to remain committed to an integration strategy, and yet sensitive to the needs for compromises with host governments and unions.

Fostering Unity: Building Communication Channels

Beyond the conditions reviewed above, however, country managers also need to be heard by top management. In an integrated business, where global competitiveness priorities permeate from headquarters, this may be difficult. Executives who manage the integration, and whose central power is rooted in controlling interdependencies among subsidiaries, may not listen carefully to dissenting voices. They may also fear that subsidiary managers may develop self-serving arguments against integration, rather than well-founded ones.

National subsidiary perspectives can be put forward and heard in different ways within the integrated MNC. First, there exist functional channels for such issues as product development, manufacturing, and marketing. Second, access to top management is often critical. Third, conflict resolution mechanisms can force consideration of national perspectives. Fourth, senior level corporate executives can be made advocates of national subsidiary perspectives to top management.[25] Finally, over time, the corporate culture can be made to support a balance between global and local considerations. These means are reviewed below. Collectively, they provide for national subsidiary influence on the overall integration strategy.

Functional channels

As we discussed earlier in this chapter, national subsidiary managers provide numerous functional inputs: feedback on market performance of existing products, requests for new products, review of development projects, distinct functional committees between operating managers from subsidiaries and corporate staff managers may provide a formal discussion arena for functional issues. Functional inputs have their limits, however. By providing only a specialized channel—where subsidiary specialists talk to headquarter specialists—they may stifle the emergence of a country-centered perspective on key competitive, political or social issues in the country. The perspective conveyed to headquarters reflects functional specialization. Headquarter specialists are likely to be more knowledgeable in their own discipline than country specialists (perhaps only because they have more data) and may dominate national subsidiary managers. Indeed, in at least two situations studied in detail, functional channels were used by headquarter executives to bolster their control over subsidiaries.[26] This, in turn, leads functional specialists in the subsidiaries to see their future, and the sense of their legitimacy, with functional counterparts at headquarters rather than with the subsidiary general managers. Beyond specific inputs, functional contribution from subsidiaries could seldom be pulled together into specific plans or action programs under the leadership of management.

Interface with senior management

Such interface may be formal and informal. The formal planning system may make provision for it. At IBM, for instance, specific areas for improvement (e.g., field sales force productivity) were the object of "program plans". Implications of these programs for individual countries were discussed well in advance; for example, in terms of hiring and retraining of personnel. Countries could also propose "environmental" strategies, in response to important conditions in the national environment, such as workers' codetermination in Germany. Such significant national issues were often discussed by the Corporate Management Committee. An individual subsidiary could also sponsor specific functional strategies aimed at improving relationships with its government, like the construction of plants in his country. In such cases requests are put forward by the subsidiary management. Should the corporate manufacturing staffs oppose them on economic grounds, the country manager can take his case to the Corporate Managing Committee. Decisions on whether to risk losing some government business or to risk having excess capacity locked in the country belong to the CMC.

In some cases, individual subsidiaries could depart from corporate patterns in the ways in which they operated and in their own internal organization. IBM Japan, for example, enjoyed considerable autonomy and adopted policies more suited to its national environment than to interfacing with headquarters.[27]

Informal aspects of access to top management are equally important. Top managers of integrated MNCs travel extensively to gain first-hand knowledge of subsidiary operation; so do their staff assistants. Subsidiary managers visit headquarters often, and gatherings of executives are frequent. These meetings provide opportunities for off-the-record discussions between senior executives and subsidiary managers.

The danger here is that preoccupation of successful interaction with headquarters takes precedence over success in the national environment. In our research we observed several subsidiaries whose management was more preoccupied with seeking corporate approval of all actions than with taking actions that were appropriate for the subsidiary. The internal organization of these subsidiaries usually mirrored that of head offices, to "facilitate" communication. Looking toward headquarters, their managers lost touch with their markets and national conditions.

Issue resolution processes

Top managers cannot deal directly with all the issues that come up in the operation of the integrated network. IBM set up a system, internally known as "contention process", to encourage resolution of intersubsidiary or interunit conflicts by middle managers. Each year, managers from any operating subunit could object to the plans and budgets of any other subunit, the budgets of which could adversely affect it. The objecting subunit could demand a joint working party to reach some mutually agreeable resolution of the difference. Should the working party fail, the subunits could duly register their difference as a "nonconcurrence" with the budget of the other subunits, for resolution by a higher level of management. Each year, about 200 of these "nonconcurrences" eventually reached the Corporate Managing Committee for final decision. Before reaching a decision, the CMC usually set some new high-level working party under the chairmanship of a senior executive (typically a vice president) of a major operating unit. Most "nonconcurrences" were resolved by the first working party, and thus never reached the CMC.

Once approved, budgets served as contracts between subunits. Should a unit fail to live up to its budgeting commitment, managers from adversely affected units were expected to apply pressure on the defaulting unit and work with its managers toward solutions that would make the achievement of the budget feasible. Subunit managers thus carefully avoided commitments they might not be able to honor. Strong peer group pressure applied.

This process led subsidiary and subunit managers to strive on their own for a balance between local and global considerations: should other units negatively affect their own operations, they could object to their plans, but they were also commited to provide goods and services at specified conditions, and to achieve certain financial and operating results within the integrated network. In watching other units' plans they took a national perspective; in committing to serve them they took a network perspective.

Advocates of localism

Some integrated companies assign to key senior executives the representation of key subsidiary or regional interests at headquarters. This usually corresponds to top management's concern that control of foreign operations by headquarters product executives may stifle national perspectives. Texas Instruments' European semiconductor business may serve as an illustration of the need for such an advocacy position. In 1978 a corporate vice president was appointed to head the semiconductor operations in Europe, breaking a hitherto monolithic worldwide product group structure. He commented:

> Involving a corporate officer locally in Europe changes the operating environment; there is more of a power base in Europe. Prior to my appointment here there was little counterweight to balance the worldwide product manager. Operating managers in Europe now have a more sensitive audience—and a less difficult one—than they had by going directly to Dallas. We now have some combination of product and regional perspectives. Legally, all European subsidiaries report to me. This enables top management to decide on an ad hoc basis to involve me in any decision.
>
> My appointment was made partly in response to needs to become more sensitive to increased government intervention. Hitherto, the quality of our product made us good citizens and gave us some share in the military market. Semiconductors have now stepped up in importance to host governments. This creates a need for more attention to broader government demands.[28]

Corporate culture

In addition to the dominant international view, it is possible to build within the network's ranks sensitiveness to local conditions. The periodic return of IBM's executives to assignments in their home country contributed to such a sensitiveness. Some integrated MNCs relied on expatriates from the home country on long-term detachment to a country. This long-term perspective enabled them to gain an understanding of the local culture and provided an incentive to integrate the subsidiary's operations into the host country environment. Some other MNCs tried to hire cultural deviants whose past experiences made them more attuned to multiple approaches and cultures.

These various mechanisms to ensure that national perspectives are not stifled within the integration network are complementary: all can be used by the same MNC. The difficulty for any MNC is to blend them in such a way as to provide for an appropriate balance between localism and globalism.

Localism and Globalism

Without the counterforce of localism, integration may run in a vicious circle that may explain the disappointment sometimes felt by corporate executives about the performance of worldwide product groups, on the premises that (1) in-depth product competencies are needed to sell their products and (2) local sales subsidiaries reporting to a multiproduct division lack needed competencies.

In summary, the successful management of integration strategies requires that visibility be brought to the performance of the various subunits and also that a balance be found, in the communication channels that underly decision processes, between the overiding concern for integration and the need to take into consideration nationally required adaptations to the integration strategy.

Formal Management Structures

The formal structure of the MNC within which integration takes place is of comparatively lesser importance. Its main role is to constrain and orient management processes. It conveys a dominant strategic orientation to the firm's business. Integration strategies are usually run with a strong functional emphasis, since the management of integration essentially takes place at the functional level. Furthermore, the extent of integration usually varies among functions, with product development and manufacturing usually more integrated than marketing.

Early single business integrated MNCs were usually organized by function internationally, with Singer providing a classic example. Others were Deere or, later, Caterpillar. In diversified MNCs, integrated businesses tend to be predominantly run via worldwide product divisions or functionally structured international companies or divisions.

These worldwide product divisions, usually themselves organized by functions and countries, seem to result in a decline in international development, at least in the case of U.S. companies. The underlying reasons seem to be the fragmentation of the firm's international experience between discrete product units and the relative loss of power of international executives. In U.S. divisions where international sales are not dominant compared with domestic sales, divisional executives may well perceive bolstering their U.S. position to developing foreign market presence.[29] Western European MNCs, usually with a much larger percentage of their sales abroad, are less exposed to this syndrome and seem better able to manage a worldwide operation through product organisations. European companies seldom had strong product executives, at home, and those they appoint usually are world-oriented executives with broad international experience.

Some integrated MNCs, both to maintain their international entrepreneurial spirit and to manage the interface between unequally integrated functions, have sometimes made multiple independent units full profit centers, measured and evaluated on their own result. Swedish companies, such as Atlas Copco and Trelleborg, seem to resort to this approach. While it clearly maintains entrepreneurial spirit in foreign sales subsidiaries, this approach makes the overall implementation of a corporate strategy difficult. Trelleborg, for instance, complemented its multiplicity of strong profit centers by "profit center boards" (even when profit centers were not separate legal entities) to ensure that the free bargaining between sales subsidiaries and manufacturing divisions did not lead to outcomes contrary to corporate policies and strategies.[30]

Other companies, such as Ford, use series of committees to manage the interface between unequally integrated functions and to ensure that inter-functional trade-offs take into account the overall strategic priorities.[31]

Concerns with the need to remain sensitive to host country constraints and also to maintain international entrepreneurship (rather than drive integration exclusively from the center) seems to have led a number of U.S. MNCs to abandon the simplicity of clear product structures. Many U.S. MNCs, with integrated operations, have adopted some form of "matrix overlays" whereby product managers have primary responsibility, but strong international groups remain, at least as corporate staff units.[32] These units enjoy close links with the CEO and usually review major decisions affecting international operations (such as investment requests and key appointment proposals) with advisory or veto power. They also provide an alternate channel for country managers to be heard at head-quarters.

Conclusion

Discussing structural issues brings us back to our starting point in considering integration strategies: their objectives. If the objective is mainly defensive—i.e., bolstering the competitiveness of a mature business so as to resist inroads from new competitors in well-established mature markets—product structures may be adequate. Where fostering and acce-lerating foreign expansion is the driving logic, then it seems that ensuring a strong voice to country executives is essential.

Managing an integrated network therefore implies two very different tasks: managing for operating efficiency within the network, and managing for effectiveness at its margins. Whilst the first task calls for coordinated operations and centralized decision making, the second calls for entrepre-neurship and careful listening in the outposts. The former—efficiently managing the manufacturing and logistics network—is easier and more obvious than the latter—ensuring effective representation of multiple "local" perspectives in central decisions.

They also conflict, and for such conflict to be handled constructively certain conditions must exist, in particular some clarity of information and motives, and multiple channels for conflicts to be voiced and managed.

This chapter has deliberately treated some of the least obvious aspects of managing an integrated MNC extensively, and been less detailed on the most obvious ones. Providing an effective representation of national interests—so they are both identified and heard—and using a structural form which maintains entrepreneurships at the national level are two less obvious critical issues that top managers of integrated MNCs should pay attention to. Integrated MNCs may remain acceptable to host governments only insofar as they become increasingly adaptive—rather than centrally run bureaucratic monoliths insensitive to market diversity and host country heterogeneity.

References

1. See *Ford in Spain (A)*. Available from HBS case services, No. 4–380–091, and *Ford Bobcat (A1) and (A2)* No. 4–380–093 and 4–380–094. GM data *provided to the author* remain unpublished.
2. A similar argument, for domestic investment decision processes in large domestic firms, was first made in J. L. Bower, *Managing the Resource Allocation Process* (Boston, Division of Research, Harvard Business School 1970).
3. See J. J. Boddewyn, "Disinvestments: The Managerial Dimension" (Baruch College Working Paper, November 1977) and D. Van den Bulcke et al. *Investment and Divestment Policies of Multinational Corporations in Europe* (London: Saxon House, 1979).
4. For some summary evidence see S. Young and N. Hood "The Strategies of U.S. Multinationals in Europe", in *Multinational Business*, Vol. 2, (1980) pp. 1–19. Indirect evidence also suggests a link between divestment and the development of regional or global integration strategies. See for instance Lawrence G. Franko *Joint Venture Survival in the Multinational Corporation* (New York: Praeger, 1972), and J. J. Boddewyn, *International Divestment: A Survey of Corporate Experience* (New York: Business International S.A., 1976).
5. J. J. Boddewyn, "Disinvestments . . .", *op. cit.*
6. See Brent D. Wilson, "The Disinvestment of Foreign Subsidiaries by U.S. Multinational Companies", unpublished doctoral thesis, Harvard Business School, 1979. Fagre and Wells found similar results in Latin America, see N. Fagre and L. T. Wells (Jr) "Bargaining Power of Multinationals and Host Governments", in *Journal of International Business Studies*, Vol. 3.2, Fall 1982.
7. J. N. Behrman and W. A. Fisher, *Overseas R&D Activities of Transnational Corporations* (Cambridge, Mass: Oelgeschlager, Gunn and Hain, 1980).
8. See T. Wise, "The Rocky Road to the Market Place", in *Fortune* for the IBM 360.
9. J. N. Behrman and W. A. Fisher, *op. cit.*
10. Author's interviews.
11. Y. Doz, Forthcoming "IBM Profile" case.
12. See J. Jublin and J. M. Quatrepoint *French Ordinateurs* (Paris: Alain Moreau, 1976).
13. See Elizabeth R. Jager "U.S. Labor and Multinationals" in Duane Kujawa (ed.), *International Labor and the Multinational Enterprise* (New York: Praeger, 1975) pp. 22–41.
14. For a summary conceptual discussion see Robert G. Hawkins and Michael Jay Jedel "U.S. Jobs and Foreign Investment" in Duane Kujawa (ed.), *International Labor and the Multinational Enterprise* (New York: Praeger, 1975). For empirically based studies see, for instance, U.S. Tariff Commission, *Implications of Multinational Firms for World Trade and Investment and for U.S Trade and Labor*, Report to the Committee on Finance of the U.S. Senate and its subcommittee on International Trade, 93rd Congress, 1st Session, 1973 (Washington D.C.: U.S. Government Printing Office 1973) and Robert B. Stobaugh *et al.*, *Nine Investments Abroad* (Boston: Division of Research, Graduate School of Business Administration, Harvard University).
15. See John M. Stopford "The Impact of Foreign Direct Investment on U.K. Employment in Manufacturing" (International Labor Organization mimeo, 1979). Research is in progress in Sweden, under the auspices of the Committee for Direct Investment at the Stockholm School of Economics under the direction of Professor Jan Erik Valhne.
16. This case is discussed in . Van den Bulcke *et al.*, *Investment and Divestment Policies of Multinational Corporations in Europe* (London: Saxon House, 1979).
17. See Duane Kujawa, "Transnational Industrial Relations: A Collective Bargaining Prospect", in Duane Kujawa (ed.), *International Labor and the Multinational Enterprise* (New York: Praeger 1978), pp. 95–137.
18. See Patrick Fridenson, *La Forteresse Ouvrière Renault* (Paris: Fayard, 1971).

19. J. Peel *The Real Power Game* (Maidenhead, UK: McGraw Hill, 1979).
20. See Duane Kujawa, *International Labor Relations Management in the Automobile Industry* (New York: Praeger 1971).
21. See Renato Mazzolini, "The Influence of European Workers over Corporate Strategy", in *Sloan Management Review*, Vol. 19, No. 3, Spring 1978, pp. 59–81.
22. Personal communication to the author.
23. Ibid.
24. Ibid.
25. See Malcolm S. Salter, "Manpower Priorities in Emerging Multinationals", paper presented at the Academy of International Business 1974 Annual Meeting (San Francisco, 28–29 December 1974).
26. See *Corning Glass Works International* cases available from HBS case services, Boston, HBSCS Nos 0–381–160, 161, 162, 163, 164, and 112, and *Rank Xerox (A), (B1) and (B2)* (available from INSEAD).
27. K. Komahashi, "IBM Japan, Ltd.: Naturalizing for a Rollback?", *The Orient Economist*, June 1982, pp. 16–19.
28. Research communication to the author.
29. See W. H. Davidson and P. Haspeslagh, "Shaping a Global Product Organization", in *Harvard Business Review* Vol. 60, No. 4, July–August 1982, pp. 125–132.
30. "Operational Goals and Guidelines" (a brochure circulated by Trelleborg Co.). In the difficulties faced by a divisional and subsidiary profit center, see *Naval* (Case Study available from the Institute of International Business, Stockholm, Sweden).
31. See *Ford Bobcat (B)*, HBSCS No 4–380–100.
32. See Business International, *New Directions in Multinational Corporate Organization* (New York: Business International Corp., February 1981), pp. 30–43.

8

Managing a Nationally Responsive Multinational Business

Issues and Tasks

The analysis of national responsiveness strategies in Chapters 1, 2 and 4 suggest that the key managerial issue for a nationally responsive multinational business is to make headquarters enhance the competitiveness of national subsidiaries without compromising the subsidiaries' ability to respond autonomously to host country demands. A motley collection of autonomous subsidiaries may survive on their own peculiar strengths and resources, each taken in isolation; yet without intersubsidiary coordination the nonintegrated MNC may lose its edge over purely national competitors.[1]

In Chapter 1 we argued that intersubsidiary coordination in selected domains allows nonintegrated MNCs several advantages over national firms: (1) the ability to pool risks and centrally allocate resources among subsidiaries; (2) the ability to avoid duplication of costly research and development and to spread the amortization of R & D costs over the larger production volume provided by several subsidiaries; (3) the coordination of exports from subsidiaries producing similar equipment to increase the overall MNC export volumes; and (4) the transfer of manufacturing expertise and other skills among subsidiaries.

Managing national responsiveness therefore hinges on a paradox: intersubsidiary coordination provides subsidiary managers with the means to improve their competitiveness and yet it limits their freedom to be successful in their own particular national environment. National responsiveness pulls the subsidiaries apart, toward full local autonomy, strong concern with their national environment, and little concern for the overall interests of the parent MNC. Intersubsidiary coordination thus has to be managed against this centrifugal pull, and yet it has to adapt to it. The extent of coordination is a dilemma for executives of nationally responsive MNCs. Whereas the integrated MNCs analyzed in Chapter 7 have a strong centrally set strategy, the strategy of nationally responsive MNCs is necessarily less clear. Headquarters do not exercise enough control over the

191

subsidiaries to have a central strategy. Yet headquarters ought to support the various strategies to make the whole more than the sum of its parts.

This chapter analyzes the administrative means used to take advantage of the firm's multinationality without compromising the responsiveness of its national subsidiaries. The first section examines the ability of headquarters to allocate resources among subsidiaries. This involves the development of information and motivation systems that enable the comparison of plans, proposals, and actual performances between subsidiaries, and provide the basis for an effective resource allocation process.

The second section describes the approach of major nationally responsive MNCs to the management of technology. The desire to avoid duplications and to spread the amortization of development costs over larger production volumes conflicts with the need to adapt products to the various national markets. To a large extent, the issues faced by nationally responsive MNCs are not fundamentally different from those discussed in Chapter 7. Only the willingness of host governments to subsidize R & D carried out locally often further complicates the issue.

The third section analyzes the potential of export coordination among subsidiaries. Judicious allocation of export contracts and export markets to one subsidiary or another may increase the MNCs overall export volume and success rate on export bids.

The fourth section examines the transfer of knowledge and skills.

Finally, national responsiveness raises an intriguing issue: what determines the division of responsibilities for strategic decisions between the headquarters and subsidiaries. In other words, how decentralized should nationally responsive MNCs be and what does "decentralization" mean in a nationally responsive MNC?

As in Chapter 7, extensive references will be made to selected companies, and at various points we shall examine in detail some aspects of their operations to illustrate and clarify the argument.

Managing Resource Allocation

Effective allocation of resources within a firm usually calls for clear comparisons of alternative uses of funds. In such large complex organizations as MNCs, resource allocation is also a social and political process among managers. Beyond the analytical aspects, it calls for means to motivate managers and to assess both their inputs in the process and the effectiveness with which they are likely to use allocated funds.

Many obstacles stand in the way of effective resource allocation among the subsidiaries of a nationally responsive MNC. First, different accounting standards and practices among countries may distort measurement tools and criteria. Second, different investment and tax regulations make it attractive to vary the capital structures of subsidiaries, and blur intersubsidiary comparisons. Third, high inflation rates and the corporate desire to hedge against currency fluctuations may further confuse the measurement of operating performances. Geographic distance, few interdependencies among subsidiaries and little headquarter control make the development of an effective coordination process unlikely. This section describes four complementary approaches used by top management of nationally responsive MNCs to address these difficulties: (1) uniformity of planning, budgeting, and control systems, (2) measurement and incentive systems, (3) peer control and, (4) direct top management involvement.

Uniformity of Planning, Budgeting and Control Systems

Though they recognize the primacy of adaptation to national conditions, most nationally responsive MNCs try to implement similar accounting and control systems in all their subsidiaries. Brown Boveri, for instance, developed similar planning frameworks for its major national affiliates.[2] Plans remained primarily a responsibility of the national companies, however; the only corporate inputs were guidelines for return on equity, return on sales, cash flow, a balance between long-term and short-term liabilities, and capital expenditure as a percentage of cash flow. The guidelines reflected top management's expectations about each subsidiary and justifications were sought from subsidiary managers should their own plans deviate substantially from these guidelines. BBC also created a corporate controller's office to monitor the performance of the various affiliates which submitted standard monthly comparisons between actual results and budgets.

Common formats for planning, budgeting and control do not solve all problems, however. The underlying data are not necessarily comparable, and it is difficult for corporate executives to check on their quality, particularly in European multinationals which do not consolidate all international results. Partly because of more stringent consolidation and disclosure requirements, U.S. companies are more concerned than European ones with achieving full accounting and control comparability between subsidiaries. As a result, U.S. subsidiaries often developed two sets of accounts: one according to the national requirements, the other according to those of their headquarters.

The control function can be entrusted to a specialized headquarter group. Individual subsidiary controllers often report to this central group, rather than to the subsidiary's managing director, and seldom are local nationals. At ITT, for instance, each subsidiary controller supplies a monthly variance report to a headquarter director of financial control.[3] This report comments on the strengths and weaknesses of the subsidiary management's forecasts and results. These reports are also filed and discussed by the national controller with the subsidiary management.

Despite these attempts to bring clarity to the data and to the planning, budgeting and control processes, resource allocation in nationally responsive multinational companies remains an act of trust in the judgement of subsidiary managers. The primacy of national strategies, the scarcity of interdependencies between subsidiaries, and the lack of substantive headquarter control over the subsidiaries give the subsidiary managers considerable power in the firm's decisions. At Brown Boveri, for instance, such power was acknowledged in the composition of the Corporate Managing Committee: besides the chairman of BBC the other members were the heads of the three largest national subsidiaries (Germany, Switzerland, and France) and the head of a group of medium manufacturing subsidiaries. The nationally responsive MNC, in contrast to the integrated one, often depends much more on personalities than on formal administrative systems, much more on cooperation than on control systems or dependencies. This makes the question of incentive for cooperation particularly critical in the nationally responsive MNC.

Measurements and Incentives

Measurement

Nationally responsive subsidiaries are usually set as separate profit centers whose performance is measured in local currency.* Translation into a single currency is undertaken for central consolidation purposes. Financial rather than operational criteria are most often used, in line with the strategic autonomy and operating independence of the subsidiaries.

Evaluation of performance

Since subsidiaries of a nationally responsive MNC are essentially self-contained, it is possible to measure each subsidiary individually and to ignore interdependencies. The types of problems faced by Ford or IBM in assessing the consequences of subsidiary marketing decisions do not exist in a nationally responsive MNC. Performance of each subsidiary can be evaluated independently.

Furthermore, since subsidiaries are usually free to set their own plans— with only very broad corporate guidelines and unassertive central staff comments—they can be evaluated against their own choices. The process at Nestlé is fairly typical of that observed in other nationally responsive MNCs.

All the marketing planning, including the budget, is done by each of the companies. Each

---

*To evaluate the operating results of the subsidiary rather than the financial acumen of its managers in forestalling currency translation losses.

year, they come to a meeting in Vevey with a budget for the year, and they discuss it for two or three days with our specialists. It is discussed to get an explanation of why it has been proposed, not at all with the idea of having it changed or of imposing something of our own. Rarely does it happen that in one or another country we decide we are making an important mistake and then ask the managers of the subsidiary to change their plans. Sometimes we make small alterations, but we can reckon that 95% of the budget will not be changed. Everday operations are controlled abroad. We have the usual flow of information, all the charts, and at any moment we know exactly what is going on. So if anything is done wrong, we are in a position to intervene at once and not wait until the disaster of finding out that the business is badly run.[4]

Evaluation of subsidiary performance against their own plans and budgets avoids the difficulty of developing meaningful common yardsticks, and acknowledges the diversity of circumstances faced in the various countries where the company is active. Contrary to integrated MNCs, interdependencies between subsidiaries are not critical enough to impose a need for common yardsticks.

The long tenure of subsidiary managers guarantees they develop plans in the best long-term interest of their subsidiary.

Career paths and rewards

In nationally responsive MNCs, local nationals usually manage the subsidiaries, careers are primarily national in scope, and senior positions in subsidiaries carry much clout, as in a purely national company.

National focus in career paths have several consequences. First, subsidiary managers develop a long-term perspective: they live with the long-term consequences of their decisions. Second, headquarters positions are not coveted by younger aspiring national managers—these positions are few and often carry little power. Promotions beyond the national subsidiary are unlikely as are moves to other subsidiaries. Younger managers thus see the development of their career in a national perspective, not in terms of contribution to the overall results of the MNC. Furthermore, national affiliates often establish their divisions as strong profit centers, a move unlikely to encourage cooperation with sister divisions in other subsidiaries, unless such cooperation serves their immediate interests.

Some nationally responsive MNCs have tried to counterbalance their staffing national and promotion practices by tying financial rewards to corporate performance. Yet, these financial rewards seldom balance the long-term national focus of subsidiary executives.

Peer Control

Unable to control subsidiaries fully from headquarters, or to counterbalance the bias toward subsidiary autonomy built into the promotion and reward systems, corporate managers of nationally responsive MNCs have sometimes acknowledged the collective responsibility of subsidiary managers by submitting their plans and resource allocation requests to peer approval.

"Business teams" or "product teams" may regroup the managers in charge of the same business in different affiliates. Corporate staffs may also have representatives on each team. The tasks of these teams may include the formulation of corporate-wide product line objectives and business plans to ensure the best exploitation of opportunities for coordination of activities between the various affiliates and more specifically to review the product specifications, development budgets, and capacity increases suggested by their members for their own operations.

Yet operating such coordination teams successfully meets difficulties of several natures. Members are submitted to profit pressures (typically they head profit centers within their own subsidiary) but may not be high enough in the hierarchy of their subsidiary to commit themselves to product or business team proposals. At Brown Boveri, for instance, such teams were useful forums to exchange information, but did not readily evolve into decision-making bodies.[5] Too many pressures worked against BBC's teams for them to be effective: profit center measurement and reward in the affiliates, little central management support, the primacy of state-controlled customers in most of BBC's businesses, the lack of team integration into other management processes (e.g., planning, and budgeting which continued to remain largely national), and national career patterns.

ITT's top management had recognized these difficulties in coordinating subsidiaries. Peer control took place where the power was: for instance, among the heads of the major telecommunication equipment subsidiaries, through frequent informal meetings. In addition, ITT's top management was more closely involved in the coordination process than BBC's; meetings were held frequently between top management and subsidiary executives.

The quality of peer control may thus largely depend on the top manager's ability to monitor the process effectively. Peer control worked well at Brown Boveri for businesses of which top management had direct experience and indepth knowledge. At ITT, staffs were involved in the making of decisions which BBC would have delegated to the business teams. Both BBC's new coordination level and ITT's top management intervention relied on personalities more than on systems.

Direct Top Management Involvement

Direct top management involvement was often the key to effective blending of national responsiveness and intersubsidiary coordination. Geneen's management of ITT best exemplifies this approach. Once a month he and his staff spent the better part of a week at ITT's European headquarters in Brussels. The European Vice President and his staff were with Geneen the whole week. The first day was basically a policy-making session, subsidiary by subsidiary. The heads of the national subsidiaries were present, assisted by their staff as needed. The second day was devoted to "Product Strategy and Action Board" sessions. Managers from regional headquarters and from subsidiaries attended according to their involvement with the products being discussed. Subsidiary managing directors attended as needed. Geneen and his corporate staff were available for problem-orientated discussions on any topic during the last three days. Typically, individual subsidiaries would be discussed by the subsidiary controller, and the monthly meetings in Brussels (plus bimonthly budget reviews in New York) all contributed to Geneen's ability to stay personally on top of ITT's operations.[6]

At few other multinational companies was top management so close to subsidiary operations, and so involved in the detail of resource allocation decisions as was Geneen at ITT. His uncanny ability to lead large meetings and absorb data made such involvement productive; to many other CEOs it might not have been. Yet personal involvement may be the most effective way to ensure central guidance without stifling the national responsiveness of subsidiaries.

Conclusion

In this section we have discussed some means used by corporate managers of nationally responsive MNCs to ensure effective resource allocation in their subsidiaries. Uniformity of planning, budgeting, and control systems, measurement and incentive systems, peer control and top management intervention can all play a role in making intersubsidiary resource allocation more effective. Yet they face formidable obstacles: headquarters have little concrete substantive power on subsidiary operations. Thus, cooperation is based more on persuasion and shared short-term interests than on central authority. The ability of the corporate level to allocate resources centrally is also limited by the fragmented nature of the strategy; there is no central comprehensive strategy to provide a clear guidance to resource allocation decisions.

Some companies parallel this strategic fragmentation in their resource allocation process: instead of allocating resources centrally they let each subsidiary develop without corporate funding. Brown Boveri, for example, provide corporate funds to very rapidly growing subsidiaries only, e.g., Brazil. Subsidiaries usually retain their earnings, their share of corporate expenses being covered by technology royalties and other such charges. Though it decreases the firm's flexibility in deploying resources, this approach obviously minimizes corporate headquarter's involvement.

In some domains, however, headquarters can work in the shared interest of the subsidiaries and, in the process, acquire a basis for some concrete substantive control over the subsidiaries. One particularly important domain is the coordination of research and development and the management of technology transfers between the subsidiaries.

Management of Technology

Managing the technology within a nationally responsive MNC is complicated by (1) the geographical dispersion of activities (2) the demands of various national markets for adaptations to products and processes and for the development of new technologies, and (3) the need to transfer technology between subsidiaries and minimize wasteful duplications. These conflict and create a difficult choice between central R & D and autonomy of subsidiary R & D efforts. In this section we first examine the impediments to the central management of R & D, then we consider the solutions adopted by ITT and Brown Boveri, and finally draw some implications.

Impediments to the Central Management of Technology

Dispersion of activities

When products require adaptation to diverse local needs there are strong benefits to locating R & D activities in subsidiaries where engineers and scientists can interact directly with customers whose needs they expect to satisfy. Host governments may also grant R & D subsidies to nationally responsive MNC subsidiaries, provided the work is done in the host country. Nationally responsive MNCs are thus likely to carry out R & D work in various countries.

However, host governments also often expect technology to be transferred into their countries from other subsidiaries—some extent of integration—but governments are unlikely to tolerate tight integration of R & D because they wish subsidiaries to remain able to engage in R & D locally at the government's request rather than under the full control of foreign headquarters.

Partially integrating geographically dispersed R & D efforts is no easy task. First, managing technology in any setting is difficult; it hinges more on creating propitious conditions than on managing in a conventional sense.[7] The circulation and exchange of technology is an informal process depending upon personal relations of the involved persons. Uprooting individuals may destroy their creativity. This suggests that multinationals technology coordination may be difficult beyond a limited geographical distance.[8]

Companies sometimes concentrate a research team working on a specific project in a single location to increase the efficiency of informal communication among the involved specialists. But engineers and scientists are not always extremely mobile internationally. Some companies, therefore, assign particular product lines to individual subsidiaries on a long-term basis so that the most critical integration is done locally, with lesser needs for intersubsidiary coordination.

Diversity among markets

Subsidiary executives want to serve best their local market needs. This legitimate desire leads to the proliferation of R & D projects in response to local demands for adaptations of new products. Such proliferation may undermine the MNC's key competitive advantage of spreading R & D costs over the large production volumes provided by sales of uniform products to several national markets. Corporate managers therefore usually strive to limit uncoordinated national R & D projects and to increase coordination.[9] A recent study of fifty MNCs suggest that more technology intensive MNCs exercise more central control on R & D activities in the subsidiaries and less easily let these subsidiaries engage in new product development efforts, ten in line with the expectation that massive R & D commitments would be made centrally.[10]

Difficulties of technology transfer

Though technology transfers among subsidiaries of the same MNC are easier than between independent parties, they still involve considerable costs and efforts. First, the transferring subsidiary may not be interested, fearing it will create an internal competitor. Second, the managerial structure for the exchange of technology may not be in place.

These three difficulties—dispersion of activities, fragmentation forces requested by the diversity among markets, and obstacles to technology transfer between subsidiaries—have to be overcome for the management of technology to be effective. We can now revert to our examples of high-technology nationally responsive MNCs, ITT and BBC, and describe how they have addressed these difficulties.

Two Examples: ITT and BBC

ITT

ITT had achieved a relatively informal process of coordination of product development and technology transfers among its European telecommunication equipment affiliates at least for routine developments, if not for major efforts as the "1240" switching system. An ITT-Europe Technical Department in Brussels (subdivided into a series of product-line services for main exchanges switches, transmissions, business systems and PABXs, and station equipment) was in charge of coordination. Its director reported to the R & D and engineering services of the worldwide telecommunication equipment group at corporate headquarters in New York. Each product-line service interfaced with the chief engineers of ITT's subsidiaries in Europe, but had no direct authority over them. A simplified sketch of the organization is presented in Fig. 8.1.

The actual influence of ITT Europe's technical department varied between product lines. PABX were more centrally managed than main exchanges, for instance. As reported in Chapter 4, ITT's subsidiaries often produced somewhat different versions of similar equipments. This often enabled ITT to select the best features from each variant and to improve their overall design over time. It also provided new ITT customers with a choice of equipment offering slightly different specifications and interface characteristics.

This process balanced conflicting demands: it provided for the diversity of products needed to serve differentiated markets and yet avoided major duplications. It protected the technical proficiency of the subsidiaries

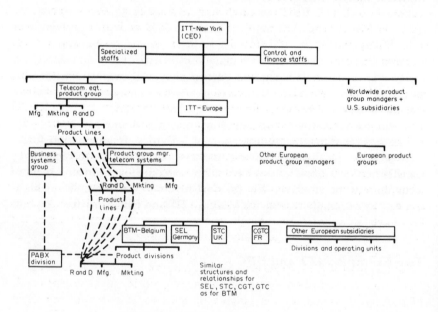

Fig. 8.1.   Simplified sketch of ITT structure
Source: Compiled by author.

without resulting in unduly large technical staffs. Projects could be shared between the subsidiaries, major programs such as the development of electronic switching systems drew on personnel from most subsidiaries. Yet, coordinating the various tasks, particularly since the switching system selected for development stemmed from U.S.-based research was difficult and costly.

Intersubsidiary cooperation sometimes remained difficult, however. When large potential export sales or license fees are involved, subsidiaries may be reluctant to share their knowhow. Product specifications were not always circulated among subsidiaries and each kept "black books" of minor modifications introduced on the shop floor that never found their way into official equipment descriptions, and were not passed on to sister companies.[11] Consideration had been given to carrying out all electronic switching R & D in the United States, but action never followed. ITT executives, however, felt that some duplication of R & D efforts was inescapable, given the demands for national technology put forward by various PTTs.

BBC

Coordination of R & D at Brown Boveri was carried out by business and product teams. BBC had always been a technical leader in the European electrical equipment industry and its success remained partly based on technical excellence. BBC's research activities had originally been concentrated in Switzerland, but more balanced R & D activities evolved over time among the major affiliates. In addition to the Swiss laboratories, research was carried out in Germany and in France.

One affiliate assumed leadership for each domain of applied research. In most cases such leadership resulted from history rather than from deliberate specialization. Germany, for instance, had become the technological lead house for nuclear energy, Switzerland for turbines and alternators, and France for electrical motors.

Adaptations of specific technologies or modifications to products were made for its own needs by each affiliate in national development centers. Though the core competence to develop a technology clearly belonged to one affiliate only, others could also gain some depth of knowledge through the adaptations they made. Adaptation of new products or processes for market introduction was generally carried out simultaneously in several national companies.

Financing of R & D was decentralized. The company using the technology, product or process under development paid its development costs. When several companies were involved, costs were shared among them according to agreed-upon estimates negotiated by an intersubsidiary research committee. In all cases the national affiliate initiating the project remained responsible for the appropriation of funds, not corporate management or other beneficiary affiliates. An affiliate could not proceed on its own with a new development project, however. It had to present to the appropriate business team a proposal outlining the expected results of the project, a schedule, and an expense budget. Approval by the business team was required for the project to proceed. Team members considered the potential of a project for their own subsidiaries in approving a project.

The negotiation, review and approval process by the business teams, as well as their subsequent reviews of ongoing programs, also provided support for, and consensus on, the sharing of costs. Corporate managers also hoped such a process would keep "creeping diversification" in check and limit R & D duplications.

Still the R & D coordination process did not draw unreserved praise from BBC's top executives, one of whom commented:

> In some business development coordination works well, in others not so well. There are some systems for which the specifications are rather obscure, and a "business team" has a hard time judging the development and understanding the motivation behind it. Unless the companies get directly into negotiations and agree not to oppose each other, it may be difficult to disentangle conflicts on who should develop what. Conflicts are moved upstairs, where they become more difficult to resolve. In rapidly evolving domains the "business team" response is too slow. Five or six months may elapse before a decision and you are not going to hold off a research team for that long, so development just goes on.[12]

Conclusion

National responsiveness seems hardly compatible with the tight central management of R & D, yet some R & D integration remains necessary. Both BBC and ITT were able to achieve some integration through some form of participative centralization: by and large, subsidiaries remained centers of initiative for new technology, but also cooperated to avoid duplications and share work on major projects. Since each subsidiary also adapted equipment to the idiosyncracies of its national market, it maintained a broad base technological competence and satisfied customers' needs for differentiated products. Broad base subsidiary competency also facilitated the technology transfer process. Though in the perspective of pure economic efficiency this loose coordination of R & D was probably not optimal, it constituted a workable compromise between economics and imperatives. Another key area for intersubsidiary coordination was that of exports: there, however, the economic and political imperative more closely coincided than in the management of technology.

Exports Coordination

Export Coordination as a Source of Competitive Advantage

Nationally responsive MNCs manufacture comparable products in several countries. By letting technological, financial and political considerations decide from which subsidiary to bid for a contract or to serve an export market the nationally responsive MNC can offer a better choice to customers than integrated MNC and national companies whose equipment is available from one national source only.[13]

Coordinating Exports

The difficulty of coordinating exports varies mainly with the frequency of separate export contracts and the nature of the selling task. When export contracts are large, few, and far between, *ad hoc* informal allocation of bids may suffice. When contracts are more frequent, the allocation and coordination process may need to be formalized. When the selling task is extensive and requires the development of long-term links with many customers or distributors, a permanent allocation of export markets to individual subsidiaries may be required.

Informal allocation of export bids

With few large export contracts, and relatively little product diversity, ITT's major European subsidiaries could coordinate their exports informally. In their frequent meetings the subsidiary managing directors regularly discussed the allocation of responsibility to negotiate with potential export customers. Since ITT did not maintain an extensive network of overseas offices, allocation could remain flexible. At the initial stages of contract negotiations, ITT Europe's staff or the managing directors of the major subsidiaries could direct potential customers toward one subsidiary or another. Customers could also evaluate the equipment of several subsidiaries. When interest firmed up, responsibilities for detailed negotiations, proposal preparation and contract implementation were allocated to one of the subsidiaries.

Formal coordination of export activities

When export contracts become more numerous, products more diverse, and local selling task more permanent, informal *ad hoc* allocation is no longer sufficient. With the exception of a few businesses—e.g., turbogenerators—for which informal coordination could work, BBC had to resort to a more formal process.

The choice of which major affiliate to select as a supplier was not left to sales subsidiaries or external agents. Corporate marketing staffs coordinated BBC's export efforts and drafted an annual export budget for each major affiliate. The budget tried to reconcile order forecasts received from the sales subsidiaries with export expectations submitted by the major national affiliates as a result of their own capacity and load planning. A coordinated tendering program was developed as a basis for the affiliates' final export budgets. These proposed budgets were circulated and discussed in a Marketing Committee until agreement was reached. This committee regrouped the heads of the three major corporate marketing departments (heavy equipment, complex systems, light equipment), the heads of marketing staffs in each of the major affiliates, and corporate executives overseeing sales subsidiaries and smaller manufacturing subsidiaries. Once approved, budgets provided a basis for corporate marketing staffs to allocate customer inquiries to the various affiliates. A corporate marketing manager commented on the process:

First, we avoid duplications. We then consider available capacity, if any choice is left by external conditions. We seldom, almost never, have complaints made about individual allocations of inquiries. This reflects the fact that each company is well aware of the importance and complexity of our task. Our key role has been recognized largely because we are able to promote the overall business very successfully. We always try to improve, find what should be done, look for information, work closely with everyone.[14]

Over the years, Brown Boveri's exports had grown steadily, despite the revaluation of the currencies of countries from which it exported. In the 1975–76 recession, in particular, BBC had more than offset the decline of its home markets through much higher export volumes. This growth in exports provided corporate marketing managers with some influence over the national affiliates. One of the marketing managers commented:

Because we coordinate export orders, we have some control. Affiliates know how important it is to be on good terms with us. It is not that we are higher than any profit centre in the organization or that we run the show all by ourselves. We are at the crossroad, a policeman of business traffic, and it is only the authority given to us by the managing committees that enables us to do the job.[15]

Once responsibility for a contract had been allocated to an affiliate, it became responsible for its successful implementation. It could subcontract part of the contract to other BBC companies, but was under no obligation to do so.

Permanent allocation of export markets

Coordination of exports becomes more difficult when contracts are small and numerous and when success implies the development of extensive distribution channels within the importing country. *Ad hoc* allocation or central coordination becomes difficult. One possibility is to use permanent allocations of export markets among the exporting subsidiaries. For industrial products at BBC, France could have first pick on all exports to Poland, and Germany to Turkey, for instance. Technical and financial factors can be reviewed periodically instead of contract by contract, and cultural and political affinities are taken into account once for all. This provides the exporting subsidiary with a long-term incentive to serve the market well and develop permanent sales and service networks.

There is clearly a trade-off between the advantages of maintaining the flexibility of allocation and the need to set up permanent export distribution channels. Unless the subsidiaries enjoy a clear long-term priority in serving one market or another, their managers may be reluctant to commit the necessary resources and time to cultivate the market. A "free for all" approach in which the subsidiaries compete against each other—the situation at BBC prior to 1970 and sometimes still the situation at ITT— has numerous drawbacks. Most serious were the ability for customers to lead subsidiaries to compete on prices and the danger of aggravating customers by numerous uncoordinated subsidiary approaches. When contracts are large in numbers but small in unit amount and when a permanent local sales and service field force is needed, a clear allocation of export markets among affiliates thus provides the most effective solution.

The three coordination approaches also lead to quite different extents of headquarters control over the subsidiaries: whereas *ad hoc* contract allocation by the subsidiary heads themselves or permanent market allocations leave little room for headquarters influence, more formal but flexible allocation confers them great power. There is no question, for instance, that the BBC's headquarters marketing staff executives gained much power over affiliates through their ability to offset faltering domestic markets with large export gains. The growing reliance of affiliates on exports for a sizeable part of their revenues, and their dependence on flexible central allocation, led them to closer cooperation. Permanent allocation of markets, however, removes a key leverage point from headquarters control.

Transfer of Knowledge and Skills

The transfer of knowledge and skills can be ensured in several ways. Nationally responsive MNCs usually have at least "product teams", where the managers responsible for a particular product in each subsidiary get together periodically to exchange information. Such "teams" can be headed, or coordinated, by a headquarters specialist, or several such executives. BBC, for example, used marketing coordinators to head the teams. Product teams were exchanging information in market, manufacturing technology, product applications, quality and reliability, new designs and so forth.

Many companies also have extensive corporate service staffs that can provide advice to national subsidiaries in such areas as plant engineering and process layout, marketing and merchandising techniques, administrative procedures and data processing, among others. Their services may be imposed by headquarters—e.g., all new plant investment proposals need to be reviewed by manufacturing—or merely made available to the subsidiaries whose management may or may not use the service.

Improved technologies for rapid communications also allows the building of control data bases, or engineering services, that can be accessed by the various subsidiaries. Nationally responsive subsidiaries which supply systems often tap into central engineering and design services. The same is true for custom-made products requiring extensive engineering.

Decentralized Strategy and Headquarters Control

Despite central influence in a few domains such as resource allocation, management of technology, and export coordination, nationally responsive approval of the divisional plans and budgets within each subsidiary clearly was the key stage in the planning process. The composition of the Corporate Managing Committee acknowledged the autonomy of the subsidiaries: it was composed of five geographic executives and of the president. Geneen's personal involvement notwithstanding, the strategy of ITT's subsidiaries remained primarily responsive to local conditions. In the telecommunication equipment business at least, intersubsidiary coordination remained largely informal and was entrusted to subsidiary heads rather than corporate or regional management.

The Pitfalls of a Decentralized Strategy

Such lack of headquarters control may lead to serious problems, despite its obvious congruence with short-term national responsiveness. First, possibly relevant alternate strategic views were ignored. Corporate levels could hardly develop perspectives different from those embedded in the geographic structure. Comments by a senior executive in a food company illustrate these difficulties:

Allegedly there are product strategies for Europe which give a basic line of direction. But each of these is largely an aggregation of individual country strategies, and it is not specific enough to provide the background for making tradeoffs between countries or products. Another problem is lack of facts, or data, to consider business from a global perspective. Corporate finance staffs put together the numbers but the quality and comparability of the underlying data are still debated.[16]

Given market diversity, political imperatives, the difficulties of making data really comparable between countries, and the relative small size and weakness of headquarters or regional staffs in nationally responsive MNCs, managers tend to ignore opportunities for coordination and partial integration.

Second, tacit coalitions between national subsidiaries and local parties further reinforce national concerns. Subsidiary managers see their future as dependent on these coalitions, not on the maintenance of international competitiveness. When the two conflict, political imperatives are given priority.

Third, the goals of the subsidiaries and that of headquarters may differ. A subsidiary may diversify away from areas of its parent's competence, driven by local competitive conditions. An example is provided by the German affiliate of Brown Boveri, BBC-Mannheim, which in the 1950s and 60s diversified on its own into a wide range of high technology growth industries. BBC-Manheim often matched Siemens' own diversification moves, for instance into computers (where BBC-Manheim acquired the independent German firm Zuse), electronic components, and nuclear reactors. Such diversification may have been a legitimate way to compete with Siemens, but it did not much capitalize on BBC's strengths as a multinational.

In some cases headquarters executives may fear that such diversification is guided by the local managing director's desire for autonomy. When the French aluminium company Pechiney hired a former conglomerate executive to head its U.S. acquisition, Howmet, Pechiney executives found it hard to decide whether Howmet's diversification was driven by competitive demands or personal ambition.[17] In doubt, they fired Howmet's manager. Subsidiary executives may also strive for quick growth, at the expense of profits, whereas headquarters demand profits.[18]

Finally, and most critically, lack of headquarters control makes the emergence of a new strategy in response to changing industry conditions extremely difficult. Let us take an example: one food company whose subsidiaries had been extremely autonomous attempted to exercise more selectivity in its allocation of resources. The company enjoyed a leading market share in major business and was quite profitable. The issue thus was not resource scarcity, but the lack of large investment opportunities with good profit potential. Top management had set up various worldwide business boards where the five key executives for a business (usually the United States and four overseas regional heads) met to develop new strategies. It was decided that new product ideas and new business opportunities would be submitted to these business boards. The boards would collect all pertinent information needed for a thorough understanding of each business and for a determination of the long-term implications for the whole company. After a period of several years the results were disappointing. Some new businesses had been developed by one subsidiary or another, but these innovations had almost never moved from one country to another. Coordinated resource commitments to the same business in several countries were not made. A manager summarized the issues in the following way:

Traditionally our strength comes from the diversity and flexibility provided by local subsidiary autonomy. We have mature products and markets, and not that much in the technology pipeline. The boards do work to try to look ahead, but they have no grip on the organization. The corporate people have the illusion of power: they believe that once they put something on paper it is understood and followed. Many businesses would in fact require more central effort: technology has to be acquired or developed centrally and trade-offs between risky investments should also be made centrally. The business boards are opposed by regional and national managers, who see them as a threat; their task is not defined with clarity, the power of the top is not behind them, commitment is lacking.[19]

We have discussed Brown Boveri's similar difficulties with the business and product teams. These difficulties made it impossible for BBC to shift to a strategy of integration in businesses where this was needed, such as for small motors. In the late 1960s severe price competition from Eastern European and Eastern suppliers eroded the profitability of BBC's small motor business. Even though motor production was quite sensitive to economies of scale and experience, several of BBC's European affiliates each manufactured a full line of motors in small volumes. Corporate staff prepared a rationalization plan in 1971; it was quickly approved by the Corporate Managing Committee. Five years later, in 1977, the plan was only partially implemented. Lack of sufficient headquarters control had put the plan into jeopardy, and the predominance of national perspectives was strong enough to prevent its implementation. Subsidiary managers feared any step toward integration would compromise their relation with large public sector customers who provided their prime markets. As we discussed already, the formal administrative systems all sustained a purely national perspective.

The difficulty BBC and the food company faced is common to all nationally responsive MNCs: how to influence the subsidiary managers and limit their autonomy without appearing to threaten their power. In some cases this can be achieved informally, e.g., between ITT's telecommunication equipment companies. The relationship between the subsidiaries and their national PTT customers may be close enough to instill confidence in their managers *simultaneously* to manage strong relationships with both national customers and multinational headquarters.

Central Management Overlay

Some companies, however, were not content with decentralized strategies and weak headquarters. They wanted to develop a central strategic management capacity and, to preserve the dominance of geographic subunits. A typical approach, then, was to overlay a product-function corporate group on the geographic structure, and give it some power.* Dow Chemical provides an example of such an approach.[20] After experimenting with various kinds of structures, Dow Chemical was organized by 1975 into five autonomous regional companies: Canada, Europe, Latin America, Pacific and United States.[21] Corporate headquarters did not total more than 250 employees. In order to establish priorities in resource allocation between areas, Dow had developed a Corporate Product Department (CPD).[22] One of the Corporate Product directors commented:

---

*The worldwide telecommunication product group in New York and European staffs in Brussels assumed such a role in ITT, but had little clout over the heads of the major national subsidiaries.

Part of my job is to go around and help the areas develop profitable projects in plastics, and in general the Department's assignment has been to do that—to build product business around the world and to do it profitably. We do this by suggestion and salesmanship, backed up by agreed-upon product strategies, but never by fiat. We've always worked closely with the directors of business development in the areas toward a strategic consensus.[23]

Product teams* had been set up between product managers of the different regional companies and the relevant CPD members. According to CPD's management, three elements contributed to the success of the product teams:

(a) The companywide economic evaluation system makes alternatives explicit, visible and understandable and allows managers from different units to co-operate in joint economic studies.

(b) The integration of the functions' needs and contribution around the product supports worldwide product management.

(c) The reward system does not stress profits in a particular area, but the overall results of Dow. The performance of individuals is evaluated, and discussed and rewarded against specific missions, not local profits.[24]

The CPD's role was not to second guess the areas, but to make sure that their investment analyses and strategy studies were done objectively. A set of check and balance mechanisms provided such objective assessments of area plans. A senior CPD commented:

The central group has all information collected on alternatives, ratios, spendings, methods, and much information on the specific situation and its experts in economics; marketing or technology can raise questions and challenge the numbers. Simply by being there we create the need for objective studies.[25]

Each CPD director was in charge of the long-term success of his business worldwide; he was not, however, a profit center for his product group. His direct influence on the areas came from his control over capital appropriation programs: each CPD director had to approve all resource allocation requests for his business together with the presidents of areas where investments were to be made. Direct access to the company's president also yielded informal influence. Corporate services also coordinated technology development and transfers among areas. Technological intelligence in company experience and assistance to plant start-up were coordinated centrally.[26]

The CPD was supported by reward systems based on Dow's overall performance, rather than of individual subunits, and by a culture of open communication.[27]

Another key role of headquarters management in the nationally respon-

---

*As in Brown Boveri & Cie, there were two levels of teams: product teams with a range of products, e.g., styrofoam, where specific product marketing strategies were worked out, and business teams, e.g., plastics where overall business strategies are formulated.

sive MNC is to provide cultural norms, organization beliefs and behavioral standards. At Dow, top management inspired the open communication culture. In the food company studied in detail, the chief executive had a tighter more withdrawn style than corporate executives at Dow. Even though the substance of subsidiary strategies is but little influenced by corporate management, the power of symbols, beliefs and norms in holding the nationally responsive MNC together may be considerable. Dow, for instance, had developed the "International Business Principle" to promote good relationships with host governments, and had expressed support for the OECD guidelines for international investments and multinational enterprises.

At Dow, too, strong corporate identification with the CPD provided for power to coordinate the areas. Dow's President confirmed the role of the CPD:

> All the areas have to participate with you in coordinating Dow strategies. You must help to stimulate our people in the various areas to drive for continued growth in sales and profit by keeping them informed of what we have to contribute, even though the strategies for individual area growth must be left to the areas. We want you to serve, where necessary, as catalysts in starting new business action and in helping to communicate good and practical ideas. Dow will continue to pioneer in new geographical areas and you should assist effectively in this endeavour.[28]

Indeed, Dow's CPD, or Brown Boveri's corporate marketing department, were effective because the geographic manager could see their usefulness. Beyond coordinating the strategies of the various areas along product lines, the CPD was useful in (1) allocating products in short supply between the areas, (2) maintaining price consistency among the areas, (3) balancing excess capacity, and (4) serving as a clearing house for technical, financial and competition knowledge and knowhow. Similarly, the key role of BB's corporate marketing managers was well recognized by the major exporting affiliates. These managers helped the affiliates increase their export volumes and adjust their use of their capacity. At the same time they could provide a worldwide product perspective without removing the strategy making responsibility from the field nor getting directly involved in subsidiary operations.

The Need for Central Guidance

Overlay structures such as Dow's CPD do not imply that the firm moves away from autonomous national responsiveness and toward integration. The national responsiveness perspective may well remain dominant, but it is submitted to constant challenge by headquarters executives whose jobs are defined in a worldwide product focus.

When these headquarters executives can make substantial contribution to the national subsidiaries or regional operating units they acquire influence. Their contribution is based on the potential pay-offs of central coordination. In the case of the food company, with mature nationally differentiated markets, there were few opportunities for central coordination to bring substantial advantages. By contrast, at BBC, ITT and Dow, the advantages of central coordination were very significant. Market evolutions at BBC and ITT further increased the importance of central coordination. As European countries increasingly developed national champions, and as developing countries expanded their telecommunications and electricity distribution networks rapidly, export markets came to represent a much larger share of total sales at ITT and BBC. As the technologies evolved more rapidly, subsidiaries also became increasingly dependent on coordinated R & D and technology transfers. Corporate staff's power increased with this growing dependence of subsidiaries. At Dow, overcapacity and free trade put stronger economic pressure on host regions and forced their managers to turn to headquarters to improve the efficiency of operations.

One can thus consider the nationally responsive MNC as a self-regulating system: the affiliates turn to the headquarters when they need them, and away from them when they do not. Yet, even though the need for their services varies over time, headquarters staffs remain able (1) to develop an alternative perspective on the company business to that of national subsidiary managers, and (2) to act as a clearing house for specialized knowledge. Central analytic capability and some basis for headquarters control may be precious when a strategic shift becomes needed. They can quickly contribute to the strategic reorientation of certain business away from national responsiveness. At Brown Boveri, for instance, the corporate marketing staffs provided the nucleus for an emerging worldwide product management role. Dow's CPD directors could play the same role almost overnight, should the need to coordinate and integrate the operations of the areas appear. Without such a nucleus, a strategic reorientation away from national responsiveness may be extremely difficult to implement. Even though there may be no pressing need for central guidance, maintaining a corporate capability for such guidance may be needed.

Conclusion

Nationally responsive MNCs face a three-way trade-off between (1) the national orientation of subsidiaries, (2) the effectiveness of intersubsidiary coordination, and (3) the complexity of central management's tasks. The trade-off is difficult because it rests on a paradox: subsidiaries must be responsive, but in order to be competitive with larger national champions they also need to draw on corporate or sister companies' competencies. Developing an ability to pool competencies without unduly constraining the strategic autonomy of the subsidiaries is a difficult administrative task. Administrative procedures alone will not do it; it is also a matter of creating a climate and a set of incentives conducive to the sharing of knowledge within the organization. Central allocation of strategic resources is even more difficult. A number of nationally responsive MNCs just ignore the issue, and require that each subsidiary stand on its own feet. This is hardly satisfactory in strategic terms, but generally simplifies top management's tasks. Others develop corporate services to coordinate and monitor the deployment of funds. A notable example is Dow. Their problem is the converse of that of integrated MNCs: to maintain a worldwide product-oriented perspective in a company dominated by varied national priorities.

Some companies, concerned with the difficulties of developing consistent business strategies among a collection of nationally responsive subsidiaries, go one major step further; strategy, instead of being primarily the result of subsidiary decisions, becomes the outcome of a negotiation process between headquarters and subsidiaries. In some cases independent national strategies emerge, in some others worldwide strategies. In prior chapters we referred to these strategies as multifocal: part subsidiaries, part headquarters. In the following chapter we explore the managerial process through which these ambiguous strategies are defined and implemented.

References

1. This is a key premise of Hymer's work. In order to overcome the inherent disadvantage of lack of familiarity with foreign environments and foreign markets a firm investing abroad ought to have some unique capabilities, for instance superior technology when each national market is closed. The larger body of empirical data subsequently gathered by the Harvard Multinational Enterprise project supports this proposition. See S. H. Hymer, *The International Operations of the National Firm* (Cambridge, Mass.: MIT Press, 1976), based on the author's 1960 Ph.D. dissertation.
2. For a detailed description of Brown Boveri's structure and management processes, see Y. Doz, *Government Control and Multinational Strategic Management* (New York: Praeger, 1979), pp. 183–208.
3. See M. Y. Yoshino and A. Mahini, *International Telephone and Telegraph*, Harvard Business School case study, available from the Intercollegiate Case Clearing House (ICCCH no. g–380–045).
4. See "Nestlé at Home, Abroad", in *Harvard Business Review*, November–December 1976, pp. 80–88. Quoted from Mr. Pierre Liotard-Vogt, formerly administration délégué of Nestlé.
5. Some of their difficulties are presented in greater detail in Y. Doz, *Brown Boveri & Cie*, Harvard Business School case study, available from the Intercollegiate Case Clearing House (HBSCS no. 4–378–115).
6. G. P. Dyas, "ITT: Strategy and Structure, an Overview" (mimeo, INSEAD), 1979.
7. For a summary critical review of the available literature, see Richard S. Rosenbloom, "Technological Innovation in Firms and Industries: An Assessment of the State of the Art", in P. Kelly and M. Kranzberg (eds.), *Technological Innovation: A Critical Review of Current Knowledge* (San Francisco: San Francisco Press, 1978). For analyses of the role of multinational enterprises, J. E. Parker, *The Economics of Innovation: The National and Multinational Enterprises in Technological Change* (London: Longman, 1974) and E. Mansfield, "Technology and Technological Change", in J. H. Dunning (ed.), *Economic Analysis and Multinational Enterprises* (London: Allen and Unwin, 1974), pp. 147–183.

See also Alan Kantrow, "The Strategy-Technology Connection", in *Harvard Business Review* (July–August 1980), pp.6–21.

8. See Thomas Allen, *Managing the Flow of Technology* (Cambridge, Mass.: MIT Press, 1978).
9. Lowell W. Steele, *Innovation in Big Business* (New York, NY.: Elsevier, 1975).
10. J. N. Behrman and W. A. Fischer, *Overseas R&D Activities of Transnational Corporations* (Cambridge, Mass: Oelgeschlager, Gunn and Hain, 1980).
11. See J. N. Behrman and H. W. Wallender, *Transfer of Manufacturing Technology within Multinational Enterprises* (Cambridge, Mass.: Ballinger, 1976), pp. 138–148.
12. Personal communication to the author, quoted from *Government Control and Multinational Strategic Management* (supra), pp. 198–199.
13. For a description of a land-mark case, The Fruehauf Trailer Export Contract to China, see J. N. Behrman, *National Interest and the Multinational Enterprise* (Englewood Cliffs: Prentice-Hall, 1970)
14. Personal communication to the author.
15. Ibid.
16. Personal communication to the author. For a study of the food industry providing supporting evidence, see C. A. Bartlett, "Multinational Structural Evolution," unpublished doctoral dissertation, Harvard Business School, 1979.
17. See D. Zumino, *Pechiney (A) and (B)*, mimeographed cases from Centre d'Enseignment Supérieur des Affaires, Jouy-en-Josas, France, 1971.
18. For an example, see Pierre Liotard-Vogt, "Nestlé at Home, Abroad", in *Harvard Business Review* (supra), p. 84.
19. Personal communication to the author.
20. For background data on Dow Chemical's international structure, see R. Vernon and McKern, *The Dow Chemical Company: Organizing Multinationally*, Harvard Business School case study, available from the Intercollegiate Case Clearing House (ICCH no.9-371-419). See also S. Davis, "Trends in Multinational Organization", in *Columbia Journal of World Business*, Summer 1976.
21. Dow Chemical Company, *Annual Report* (1976), p. 3.
22. Ibid., p. 4.
23. Personal communication to the author.
24. Personal communication to the author.
25. Personal communication to the author.
26. Dow Chemical Company, *Annual Report* (1976), p. 5.
27. Ibid.
28. Ibid.

9

*Managing a Multifocal Strategy**

A multifocal strategy is intrinsically ambiguous: it forsakes the clarity of national responsiveness and multinational integration strategies in an attempt to trade-off their costs and benefits flexibly from decision to decision. The essence of a multifocal strategy is to offer something for everyone. It sometimes exploits opportunities for integration, sometimes leaves complete autonomy to the subsidiaries. The firm is willing to maintain significant production and R & D facilities in each market it serves, and enters into technology, production, or marketing agreements with local firms to satisfy national demands or best fit local conditions. On the other hand, it will integrate operations wherever feasible, and standardize products and processes among subsidiaries. Integration or responsiveness considerations eventually prevail for any decision, but in no systematic way, set *a priori*.

Integration or responsiveness strategies both orient the management structure of the firm in one or another dominant direction, not so in multifocal strategies: responsiveness and integration needs are weighted one against the other separately for each decision with no *a priori* assumption of dominance of one over the other. Firms follow a multifocal strategy only when responsiveness and integration are *both* comparably important and when, therefore, choices are ambiguous. A key organizational capability, therefore, is to shift the locus and logics of decision from a national concern to a global view, and vice versa, from decision to decision.

The Issues and the Tasks

More so than strategies of responsiveness or integration, a multifocal strategy calls for a complex strategic process that spans the whole firm, involving functional, product and geographic executives. Whereas the decision process is relatively centralized at headquarters in integration strategies—where the issue is to ensure effective inputs from subsidiary

---

*The contributions of C. A. Bartlett and C. K. Prahalad in helping the author clarify the ideas expressed in this chapter are dutifully acknowledged.

managers—and decentralized in national responsiveness strategies—where the issue is to ensure effective headquarter coordination of selected tasks—a multifocal strategy creates ambiguity in the decision making process, and forces it to span multiple levels and loci of influence within the firm.

As I have discussed already, there is no single vantage point, within the firm, from which to consider all needs. Needs for responsiveness typically enter the MNC via subsidiary managers, whereas needs for integration are usually more acutely perceived by headquarters executives. Closeness to market conditions and host country governments, as well as awareness to the importance of success at the local level, make subsidiary managers sensitive to needs for responsiveness. Such managers also constitute a national conduit for the expression of responsiveness needs by local officials who may meet with local subsidiary managers more frequently and more informally than with foreign corporate managers. Conversely, perceiving needs for integration usually required a multicountry view of a business, of its markets, technologies and competitors. Such a view, as well as the specialized resources (e.g., manufacturing technology staff or strategic marketing groups) needed to nurture it, are more likely to stem from headquarters than from individual national subsidiaries catering mostly to their own domestic markets. In sum, perceptions of needs for responsiveness and perceptions of needs for integration are likely to come from different parts of the organization in distant geographical locations.

These perceptions need to be confronted, integrated, and fused to reach decisions that consider in detail both responsiveness and integration needs on an *ad hoc* basis, and reflect the merits of each position as they apply to the specific decision at hand. Except for relatively simple businesses, where key decisions are few and far between, and where top management keeps a detailed understanding of the business, the difficulties of centralized decision making lead top management to seek to delegate decision making directly to the managers involved: subsidiary managers abroad and product executives at headquarters.[1] Delegating decision making without structuring its processes and rules would not work, however. The inherent tension in choosing between responsiveness and integration might lead to decisions outcomes more influenced by the personality and leadership abilities of executives, by the key resources they control directly or by the extent of uncertainty (or discretion) they represent (or can exercise) toward other parts of the organization, than by the intrinsic contribution of such outcomes towards the success of the firm.[2] Left to their own devices, for instance, subsidiary managers are likely to follow inappropriate personal strategies. Some with strong roots in their country may try to shield their subsidiary from headquarters influence and to protect their autonomy jealously. To this end, they may voice an exclusive concern for responsiveness and use incomplete or biased data to fend off any headquarter intervention. Since they often use data the accuracy of which can hardly be checked at headquarters—such as information obtained in a private lunch with a senior host government official—they can gain considerable room for manoeuvre. Conversely, a more ambitious less rooted subsidiary manager. may favor integration and bid for a leading role in it, ultimately propelling him to regional or worldwide business responsibility when such integration may not be justified. Both defense of subsidiary autonomy and integration drive often constitute unwarranted choices. Similarly, headquarter executives may be tempted to organize a self-serving integration effort, based on more or less accurate "hard" data (e.g., anticipated cost reduction) that subsidiary managers find difficult to counter given the "soft" nature of their data (e.g., country sentiments or possible loss of market share induced by a shift to standardized world products). Trade-offs between head-quarter executives' priorities for integration and subsidiary managers' concerns for responsiveness therefore need to be actively managed and balanced, if flexibility between responsiveness and integration is to be preserved.

To provide such flexibility in reaching *ad hoc* trade-offs, a multifocal strategy puts to question usual views of organization structure. The common view, as depicted in the multinational management literature, is architectural: in a search for the "right" structure, worldwide product line structures are adopted for integration, and geographic structures for national responsiveness.[3] I have shown, in the preceding two chapters, that even for clear strategies of integration and responsiveness, the issue of representing a view opposite to the dominant logic already exists. Confronting conflicting views is even more important for multifocal strategies where the outcomes may differ from decision to decision with little predictability. Neither a "product" nor a "geographic" structure would do, since no dominant view is set *a priori*. A multifocal strategy does not specify, either, a set of tasks and a clear pattern of interdependencies among subunits. It, therefore, leaves the relative criticality (and the relative power) of various executives unspecified, and variable from decision to decision. The textbook answer—equal power to contending executives in a matrix structure—would, should it work, lead to paralysis: no movement results from two equal and opposite forces. Equal power is not workable in practice anyway, and matrix structures, therefore, become unstable, unless they are actively managed.[4]

The interaction between the outcome of strategic decisions and the relative power of headquarter and subsidiary executives further complicates the management of a multifocal strategy. "Who is right" is also "who is powerful"; strategic choices and power within the organization are intertwined. Strategy here is not the consistent and harmonious determination of purposes and goals, the choice of agreed-upon courses of action, and the design and management of an organizational structure to implement the determined courses of action. It is, instead, a fragile, partial, constantly challenged temporary reconciliation of different points of view embedded in the interests of major organizational subunits and supported by powerful managers. Problems are likely to be faced as they occur, with little anticipation, no consistent plan to solve them, and little consistency in how successive problems are solved. Consequences of choices are seldom fully explored, lest they make differences in the perceptions and priorities of managers too explicit and, thus, choice more difficult.

Despite the above difficulties, constant tension between executives defending national responsiveness and executives supporting multinational integration is required to provide the basis for an advocacy process which transposes within the firm contradictions found in its environment. Variety in perceptions and adaptability is a condition for the successful adaptation of the firm to an intrinsically contradictory environment.[5] Yet this compromises the consistency of strategic choices over time. To achieve consistency in resource allocation, top management has to develop the means by which to support selectively one group or another for each individual decision and build consensus (or a dominant coalition) around key decisions. Projects may need to be approved, even though they do not draw consensus. In some cases subsidiary managers prevail, in some others worldwide product executives do. Full balance and power symmetry between the subsidiary managers (who favor responsiveness) and the product executives (who favor integration) would lead to paralysis. For each decision, power and responsibility cannot be equally shared between executives who support integration and executives who favor responsiveness. For some decisions, such as the development of new products, a global orientation may have to prevail, for some others, such as the location of new investments, a national one may be needed. Top management, therefore, has to provide flexible and selective asymmetry between multinational integration and national responsiveness.

Any choice will not please all managers; some may win, others may lose, on immediate decisions. Top management, therefore, is confronted with two more tasks: to alleviate the consequences of adverse choices on the losers, so they will consent to decisions that go against their position and not sabotage their implementation, and to modify the allocation of power, so that decisions will, indeed, be implemented.

In sum, managing a multifocal strategy involves three related top management tasks:

1. *Ensuring that relevant data are brought to bear on key decisions.* Such data are gathered, organized and analyzed, from their own perspective, by the various managers who participate in the decision process. Each of them, based on his/her own experience, background, and the information available to him/her over time, develops a cognitive map of the business. Cognitive maps in use clearly differ between head-

quarter and subsidiary managers, and also, between executives from different functions, different cultures and diverse experiences. Such cognitive variety is useful to improve the quality of the decisions by bringing together different sources of data and rubbing one against another different interpretative schemes. The diversely gathered and comprehended data they possess must be brought to key decisions to ensure all aspects are considered.

2. *Creating the conditions for a consensus among managers on key strategic decisions.* A process must exist to reduce the cognitive variety from the inputs into the decision to its outcome, and to build legitimacy to and consensus for that outcome. This implies providing both the channels and the incentives for the managers involved to cooperate rather than fight or ignore each other.

3. *Managing relative power among managers.* For the decisions to be actually implemented, i.e., for resources to be allocated accordingly and for commitments to be made, the power balance among executives involved in implementation has to correspond to the thrust of the decision. Short of such power alignment, the decision may be reached intellectually but little or no action will follow in practice.

Concretely, top management can undertake a whole range of actions to improve the above processes. Top management can structure the information channels and data available to subsidiary managers and to headquarter product executives, and differentiate them so they support strongly different orientations. Beyond providing the appropriate data, top management may also provide measurement criteria that orient managers in one direction or another. Obvious arrangements are to give profit and loss responsibility both to subsidiaries and to headquarter product managers and let them negotiate. More complex schemes may be developed, with differentiated measurement yardsticks. Widely different perspectives may develop within the firm. Three managers for the same businesss unit, for instance, viewed their business quite differently in a major European MNC:

Headquarter product division manager

In order to survive we have to be united and break through national barriers in terms of finance, marketing and technology. Consequently, we need rigorously controlled central product policy, no manufacturing duplications, and a very clear set of manufacturing policies. We want to leave very little influence to governments. The small size of national markets and the pressures of new technology will mean that a national approach cannot ever be justified; we will always have a need for strictly centralized management and strong operational interdependencies.

Subsidiary manager
The markets and national industry situations in Europe are not sufficiently homogeneous to reach similar Europe-wide solutions. The fragmentation of markets and industry creates problems. We need to create a council of the subsidiary managers and see where we can cooperate. Now it is a unilateral relationship with central headquarters, with the center pulling the strings.

Corporate manager
Our industry is considered by the governments of several countries as an activity of the highest strategic importance. In turn, our subsidiary managers are influenced by the feelings of their host government officials. This is reinforced by the financial incentives thrown in by the governments. We are thus facing a number of managerial restrictions, both internally, and in our relationship with the environment. We cannot really avoid duplication and replications. Yet, two-thirds of the industry are competitive; this creates a difficult dilemma.

Such cognitive differences are healthy, and should not be suppressed; they do reflect the intrinsic difficulty of trade-offs between responsiveness and integration in the firm's competitive posture, given the nature of the industry.

The central assumption of this approach is that superior solutions will indeed be discovered when managers with different expertise and orientation get together to thrash out their differences on a common problem. Strategic decision making is, therefore, seen as the process of finding a solution eventually acceptable to all key managers involved. Such plurality of perspectives implies the belief by top management that strategy formulation can be a process of identifying a feasible course of action which incorporates the concerns, desires and goals of all key actors who are affected by the decision.

Despite the learning implied in confronting different orientations, and the flexibility in adapting to diverse situations, the recognition of sharply different cognitive and strategic orientations makes maintaining consistency in resource allocation difficult. Too much flexibility in adaptation leads the strategy to dissolve itself into a series of uncoordinated reactive incremental adjustments. Too much clarity and consistency diminish the benefits of a multifocal approach. Therefore, top management wants the various cognitive orientations to be expressed strongly and represented credibly so that no subgroup is allowed to become a permanent coalition whose views regularly carry the day.

Successfully managing the convergence process from cognitive variety to strategic consensus is difficult. The task is not to suppress certain views, but to transcend the various views into a consistent decision process. Here, too, various tools can be used by top management. Structuring committees and task forces, multiplying meetings, working on attendance, actively participating in these meetings, and making agreements and commitments explicit are ways for top management to foster convergence toward common choices. Rewards systems based on contribution to total results rather than local results can be useful. So is the acceptance of slack. Slack can take several forms, from the classic inventories that decouple operationally product divisions and subsidiaries, to specific accounting or measurement adjustments. At General Motors, for instance, the various brands could give "area allowances" to subsidiaries to carry out measures requested by the brands that would negatively affect the performance of subsidiaries. For accounting and measurement purposes these "allowances" compensated subsidiaries for the cost (actual and/or opportunity cost) of carrying out the action requested by the brands.

In most complex MNCs, regularity in the resolution of certain issues involves the blending of administrative mechanism. For instance, planning, budgeting, measurement, and evaluation processes are coordinated to create a consistent administrative context and to provide channels for airing conflicts. Arenas for conflict resolution can also be provided, such as intersubsidiary committees, functional committees (e.g., product planning and development), administrative committees (e.g., investment evaluation) and special working parties and task forces. The selective use of administrative mechanisms enables top management to shape the cognitive orientation of individual managers, to make sure that managers most aware of certain types of risks (e.g., technological risks vs political risks) are given a stronger say in decisions where these risks are significant, and to give one or another strategic direction the upper hand in certain classes of decisions. For new product specification, for instance, worldwide product-oriented executives may have a decisive say, but subsidiary managers may enjoy veto power over integration and reallocation of manufacturing activities.

All the approaches mentioned above share the same objective: to maintain cognitive diversity while narrowing the multiplicity of strategic options by providing for their in-depth review. Yet consensus on choices does not necessarily develop; superior solutions are not always found. In these circumstances top management must resolve conflicts directly, lest conflicts escalate close to top management and stay unresolved. Therefore, top management has to retain the capability to make substantive choices at least on an exception basis.

Top management must also retain a capability to shift power selectively among managers within the firm. Selective power asymmetry guarantees against strategic paralysis. Middle managers, who prepare recommendations on decisions and investment proposals, must know that these may be approved without drawing full consensus. Projects, plans and budgets that fully satisfy both groups of executives are likely to be too few to provide a basis for long-term competitiveness. Commitments cannot be limited to what suits both sides. For some commitments power to allocate resources cannot be shared equally.

The task of top management thus becomes that of selectively creating asymmetry in the power to commit the resources of the company to specific projects. In some cases top managers agree with product executives, and commit resources in a strategic framework of worldwide integration. For other decisions top managers support subsidiary managers against head-quarters product managers, and commit resources in a perspective of national responsiveness.

Power asymmetry is also, to a large extent, regulated by the nature of uncertainties and dependencies faced by the firm. A manager's power is based on his ability to absorb uncertainty—and transmit it—from key external contingencies. Worldwide product managers may welcome the absorption by subsidiary managers of national uncertainties. Conversely, subsidiary managers may gladly defer to product executives to decrease technological uncertainties. The relationship between power and uncertainty absorption or control also contributes to set limits to asymmetry. If a product or a subsidiary executive goes too far, the multifocal management process loses effectiveness: opportunities for integration and rationalization are needlessly missed, or acceptance by host countries compromised. Managers who supported the excessive asymmetry lose face and jeopardize their power.

This puts checks on the quest for power. For instance, subsidiary managers will gain more power on decisions for which the political imperatives are most important sources of uncertainty. Reciprocally, product executives gain most power on decisions for which economic uncertainties are most critical. The process is self-adjusting: if the host government demands decrease in overall importance, product executives gain power across the board, and interdependencies are likely to increase. These interdependencies, in turn, provide a stronger basis for central control. Conversely, if political imperatives become more critical, subsidiary managers acquire power and interdependencies are likely to loosen.

Despite such self-regulation, top management must retain the capability to reallocate power, be it only because self-regulation projects today's contingencies into the making of decision affecting the future and therefore wrongly assumes the stability of these contingencies over time. Asymmetry in power must reflect future directions and forecasts of critical needs for responsiveness and integration, not today's conditions.

Top management can affect the relative power of managers in several different ways. Careful and selective career development and promotion decisions are a most obvious approach, so are other rewards and sanctions. Less obvious is to de-emphasize the importance of individual power to key managers, by decoupling prestige and recognition from current power or by developing loyalties to the corporation which transcend individual power. Building checks and balances into the decision processes constitute another way to regulate power and ensure that all perspectives are duly considered.

In summary, the strategic management tasks called for by a multifocal strategy are complex. They involve sustaining several alternate cognitive perspectives on the business and the key strategic choices that affect it, fostering a consensus (or at least a dominant coalition) on key choices, and creating selective power asymmetry to ensure the implementation of key decisions. These imply constant top management attention to the quality of decision processes, and cannot be assigned to a formal structure or to a dominant set of executives.

The next section details the tools and mechanism for top management structuring of these decision processes.

Leverage Points for Top Management

In this section I review quickly the main top management mechanisms in use within MNCs which pursue multifocal strategies, and present their use. Their mechanisms constitute a repertoire of action tools for top managers to sustain cognitive variety, develop strategic convergence and manage power asymmetry. They fall within three broad categories: managing data, managing managers and structuring conflict resolution processes (Table 9.1).

TABLE 9.1   *A Typical Repertoire of Administrative Mechanisms to Carry Out the Top Management Tasks Demanded by Multifocal Strategy*

1.   Developing and appointing managers
 ● Choice of key managers
 ● Career paths
 ● Reward systems
 ● Patterns of socialization
 ● Management development programs

2.   *Providing and analyzing data*
 ● Information systems
 ● Measurement systems
 ● Resource allocation procedures
 ● Strategic planning
 ● Budgeting

3.   *Resolving conflicts*
 ● Decision responsibility assignments
 ● Integrators
 ● Business teams
 ● Coordination committees
 ● Task forces
 ● Issue resolution processes

These mechanisms are not of equal value in carrying out all three sets of tasks, and some assist more in one task or another, according to how they are being used. Information systems, for instance, can have multiple impacts. By supplying more or less varied information, and presenting it in more or less differentiated ways, they can increase or limit cognitive variety within the organization. According to how they are set, they may also make one or another strategic alternative look better or worse against a particular set of data, thereby affecting strategic convergence. Finally, since selective access information often provides power within an organization, how information systems structure access to data within the organization also affect power. A first concern of top management, therefore, is to consider which task can be best supported by which set of mechanisms and to blend the mix of available mechanisms to the tasks to be performed. Too many mechanisms used to manage power, without power balance shifts being rooted in good data and well-considered strategic choices, could both be mistaken in substance and undermine top management's legitimacy. Conversely, too great a concentration of mechanisms towards data could yield superb analysis but little capacity for implementation.

A second concern of great importance for top managers is the strength of the mechanism and its symbolic value as perceived by middle managers. An intersubsidiary coordination committee, for instance, is of little *a priori* significance: so much depends on how it is used, and a skillful top manager may vary the use of such a committee almost from meeting to meeting with the issues at hand. Such a committee may also be dissolved on short notice, without major difficulties. In contrast, replacing a highly respected senior executive in charge of worldwide product line coordination is a stronger and more portentous move: it cannot be reversed easily without losing face, flexibility may not be very high and the symbolic value of such a change is considerable. Even more significant are patterns of career paths; they take years to shape and longer to be modified. The costs of mistakes may be extremely high: wastage of managerial talents, power struggles, resignation and high emotional and personal costs to the managers involved. Senior executive appointments and implicit or explicit career paths directly affect the perceived power relationships and are extremely strong mechanisms. Other mechanisms, such as strategic planning procedures, may not have the same strength as the mechanism described above, but may contribute to make mechanism legitimate by selectively focusing the cognitive orientations or by fostering an awareness of selected strategic opportunities or difficulties whilst leaving other issues unchanged.

Several other top management concerns may bear upon the selection and use of one mechanism or another. These are:

—*Directionality*: Does using the mechanism imply supporting a specific orientation or merely improving the capability to confront different orientations?

TABLE 9.2 Attributes of Selected Administrative Mechanisms

Mechanisms	Dimension most influenced	Strength of signal and symbolic value	Directionality	Selectivity	Continuity	Time horizon	Need for top management ongoing support
Managers' management							
1. Choice of key manager	Power	Strong	Set	Low	High	Medium	Medium
2. Career paths	Power	Strong	Set	Low	High	Long	High
3. Rewards and punishment	Power, Strategic	Strong	Modulated	Low	Medium	Medium	High
4. Management development	Cognitive	Modulated	Modulated	High	Medium	Short to Medium	Low
5. Patterns of socialization	Cognitive	Low	Implicit	Low	High	Long	High
Data management							
1. Information systems	Cognitive (Strategic, Power)	Modulated	Modulated	High	Low	Medium	Low
2. Measurement							
Business performance	Cognitive	Medium	Modulated	Medium	Medium	Variable to long	Low
Managers' performance	Power	High	Modulated	Medium	Medium		
3. Capital appropriation							
Content	Strategic	Low	Modulated	Low	Low	Short	Low
Impetus	Power	High	Modulated	Low	High	Long	Medium
Approval	Authority	High	Modulated	High	Low	Long	High
4. Strategic planning	Strategic	Variable	Clear	Low	High	Long	Medium
5. Budgeting process	Authority	High	Clear	Low	Low	Short	Low
Conflict resolution							
1. Decision responsibility assignment	Authority	High	Modulated by decision class	Low	Medium	Medium	High
2. Integrators	Cognitive	Low	Clear	High	Low	Short, Medium	High
3. Business teams	Cognitive	Low	Clear	Low	Medium	Short, Medium	High
4. Coordination committees	Cognitive	Low	Unclear	High	Low	Short, Medium	High
5. Task forces	Strategic (A), (P)	Variable according to composition	Modulated	High	VARY WITH COMPOSITION	Short, Medium	High
6. Contention process	Strategic (P), (A)	Variable	None	High	Low	Short, Medium	High

—*Selectivity*: Can the mechanism be used selectively to support different orientations for various categories of decisions?

—*Continuity*: What are the costs (emotional and personal, in terms of broken commitments, lost face or diminished power or authority as well as organization) of discontinuing or shunting its use?

—*Time horizon*: How quickly does the mechanism yield results?

—*Channel for top management intervention*: Can top management use the mechanism to intervene personally and directly in the decision made?

—*Needed top management support*: Does the mechanism require substantial top management personal involvement and direct explicit support?

Space considerations preclude a detailed analysis of each mechanism here. A summary list of mechanisms, with their main characteristics, is provided in Table 9.2. It can be used as a quick guide to critical characteristics of important tools. A discussion of the blending of tools toward building a multifocal organization is provided below.

Using Tools Toward a Multifocal Organization

In this section I review how three groups of management tools can be used to build a multifocal organization. The first group of tools, *data management tools*, provide the infrastructure for the multifocal organization. Information is critical to all three tasks. By providing alternate ways of aggregating business data, for example, they support multiple perspectives on the same business. MNCs following multifocal strategies should have *information systems* that aggregate and disaggregate accounting data both by product or business worldwide and by country, and also separate financial performance (influenced by outside conditions) from actual operating performance. The contribution of individual subunits, and the accounting consequences of decisions affecting them, can, therefore, be examined from multiple perspectives. General Motors, for instance, developed such accounting practices in the late 1970s, allowing consideration of investment or production planning decisions both within the context of one single country and within that of the worldwide manufacturing network. Information systems also affect power, in particular insofar as they provide data asymmetry. LM Ericsson, for example, used "area managers" who received detailed data both from foreign subsidiaries and domestic divisions. Divisions had no detailed data on foreign subsidiaries' performance and vice versa; area managers had an information (and power) advantage in arbitrating decisions affecting both types of units.

Information systems can also be made to broaden or narrow cognitive variety selectively. They may provide data in a single narrow perspective for agreed-upon strategies and support multiple vantage points for issues on which no position has been taken yet.

The planning process also constitutes a strong mechanism. It may be used to encourage the recognition of interdependencies among units of the company. To implement a multifocal strategy, planning cannot be of the "single future" all-encompassing traditional variety. On the contrary, it must help identify critical contingencies, and establish agreed-upon scenario and program contingent strategic responses so that a repertoire of response modes to different types of difficulties is built into the organization. Again, top management can use planning to vary the relevant cognitive and strategic scope perceived by intermediate level executives and to build consensus around key options. Active top management involvement, preselling to key managers, extensive interaction among planners from the various units, negotiations around key interdependencies, are all part of the planning process for a multifocal strategy. Planning, here, does not seek maximization but preserves a wide range of implementation options and ensures they could be pursued with the least difficulty by members of the organization.

Measurement systems can similarly be broad or narrow. They may clearly define job boundaries (the old authority = responsibility concept) or, on the contrary, by extending beyond a manager's immediate authority, force interaction and active communication among managers with overlapping responsibilities. Measurement systems can also narrowly focus management attention on very specific aspects of a business or nurture cognitive variety. Multifocal strategies tend to call for broad measurement systems, based on the performance of tasks, and on contribution to the whole, rather than narrowly on immediate self-generated results.

Resource allocation procedures affect multiple tasks. They affect power directly (obviously through the purse strings) and who is included in resource allocation processes in what capacity therefore becomes a clear signal of relative power. If a central technology group must approve all proposals from the national subsidiaries, plant investment proposals are likely to reflect technological standards set by that group. Corporate marketing staff groups may exercise a comparable influence. The process of resource allocation, therefore, can be set to act on relative power between contending groups of managers.

Defining the content of proposals may also be used to sustain a multifocal orientation. A plant investment program may have to consider alternate sourcing possibilities from other subsidiaries and assess the costs and benefits of world-scale plants compared to proposed national plants. The demands placed on the content of resource allocation requests affect both cognitive variety and strategic convergence, according to how they are structured.

Multiple checks and balances may be introduced in the allocation process, as well as escalation mechanisms toward top management arbitration of conflicts. An excessive concern for consensus in resource allocation, however, may lead to paralysis, with very few decisions drawing the required consensus. Corporate approval may be rooted in peer groups' approval, for instance through a worldwide product team regrouping all executives involved with a product. Whether such check and balance approach results in paralysis or spirited entrepreneurship depends largely on individual managers' motives and interests. Managers' management mechanisms are, therefore, critical. *Managers' management tools* are several. Foremost, and most closely watched, is the *selection of key executives*. Selection can be used to change relative power between product and country executives. Some individuals are more enterprising, more strong-willed, or more skilfull at using a power base, or at eliciting personal loyalties and commitments than others. Other things being equal, such individuals are likely to create power asymmetry in their favor. In contrast, other senior managers may have more judicial or administrative traits. By putting entrepreneurs in charge of product divisions at headquarters or in charge of regional units, and by putting administrators in charge of national subsidiaries, it is possible to encourage integration.[6]

The reverse would be true by moving forceful executives to subsidiary management positions. Alternation of key managers between the two types of position strongly encourages a multifocal orientation. Executives may professionally disagree on a choice, but have enough personal empathy to understand each others' position and transcend their differences in the search of a solution. Careful balancing of power via executive selection usually receives considerable top management attention. Top managers often see it as their most critical task. It is a constant exercise in dynamic disequilibrium, since asymmetry in power must be kept within bounds. Too aggressive product group managers might grab absolute power and move too far toward integration. Conversely, too strong subsidiary managers may lead to fragmentation. In other words, asymmetry in personality must be sought, but prevented from leading to domination. Further, since key managerial appointments can usually be rescinded only at extreme personal costs, they leave little room for mistakes. Finally, top management's attention and involvement may be needed not only in selecting appointees, but also in the latter phase of settling interpersonal relationships and modulating asymmetry.

Career paths, though less immediately visible than key appointments, have a very significant cumulative effect. Multi-country career paths were used to support worldwide integration strategies, whereas national career paths made worldwide strategies more difficult.[7] Alternating headquarters and subsidiary positions makes middle managers attuned to both integration and national responsiveness. GTE's international communication group drew its worldwide product group managers from its area organizations so they did not lose touch with regional concerns and priorities.[8] Furthermore, by appointing former key area executives to worldwide product group managers, GTE's top management was sending a complex signal: successful managers moved from area to product responsibilities, but product responsibilities were not given to managers who had no extensive area experience. This message was expected to assist top management in the difficult balancing between integration and responsiveness. Patterns in career paths also have to take into account the nationality of managers. LM Ericsson managed a difficult blend of career paths.[9] Swedes with a long experience at corporate headquarters were sent to manage foreign subsidiaries, or to hold key control positions in them. These were usually long-term assignments, and these expatriate managers were expected to develop an in-depth understanding of the national subsidiary environment, and to defend responsiveness. Their concern for responsiveness, however, was balanced within each subsidiary, by operating managers on short-term detachment from the domestic product division. Such managers moved quickly from country to country or back and forth between division headquarters and subsidiaries. Subsidiary managers had little power over these mobile managers. One subsidiary manager commented:

A division manager is sent to me to head switching operations here. Back in Sweden, he was pretty close to his division's boss. This man will see his future in switching, not in my country. I tell him, "You no longer have any master in the switching head office, you do not serve the switching division to Stockholm, but the subsidiary here." The man is likely to think, "I do my best and he will help me, if he is influential in Stockholm." . . . Unless someone develops a strong liking for the local country, it is difficult to get a high degree of loyalty.[10]

Local nationals also held significant positions in most national subsidiaries, and offered a perspective contrary to that of headquarter managers on detachment to the subsidiary. Corporate executives were directors of the various subsidiaries, and the subsidiary boards took an active role in management. Finally, area functional managers played a key role in the interface between divisions and subsidiaries.

One of them commented:

I help the local managing directors; they can call on me whenever they are concerned with a matter about which they are not too sure themselves. I get involved in a whole spectrum of questions, from late deliveries to the overall strategic coordination for one continent!

To the division, you represent the fellow in the field, and vice versa. You have to lead them to compromise. To make decisions come out in way we think best for the whole company, and acceptable for both of them! People know that if they disagree with me, they may have to present a strong argument.

In a sense it is power without formal authority. Of course, if I am wrong too often my power decreases, so I move only when I am sure of myself. Sometimes you have to give more support to the local weak company than to the big tough division, but the key to success is to remain neutral, to behave as a broker. The situation is balanced enough for that.

It's a game where there can be no winner, but where some competition between managers is built into the system. A manager out in the field cannot pull all the strings himself nor can a division have local "agents" within a subsidiary.[11]

Different national origins and different career patterns between the four major categories of managers involved in subsidiary management (long-

term stable expatriates, mobile operating managers on short-term detachment from domestic division, local nationals in the subsidiaries, and
corporate executives with area management or directorship responsibilities) contributed critically to LM Ericsson's ability to maintain a multifocal
strategy successfully and yet to take full advantage of the opportunities for
integration provided by the technological leadership we described in
Chapter 4.

The above descriptions of GTE and LM Ericsson suggest the importance of career paths. In many multinationals the management of careers has
become one of the tasks to which top management devoted most attention
and a key mechanism in the management process.

In common with key appointment and career paths, *reward and punishment systems* are strong visible mechanisms; yet they leave some room for
flexible use. In all the companies which used multifocal strategies, however, reward and punishment systems were multidimensional and informal. They supported different orientations and often maintained ambiguity in their criteria, some fuzziness in their use, and flexibility in
handling individual situations, but personal reward was not impersonally
tied to performance.

By providing arenas for informal convergence of group perceptions, or
leaving subsidiary managers isolated in their own environment, *patterns of
socialization among executives* affect principally cognitive variety. Many
multinationals organize large meetings and seminars during which the
common beliefs and myths of the organization are reasserted and reinforced and new strategic directions communicated. Other companies hold
many meetings in part to foster a sense of common identity and to allow
informal expressions of disagreements. Patterns of socialization among
executives may play a significant role in decreasing the need for tight
formal means of administrative control. *Management development* also can
be used to affect perceptions by managers and facilitate their acceptance of
the intrinsic ambiguity of multifocal strategies.

Beyond setting and using data management and manager's management
mechanisms, top management can also *structure decision processes and
intervene directly into them*. First, given the intrinsic ambiguity of multifocal strategies, top management may want to compensate with a strong
corporate identity the lack of clear constant operational goals. Managers'
management mechanisms can contribute to identity building. Further
contribution can be made directly via *top management use of time*: internal
events, speeches, plant, lab or sales branch tours, the articulation of
principles and values, all contribute to creating loyalty toward the corporation beyond particular goals. Extensive socialization, travel, foreign
assignments, also develop informal networks of communication within the
firm and provide alternate decision channels that can support (or substitute
for) formal decision processes and procedures.

Yet these are no full substitute for decision clarity. Shared responsibility in joint decision making involving multiple perspectives does not imply fuzziness in input and vagueness in task assignments. Several of the companies studied had developed fairly elaborate ways of *assigning decision responsibilities*. They ranged from short documents to elaborate decision responsibility grids. Such assignments formalized the decision process and ensured that various categories of decisions were handled appropriately. Individual managers' influence in specific decisions ran from "major" or "veto power" to "technical advice" or to checks on specialized aspects. In many companies, such assignments become the primary structure.[12] The formal hierarchical structure was either a rather indeterminate matrix (e.g., Philips) or its importance was played down by top management (e.g., LM Ericsson). Decision responsibility assignments can be much more selective than a formal structure or provide different directions to specific subclasses of decisions. For instance, a telecommunications equipment company could make decisions to submit bids to new foreign customers with a strong product/technology focus and close headquarter control, whereas decisions to submit bids to long-time customers are made by subsidiaries with little headquarters control.

Overreliance on these decisions assignments can be dangerous. In order to be effective, decision responsibility assignments need a lot of knowledge about what the relevant factors for the various decisions are. Thus, they may only suit repetitive, almost routine, decisions (such as submitting bids to customers). Since each manager is likely to be involved in a large number of different decisions, these assignments may provide a way to facilitate selective asymmetry by specifying the nature of their involvement in each decision separately.

Between the broad development of a corporate identity and the narrow definition of decision responsibilities, most multifocal companies adopt intermediate means of coordination: specific individuals in "integrator" jobs, business fears and various coordination committees.

Almost all companies used *integrators* to coordinate product lines, functional specialists, or specific programs among subsidiaries. Results were often mixed. Coordinators fostered strategic convergence among operating managers, but were also feared as potential key managers. Since they often lacked the personal leadership, the relevant experience, the power, or sufficient top management support, they usually confined themselves to a role of intermediary. Simply as conduits for information, and as feedback to top management, integrators can be useful. The personal costs to them may be relatively high, however, as their position is often frustrating.

Business teams. The experience of the companies studied suggests they provide useful arenas for exchanging information and sharing ideas, but little more, unless used skilfully in conjunction with a wide range of other mechanisms. Managers from the various subsidiaries defend their own interest, unless motivated to cooperate by a wide range of other mechanisms. Yet they constitute a flexible tool and a means to get operating managers involved in the subtlety of multifocal strategies.

Intersubsidiary coordination committees share many of the characteristics of business teams, but top management can usually determine their composition more flexibly. Both the business teams and the coordination committees require high levels of management involvement to go beyond the role of information exchange forums. Unless the interests of the various subsidiaries are all served by cooperation (a possible but likely occurrence), coordination committees or business teams cannot be expected to take initiative for cooperation. The very weakness of these mechanisms confers them some advantages, however: their use remains flexible, they can be reversed, or dissolved, they create no necessary assumptions of long-term change, and their symbolic value is low. They provide, however, to top management an arena for trial balloons. Their very weakness makes coordination committees a good place where to test new ideas. Top management may thus identify the origin of possible resistance, and attempt to influence early reactions and the making of commitments for or against specific decisions.

Task forces exhibit some of the same weaknesses as intersubsidiary business teams or coordination committees. Yet, being temporary in nature, not tied in their composition to any particular subgroup of managers, they offer greater flexibility to top management. They can be made weak or strong, directive or exploratory, their conclusions may be easily reserved or represent great legitimacy, their symbolic value and their visibility may be made to vary. Among all the managerial control mechanisms, they provide most scope for selective use and for direct top management guidance. In simple situations, as we discussed in an earlier section, they can provide the primary means for top management intervention. Careful selection of the members, and influence in the definition of the issues to be addressed and the acceptability of potential recommendations, are the means used by the top management to steer task forces.

Finally, specific contention procedures and corporate arbitration bodies may exist, so that conflicts and tensions are actively tackled rather than smoothed over.

The series of tools described above can be carefully blended to structure a management process that balances concern for responsiveness and concern for integration and yet is selective enough to create asymmetry in specific decisions and push them toward responsiveness or integration as is most appropriate. Yet top management tasks remain extremely complex. Mechanisms are not similar, nor interchangeable. Some mechanisms require relatively little ongoing top management involvement, but they imply great care in their design and the initiation of their use—information

systems for example. Some mechanisms are powerful, but almost impossible to reverse or discontinue without high personal costs and a loss of face
and power to the firm's top management—key executive appointments for
instance. Not all mechanisms described above may be available to the top
management of any particular company. Some mechanisms may be so
critical to the corporation unity as to be "taboo", no single manager has the
power to change them. In some cases a particular mechanism may be a
central part of a common corporate ideology or culture dating back to the
company's founders. In some other cases a mechanism may be the outcome
of prior power conflicts or bargains among senior managers, and represent
the cornerstone of internal stability. Changing the mechanism would
reopen old wounds, revive conflicts and break a power equilibrium.

Conclusion

So far I have argued that managing an effective multifocal strategy
requires that tensions in the firm's environment be incorporated in its
decision processes and that individual managers—at headquarters and
subsidiaries—hold strongly differentiated views and engage in a well-
supported advocacy process in the making of key decisions. To succeed,
top management needs to abandon the usual architectural view of management structures and consider key tasks and issues. Top management must
make sure that the requisite level of variety is incorporated in decision-
making processes to match the external variety. This implies that data are
considered from multiple points of view and perspectives; and that
cognitive variety is actively maintained in decision processes. Yet to avoid
strategic fragmentation and disjointed decisions, a process of convergence
from diverse views to common choices must be carried out for each
decision. Strategic convergence, however, must not drive out cognitive
variety, a difficult exercise in pattern building that top management often
needs to lead actively. Top management must also ensure that, as individual decisions are made with integration or responsiveness as a priority,
one view does not become so predominant, overall, as to drive the other
out. It must, therefore, maintain an overall balance between responsiveness
and integration forces and yet encourage, or create, selective asymmetry in
decision processes. This is a dynamic process in so far as asymmetry ought
not to reflect today's power structure (based on today's contingencies and
uncertainties) but a future desired outcome. The role of top management, if
the firm is to have any strategy at all, is necessarily proactive. The active
management of relative power among middle level executives is, therefore,
a key task of top management.

The experience of MNCs suggests the blending of an array of management tools to manage cognitive variety, strategic convergence and relative
power. These tools have been briefly described above; their use remains a

difficult craft. The particular historical heritage of each firm, as well as the personality of its key executives, make their use highly situational. Conditions that allow a multifocal strategy are not always present in a firm or in a management team, the possibility to build a stable multifocal organization cannot be taken for granted; nor can its building follow the same consequence from company to company. In all cases a multifocal strategy has some specific costs. The organization and the management process it requires are intrinsically more complex and more fragile than those required by other strategies.

References

1. For a description and analysis of a relatively simple situation, see Y. Doz, *Government Control and Multinational Strategic Management* (New York: Praeger, 1979), chapter 9.
2. This is implicit in the behavioral theory of the firm; see James G. March and Richard F. Cyert, *A Behavioral Theory of the Firm* (Englewood Cliffs, N.J.: Prentice Hall, 1963). It is developed in Eric Rhenmann, *Organization Theory for Long Range Planning* (New York: Wiley, 1973) and Michel Crozier and Erhard Friedberg, *L'Acteur et le Système* (Paris: Le Seuil, 1976). For some empirical evidence, see Stephen Allen III, "Understanding Reorganisations of Divisional Companies", in *Academy of Management Journal* December 1979, pp. 641–671.
3. See, for a summary, J. M. Stopford and L. T. Wells, *Managing the Multinational Enterprise* (New York: Basic Books, 1972).
4. See C. K. Prahalad, "Strategic Choices in Diversified Multinationals", in *Harvard Business Review*, September–October 1976, pp. 67–77. See also S. Davis and P. Lawrence, *Matrix* (Reading, Mass: Addison Wesley, 1977), chapter 8.
5. See C. K. Prahalad and Y. Doz, "Strategic Management of Diversified Multinational Corporations", in A. Negandhi (ed.), *Functioning of the Multinational Corporation* (New York: Pergamon Press, 1980), pp. 77–116.
6. See Anders Edstron and Jay R. Galbraith, "Transfer of Managers as a Coordination and Control Strategy in Multinational Organisations", in *Administrative Science Quarterly*, June 1977, Vol. 22, pp. 248–263, and A. Edstrom and J. R. Galbraith, "Alternative Policies for International Transfers of Managers", in *Management International Review*, 1977, Vol. 17, pp. 11–22.
7. Ibid.
8. See "General Telephone and Electronics International" (Harvard Business School Case Study, distributed by HBSCS, No. 2–379–061).
9. See Y. Doz, *Government Control* . . ., op. cit., chapter 9.
10. Personal communication to the author.
11. Ibid.
12. For an example see "Corning Glass Works International" (B1 and B2) (Harvard Business School Case Studies, distributed by HBSCS No. 0–381–161 and No. 0–381–162).

10

Conclusion: Strategic Control and the Future of Multinational Companies

We have argued that the success of multinational companies was based on a mix of substantive and management skills, and that both were needed. Management skills become more critical over time. Early success was based on specialized, often technical, substantive skills applied subsidiary by subsidiary as the MNC invested into more and more countries, or transferred new products, or applied new processes in existing subsidiaries. Substantive skills, embodied in new products and processes, sophisticated marketing methods and shrewd financial management, drove the expansion of MNCs. These skills allowed innovation, product differentiation, large-scale, low-cost production and mass distribution; the basis for the development of large firms, first on domestic markets, then abroad.[1] Overall management skills were not critical. Interdependencies among subsidiaries were minimal, and substantive skills could be depended upon to acquire a low cost or a differentiated position in each country separately.[2] As subsidiaries and products proliferate, the complexity of headquarter operations increases. Control over the subsidiaries has to be institutionalized through corporate staffs. General management skills, both within the subsidiaries and at headquarters, become more important.

The quickening of international competition demands fast responses on such issues as new product transfers to foreign subsidiaries. The lower cost of communications allows closer exchanges between subsidiaries and headquarters. Interdependencies among subsidiaries, within the MNC, are likely to increase and may reach the integration of major functions such as manufacturing or R & D. The growing competitive interdependence of competitive moves and countermoves in multiple geographic markets, and between product lines in a corporate product portfolio, also call for increasingly coordinated global strategies between the MNC subsidiaries. Global competition, even in the absence of operational integration across borders, calls for managerial capabilities unavailable in the traditional

234

MNC which merely transferred skills and, occasionally, products abroad. Successful responses to the economic imperatives thus call not only for substantive skills, but also for managerial skills.

Dealing with the political imperatives calls for an even higher order of managerial skills. Short of granting full autonomy to the subsidiaries, a balance constantly has to be found anew between opportunities for integration and demands for responsiveness. Governments are not only impediments to globalization and free deployment of resources, they are also often allies who create new bases for market segmentation and strategic differentiation. Exploiting to one's advantage the market imperfections maintained by government calls for complex analytical and negotiating skills. As governments become more sophisticated in handling MNCs, substantive skills alone are increasingly insufficient. As we have shown in Chapter 9, developing an appropriate and flexible balance is administratively very demanding. Managerial skills are essential.

The maturing of an industry over time further contributes to the erosion of the advantages to be gained from substantive skills. Host countries can procure these skills from more and more diverse sources, and this provides them with increasing bargaining power over MNCs. Decreasing MNC bargaining power, in turn, makes the political imperatives increasingly critical, and thus enhances the need for managerial skills.

The erosion of MNC bargaining power we described in the case of the telecommunication equipment industry also affects most MNCs whose subsidiaries are not integrated. As their operations develop, and as they mature, subsidiaries become increasingly self-sufficient. Their dependency upon corporate or product group headquarters decreases. As their industry matures, national companies may catch up with whatever technical lead the multinational company had, and the bargaining power of the MNC wanes. As a result, the subsidiaries have to become increasingly responsive to national conditions. This further contributes to weaker headquarters' control over subsidiaries. Eventually, as in the case of LM Ericsson in France, the subsidiary may be acquired by national interests or be forced to become a locally controlled joint venture.

MNC efforts to maintain technological leadership may sometimes stem such development, but seldom reverse it. Unless strong patent protection exists, control over technologies seldom can be kept for long. Government can turn to alternate forms of technology transfer. International contractors, national companies unconcerned by technology exports or smaller MNCs whose management welcomes alliances with national partners, may all be suitable alternatives to MNC direct investment.

The erosion of the distinctive nature of their substantive skills puts into question the long-term viability of MNCs. New technologies, however difficult they are to keep exclusive, often help multinationals by increasing the efficient size of manufacturing activities. Products and processes of a number of industries become so costly to develop and so complex to manufacture that only access to a number of national markets can provide the large sales volumes necessary to amortize initial development costs and to achieve low-cost production.

Multinational integration thus provides multinationals with a new competitive advantage in mature industries: low costs through large scale. As we discussed in Chapters 2 and 6, not all industries offer the same potential for integration, and the balance between needs for integration and demands for responsiveness varies in predictable ways with the structural characteristics of an industry.

Successful implementation of integration strategies, however, demands extensive managerial skills, as we discussed in Chapter 7. The inheritance of national responsiveness is likely to make integration difficult. Past commitments and existing power structures defend status quo, and are difficult to overcome.[3]

As industry maturity decreased the dependence of national subsidiaries on headquarters, subsidiaries became more difficult to influence. Since early in the development of the MNC the provisions by headquarters of substantive skills to subsidiaries was enough to control the subsidiaries, strong management mechanisms are not likely to have been developed. Entrepreneurial subsidiaries and headquarters, concerned with the quick exploitation of an innovation abroad, may also have evidenced little concern for, and devoted no time to, the development of effective administrative procedures. The typical European multinational "mother--daughter" structure, in which subsidiaries report directly and informally to the parent, reflects such a situation: a strategy of national responsiveness at the subsidiary level coupled with headquarters' supremacy in R & D, manufacturing methods, and marketing approaches makes refined administrative mechanisms unnecessary.

When the substantive dominance of headquarters over subsidiaries weakens, administrative mechanisms are not available when they become needed to implement an integration strategy, and the tradition of national responsiveness lingers on.

The managerial mechanisms described in Chapter 9 provide the means for a shift from headquarters control based on subsidiary dependency to strategic control based on the structuring of decision contexts within the firm. If these managerial mechanisms are developed early, before a pressing need for them develops, the nature of control merely shifts over time. If they are not developed, the substantive influence of headquarters is eroded, and the more difficult it becomes to regain control over subsidiaries.

Short of a deep crisis affecting all subsidiaries, subsidiary managers may not be able to agree on integration or to relinquish some of their power to headquarters staffs.

Multifocal strategies and strategic diversity among businesses demand even more exacting managerial skills. The various administrative mechanisms must be combined to create consistent decision contexts appropriate to each business and to manage interdependencies selectively.

The long-term success of a MNC thus usually involves the development of both substantive and managerial skills. Substantive skills are needed for the initial establishment of the MNC, managerial skills are needed for its continued success once the substantive superiority of headquarters weakens and success becomes based on effective coordination and integration of like activities in different subsidiaries. In fact, the outstandingly successful MNCs combine both. Their success was based on superior substantive skills, but they also developed over time a repertoire of management mechanisms that allows their top management to associate subsidiary managers to the definition of major strategies and to ensure the control of their implementation by the various subsidiaries. Examples of such companies are IBM and Texas Instruments among integrated MNCs and ITT among nationally responsive ones.

In companies such as IBM or TI, such mechanisms could be extremely effective because they were used within a relatively narrow range of diversity. Subsidiaries and businesses could be treated in the same way, and the company made a clear strategic choice not to engage in activities nor to be present in countries which would require a major departure from its dominant *modus operandi*.

As governments become increasingly active partners in the implementation of their industrial policies, and as mercantilism may replace free trade, the maintenance of strategy simplicity and administrative uniformity may be unacceptable to more and more countries which will want to impose their own terms on the MNCs. As the scope and variety of host government regulation and intervention increase, and as the forms of direct cooperation involve more complex arrangements, a greater variety will have to be tolerated by MNC managers.

Host governments' interventions also blunt the efficacy of managerial mechanisms. For instance, governments may increasingly constrain managerial appointments in subsidiaries, making the central management of career patterns within the MNC increasingly difficult. Patterns of integration may have to be adjusted to fit the mercantilistic policies of a number of host governments, and be renegotiated, from time to time, to fit shifting national priorities. Host government officials, or workers' representatives, may sit on subsidiary board and in subsidiary's planning meetings, making the central planning of an integrated network impossible. Such interventions represent a shift in host government policies from limiting the strategic freedom to attaching the strategic autonomy of MNCs. Host governments not only exclude certain outcomes of MNC decision-making processes, they also attempt to penetrate the decision process itself and influence decision contexts directly.

Strategic control can be preserved, but at a growing cost. It involves maintaining a costly, and always uncertain, technological leadership, and forsaking participation in countries whose governments would not tolerate MNC headquarters control on the local subsidiaries. In the telecommunication equipment industry, maintaining strategic control may involve concentrating sales and investments in developing countries which cannot seriously consider an autonomous national industry. In computers the protection of strategic control may involve concentrating resources on developed countries formally committed to free trade and forsaking market participation in countries such as Brazil, India or Nigeria, whose governments want to share control of the computer industry with MNCs. As we stressed in Chapter 4, the trade-off between market penetration and strategic control is also viewed differently by managers in different firms, according to their competitive posture. IBM's managers may oppose any loss of strategic control, Honeywell's managers may welcome a privileged access to the French market, even at some loss of strategic control.

Administrative complexity may contribute to maintaining strategic control, but again at a cost. The transition we described, from substantive skills to managerial mechanisms, as the basis for subsidiary control is a first major step toward administrative complexity. In the same way as industry maturity jeopardized control based on substantive skills, host government sophistication may, in turn, compromise the use of managerial skills as a basis for control. To some extent more and more complex and less formal administrative mechanisms, such as influence through acculturation, may maintain the basis for control. A use of mechanisms individually tailored to different countries and different businesses can also help, but at the cost of increasing the administrative diversity faced by top management in considering the firm's various activities. If these activities can be clearly separated, variety may not create problems. If, however, activities are closely related and interdependent, and still managed and controlled in different ways, the task of managing interdependencies among them may tax the capabilities of almost any corporate management.

Relinquishing strategic control and tolerating administrative diversity maximizes market penetration. But the long-term benefits to the MNC may be minimal: weak strategic control and high administrative variety may make the MNC a soft partner in dealing with government and a weak opponent in facing international competitors. Noninvestment, nonequity forms of foreign market participation, may in such cases be more attractive than straight direct investment. Between licensing turnkey contracts, management contracts, trading arrangements and quasi-integration approaches, a number of opportunities exist for firms to participate in international markets without investing and without having to keep full strategic control.

The research summarized in this book casts some light on the difficult choices outlined above; these choices are the most critical issues confronting MNC managers in the 1980s. The shift from control based on substantive skills to control based on administrative skills was the major challenge faced by MNCs in the 1970s; the administrative heterogeneity imposed by the diversity of government intervention may be that of the 1980s.

References

1. See S. H. Hymer, *The International Operations of National Firms* (Cambridge, Mass.: MIT Press, 1976). For empirical evidence on domestic firms see A. D. Chandler, Jr., *The Visible Hand* (Cambridge, Mass.: Harvard University Press, 1978), A. D. Chandler, Jr. and H. Daems (eds.), *Managerial Hierarchies* (Cambridge, Mass.: Harvard University Press, 1980). For empirical evidence on multinational firms see R. Vernon, *Sovereignty at Bay* (New York: Basic Books, 1971), and Mira Wilking, *The Emergence of Multinational Enterprise* (Cambridge, Mass.: Harvard University Press, 1971), and *The Making of Multinational Enterprises* (Cambridge, Mass.: Harvard University Press, 1974).
2. Low cost and differentiated positions in a market are usually sources of competitiveness and high profitability. For a summary analysis see M. E. Porter, *Competitive Strategy* (New York: The Free Press, 1980), chapter 3; see also for an empirical analysis W. K. Hall, "Strategies for Survival in a Hostile Environment", in *Harvard Business Review*, September–October 1980.
3. For an analysis of these difficulties see Y. L. Doz, "Managing Manufacturing Rationalization within Multinational Companies", in *Columbia Journal of World Business*, Fall 1978.

Index

Accounting, integration
    management   179–181
Algeria, ITT   106
American Motors, integration strategy   71
Australia, auto industry   80–81
AXE   103–105

Bargaining, integration strategy   40–41
Brazil
    auto industry   80
    technology transfer, telecommunications
        industry   114
Britain
    auto industry   82
    electronics industry, national policy   127
    host government policies   37–38, 41
    integration management, labor
        relations   176, 177
British Leyland, integration strategy   71
Brown Boveri
    exports co-ordination   204, 205
    national responsiveness strategy   46, 47,
        199–212
    peer control   196
    planning control   194
    R & D   201–202
    technology management   201–202

Career paths, multifocal
    organizations   227–228
Chrysler, bargaining power   157
CIT-Alcatel   94, 100, 101, 108, 111, 114,
    115
Club 4   71
Component manufacturers, electronics
    industry, government control   120
Communication, integration
    management   183–186
Conflict resolution, multifocal
    strategy   222–225
Consumer goods, product
    differentiation   22
Contention process (IBM)   185

Corporate culture, integration
    management   186
Corporate Product Development (CPD) see
    Dow Chemical
Cost of citizenship, integration
    management   39, 52

Data management, multifocal
    strategy   222–225
Decision responsibilities, multifocal
    organizations   230
Defense, electronics industry, government
    control   119–120
Distribution
    channels, strategy   24–25
    electronics industry, economic
        imperatives   122–123
Dow Chemical, centralized
    control   208–211

Employment, integration strategy   40
Executives, selection, multifocal
    organizations   227
Exports, telecommunications industry   96
Exports co-ordination, national
    responsiveness   45

Fiat
    economies of scale, production   61–63
    integration strategy   13–15
Ford
    accounting, integration
        management   179–180
    geographical expansion   73
    globalization   155–156
    host government policies   40–41
    integration strategy   13, 43, 67–69
    logistics management   169
    R & D Management   172
France
    auto industry   82–83
    electronics industry   132–134
    host government policies   37, 38, 41, 43,
        70

241

integration management, labor
    relations 176
technology transfer, telecommunications
    industry 114

General Motors
    Australia 81
    integration strategy 67–69, 72
    R & D Management 171, 172
Germany, West
    auto component suppliers 70
    electronics industry 131–132, 141–142

Heineken, product differentiation 23
High technology, government control 119
Holden (Australia) *see* General Motors
Honda
    government policies 37, 43
    integration 138
    national alliances 132–134
Host governments, strategic
    controls 237–239

IBM
    communication management 184–186
    contention process 185
    employment, integration strategy 40
    France, integration strategy 43
    integration 137–138
        control 181, 182
        management 175
    national responsiveness 142–143
    program plans 184
    R & D Management 171–172
    trade, integration strategy 40
    training, integration strategy 42
ICL, host government policies 37, 38,
    127, 131
Imports, competitive strategies, auto
    industry 58–60
Industrial relations, integration
    management 175–177
Industrial Vehicle Corporation *see* IVECO
Industry strategies, telecommunications
    industry 113
Industry structures
    electronics industry 150
    host government policies 49–52
    strategies 148–150
Information channels, multifocal
    strategy 222–225
INMOS 127
Innovations, electronics industry,
    government control 120–121
Integrators, multifocal organizations 230
International Computers Ltd. *see* ICL

ITT
    Algeria 106
    exports co-ordination 203, 205
    industry strategies 103
    integration, host government policies 38
    national responsiveness 108, 109,
        199–212
    peer control 196
    R & D 105, 107, 199–201
    strategic flexibility 105–107
    technology management 199–201
    top management 196–197
IVECO, integration strategy 13–15, 72

Japan
    auto industry
        flexibility strategies 75–77
        integration strategies 72
        national policy 77–80
        productivity 65
    electronics industry, government
        support 126, 127, 128–131
    host government policies 156–157
    motor-cycle industry, globalization 155

Klockner Humbolt Deutz, integration
    strategy 13–15
Korea, auto industry 79–80

LM Ericsson
    career paths 228
    industry strategy 93, 94
    R & D 105–107
    strategic flexibility 104–107
    technology transfer 114–115
Leasing, electronics industry, economic
    imperatives 123

Measurement systems, multifocal
    organizations 226
Monopolies *see* Natural monopolies
Motor-cycle industry 155

Natural monopolies, telecommunications
    industry 92

Organizational structure, multifocal
    strategy 215–222

Peugeot
    integration strategy 69–70
    government support 82–83
Philips, multifocal strategy 141–142
Planning process, multifocal
    organization 226
Power assymetry, multifocal
    strategy 219–222

Price competition, electronics industry 127–128
Product life cycle 30–31
Product transfers, integration strategies, auto industry 71
Production management, integration management 168–169
Program plans (IBM) 184
Protection
  auto industry 65–66, 79
  electronics industry 126–132

R & D
  electronics industry, economic imperatives 122
  integration strategy 41–42
  ITT 105–107
  LM Ericsson 105–106
  technology management 198–199
Renault
  geographical expansion 73–74
  integration strategies 71
  government support 82–83
Resource allocation, multifocal organizations 226

Siemens, government support 131–132
Socialization, multifocal organizations 229
Sony, globalization 154–155
Soviet Union, auto industry 79–80
Spain, auto industry 81
Subsidiaries
  management structures 178–182
  multifocal organizations 231
  national responsiveness 45

strategic control 235–236
Substantive skills, strategic control 234–237
Supply contracts, telecommunications industry 93
Sweden, national policy, telecommunications industry 110

Task forces, multifocal organizations 231
Taxes, differential, integration strategy 39
Technology control
  telecommunications industry 93–94, 101, 102
  see also High technology
Texas Instruments
  competitive strength 156–157
  integration 139–140
Thomson CSF, national responsiveness 46–47
Toyota, flexibility strategies 76
Trade balance, electronics industry, government control 121
Trades unions, integration management 175–177
Training, integration strategy 42

USA, national policy, telecommunications industry 110–111

Volkswagen
  economies of scale, production 61–63
  integration strategy 69
Volvo, integration strategy 72

Zenith, localization 154–155